The Knitter's Life List

To Do • To Know • To Explore • To Make

Gwen W. Steege

Storey Publishing

The mission of Storey Publishing is to serve our customers by
publishing practical information that encourages
personal independence in harmony with the environment.

Edited by Kathy Brock
Art direction and book design by Alethea Morrison

Cover photography by © John Polak, except for © Arctic
    Photo/Alamy: back flap third row left; © Jared Flood/
    Brooklyn Tweed: front flap fourth row middle; © Lars
    Dalby Photography: front flap second row left;
    © Laura A. Oda/MCT/Landov: front flap top row
    right; Mars Vilaubi/Storey Publishing: front cover
    top, back cover (author) and front flap top row mid-
    dle; © Tim Graham/Getty Images: front flap third
    row right
Interior photography by © John Polak, except as noted
    on page 310
Illustrations by © Ann Field

Indexed by Carol Roberts
Profiles written by Nicole Cusano: pages 21, 26, 30, 41,
    57, 71, 77, 110, 147, 160, 167, 170, 173, 175, 185, 191,
    247, 275, 284, and 289

© 2011 by Storey Publishing, LLC

The information in this book is true and complete to the best
of our knowledge. All recommendations are made without guarantee on the part of the author or Storey Publishing. The author and
publisher disclaim any liability in connection with the use of this
information.

Storey books are available for special premium and promotional
uses and for customized editions. For further information, please
call 1-800-793-9396.

Storey Publishing
210 MASS MoCA Way
North Adams, MA 01247
www.storey.com

Printed in China by R.R. Donnelley
10 9 8 7 6 5 4 3 2 1

Library of Congress Cataloging-in-Publication Data

Steege, Gwen W.
  The knitter's life list / Gwen W. Steege.
     p. cm.
  Includes index.
   ISBN 978-1-60342-996-2 (pbk.)
   1. Knitting—Equipment and supplies. 2. Knitters (Persons)
   I. Steege, Gwen W. II. Title.
TT820.S678 2011
46.43'2—dc23
                              2011018086

To my husband, Dick, and to our
children and their families —

Kristin, José, and Sara
Paul and Tina
Ben and Brigid

Contents

AN *Invitation*

TO THE KNITTING TRIP OF A LIFETIME

Do you ever stop to think what it is that keeps drawing you back to your needles and yarns? Do you screech to a halt whenever you see the sign "Yarn Store"? Do you drop whatever else you're doing to devour your favorite knitting magazine the minute it arrives in the mail?

For most of us it's not just one thing that keeps us coming back for more. It could be the soothing rhythm of the knitting itself, the joy of knitting with friends, the pleasure of the colors and textures of the fibers, the ultimate reward of wearing, or of giving, that finished garment. The allure is most likely a combination of some or all of these. For whatever reason, the passion is real and a very important part of our lives. We always want more, and we don't want to miss a thing!

The seed for this book came out of a casual conversation about the way knitting finds a way into so many parts of our lives, sometimes when and where least expected. Wouldn't it be fun, we thought, to create a "life list" of things to do, patterns to try, techniques to explore, places to go, movies to see — and much more — all related in some way to knitting. The result is not in any way meant to be a rigid course syllabus with a

dreaded exam at the end. Not every "to do" will be for you. In fact, you may be inspired to create your own life list with ideas that aren't even in this book. I hope you'll consider the book an exciting resource and a guide for your own knitting adventures. Use the suggestions in these pages merely as starting points and add to them to make this a truly personal journal that evolves as you discover the things about playing with sticks and string that you enjoy most.

As research for the book began, it quickly became apparent that no one book could possibly contain everything every knitter would want to try. New festivals, new books, new blogs, new yarn stores, even new techniques (or at least, new takes on old ones) are forever appearing, and that's all good news! It's also true that each knitter has different ideas of what's beautiful and useful, so rather than even attempt to include patterns for each of the styles and techniques discussed here, the book contains resource lists of books, magazines, and websites to help you tap into all that's available. Do refer frequently to the appendix for books, websites, and other resources to guide your journey. Use what strikes your fancy to create your own life list of places to go, things to learn, and patterns you hope to try some day. It's bound to be a long and tantalizing list, but how much fun it will be to add to, revise, and dream about!

To help you master new techniques and solve those pesky, persistent problems you never seem to conquer, you'll find advice from the many talented and creative fiber experts and fiber artists who have so generously contributed their suggestions and support to this project. Many, many thanks to them all! (For descriptions of some of the special interests and accomplishments of the voices that you'll encounter throughout the book, see Who's Who in This Community of Knitting Experts, page 290. For information about their books and Internet activities, see the resource lists.) For sources of patterns for designs shown in the book, see pages 309–311.

You'll learn about the many different fibers that yarns are made of, as well as ethnic traditions or specific knitting techniques that you're likely to find useful for particular projects. For example, the sweater chapter gives some background about knitting traditions from different cultures, along with a bit of their history; the scarf and shawl chapter describes some lace traditions. In the final chapter, there's even a glimpse into the "sister" crafts, for when knitting's not quite enough.

At the beginning of each chapter, you'll find checklists for everything from stitch techniques to places to visit. If you find yourself becoming goal oriented, many projects offer the chance to accomplish several new techniques at a shot. For instance, if you've never tried stranded knitting using both your hands to manage the colors, working a Fair Isle sweater might mean learning to do that, as well as knitting from the top down on circular needles with multiple colors, and perhaps steeking. And you might do all of this while listening to an audio book that features some fellow knitters as part of the plot. (Madame Defarge, anyone? Haven't you always intended to read — or re-read — *A Tale of Two Cities*?)

It might seem that one would need more than one lifetime to explore all the many intriguing patterns, luscious yarns, and various stitch combinations, to say nothing of going to all the yarn festivals and inviting yarn stores and knitting retreats that are so tempting. But won't it be an adventure to try!

I hope this book and the many creative voices who have contributed to it provide the guidance and inspiration to begin the knitting trip of a lifetime. Make it your own!

HOW TO USE THE LIFE LISTS

At the beginning of each chapter, you'll find a "life list" suggested by the topics covered in that chapter. They are roughly organized by the themes, such as Meet, Discover, Do/Try, Learn, Go, Experience — plus sometimes some for Extra Credit (just to keep you on your toes). I hope these lists will inspire you to jot down more ideas for things you want to learn and explore, as well as places to go, books to read, and patterns to try, so that this book truly becomes your own Knitter's Life List.

EXPLORE **FIVE TOP PICKS**

WHEN I FIRST BEGAN RESEARCH FOR THIS BOOK, I surveyed several hundred knitters to find out what they thought should be on every knitter's life list of things one "must" do. Each of the lists that follow includes the most often mentioned suggestions for that category. The first item in each list got the most votes.

Techniques

- ♥ CABLES AND OTHER TEXTURAL STITCHES
- ➡ Colorwork
- ➡ Increases and decreases
- ➡ Cast ons and bind offs
- ➡ Lace
- ➡ Blocking/finishing
- ➡ Circular knitting
- ➡ Fixing mistakes

Garments

- ♥ SOCKS
- ➡ Sweater
- ➡ Lace shawl
- ➡ "Something for myself"
- ➡ Scarf
- ➡ "Something designed by me"
- ➡ Mittens
- ➡ Afghan

Specific Patterns

- ♥ 3-HOUR SWEATER (1930s VINTAGE PATTERN)
- ➡ Hemlock Ring Blanket (Jared Flood)
- ➡ Flow (tank top) (Norah Gaughan)
- ➡ Clapotis (shawl) (Kate Gilbert)
- ➡ Baby Owl Sweater and Bonnet (Penny Straker)
- ➡ Baby Surprise Jacket (Elizabeth Zimmermann)

(Many of these patterns are available online. For website addresses, see the appendix.)

Yarns

Most knitters were aghast at the idea of having to say what their favorite yarn was: "Just one?!" But wool came out far ahead of all other categories, with Merino (which of course is wool) coming in second, followed by cashmere, alpaca, and cotton. Along with fiber type, a strong vote came in for hand-painted yarn. And one knitter from Australia confessed simply to liking all "yarn fondling, wool sniffing, and general adoration — gazing and basking in the loveliness."

Other Fiber Loves

- ♥ SPINNING
- ➡ Crocheting
- ➡ Sewing
- ➡ Quilting
- ➡ Weaving
- ➡ Embroidering

Penny Straker's pattern for the Baby Owl Sweater is a well-loved classic. How many babies have you knit it for?

Chapter 1

THE

yarn
LIFE LIST

For many of us yarn is what knitting is all about. Even the most frugal and normally sales-resistant person can find an excuse for buying just one skein with an undeniably beautiful color or an incomparably soft feel. If you admit that you're a pushover for yarns, here's a rundown of both common and not-so-familiar yarns that you're sure to encounter at some point. Each is worth a place on your life list. Yarn manufacturers continue to explore new processes and new blends, so you may discover additional choices when you shop. I've described only natural fibers, both plant- and animal-based, though some knitters prefer synthetics because they feel these fibers are more easily washed and may be less itchy.

MEET

- ○ Sarah Anderson
- ○ Ann Budd
- ○ Michael Cook
- ○ Linda Cortright
- ○ Kaffe Fassett
- ○ Kay Gardiner
- ○ Gretchen Frederick (Solitude Wool)
- ○ Vivian Høxbro
- ○ Marianne Isager
- ○ Brandon Mably
- ○ Clara Parkes
- ○ Deborah Robson

DISCOVER

- ○ Search out an angora breeder at a fiber fair.
- ○ Talk to breeders at fiber festivals.
- ○ Look for natural-color angora yarn.
- ○ Find the mohair goats at a fiber festival or agricultural fair.
- ○ Search for yarns labeled by the sheep breed the fleece is spun from.
- ○ Ask at your local yarn shop if they carry yarns spun at small U.S. mills.
- ○ Look for fibers you've never used before.
- ○ Look for a yarn sturdy enough to knit a leash or cord.
- ○ Enjoy armchair-traveler pleasures by checking out fiber festival photos on the Web.

- ○ Collect your favorite-color yarns, then build a project around them.
- ○ Let your mood of the moment dictate your color choices.
- ○ Choose analogous colors you love, then throw in a complementary color as an accent.
- ○ Find color inspiration in quilts, carpets, saris, and other textiles.
- ○ Find color inspiration in rusty bridges, old trucks, and industrial buildings.
- ○ Collect postcards of favorite paintings at an art museum, and base a knitting project on the colors in one of them.
- ○ Photograph landscapes and gardens (or clip them from magazines), and use the colors in your next project.
- ○ Collect clippings of textiles and pottery you like and let the colors and textures inspire your knitting.
- ○ Buy a field guide to butterflies, insects, or birds, and use the colors of one to create a palette for a project.

DO/TRY

- ○ Work a section of angora into a project as a decorative accent.
- ○ Buy yarns (and fleece) direct from the source.

- ○ Keep track of what, where, and when you purchase your yarns and fleeces.
- ○ Collect your experiments with various yarns in a notebook.
- ○ Hand paint or hand-dye some silk yarn.
- ○ Make something small with cotton, such as a washcloth or spa item.
- ○ Knit an earth-friendly hemp market bag.
- ○ Choose a cotton/linen blend and knit a cool summer top.
- ○ Work on one of Ann Budd's patterns.
- ○ Knit socks from the toe up, with nicely rounded heels.
- ○ Knit a design from one of Kay Gardiner and Ann Shayne's books.
- ○ Knit a Debbie Bliss design.
- ○ Make something Jil Eaton designed.
- ○ Work one of Vivian Høxbro's designs.
- ○ Make something designed by Marianne Isager.
- ○ Work a Kristin Nicholas design.
- ○ Recycle an old or secondhand sweater by unraveling it, and knit something new with the yarn.
- ○ Include care instructions with hand-knit gifts: you'll find them on the yarn band.
- ○ If you're a spinner, ply two or more lightweight recycled yarns together.

- Knit a pattern designed by Brandon Mably.
- Knit with two different-colored yarns held together.
- Use multiple, closely related colors in a project.
- Knit something designed by Kaffe Fassett.
- Victorians used to create flower nosegays that carried messages (love, friendship, and so on). Choose two or three colors for their meaning and knit a hat or scarf with a hidden message for someone you care about.
- If you have a PDA or iPad, use an app to keep track of your yarns, supplies, and projects.
- Sign up for Knitter's Review online.
- Knit something for yourself with special yarn that you just love to touch.

LEARN

- Investigate where your cashmere comes from.
- Read books to learn about fiber-bearing animals and the qualities of their fiber.
- Learn to spin.
- Compare yarns made of alpaca with those of llama.
- Be an armchair traveler: learn about places Linda Cortright writes about in *Wild Fibers* magazine.

- Compare mohair blends with 100 percent mohair yarns.
- Research the fleece characteristics of different breeds of sheep.
- Compare tussah silk and bombyx silk.
- Read labels and ask questions to determine whether yarns are recycled, organic, and/or fair trade.
- Sign up for workshops at fiber festivals.
- Dig through your stash and examine yarns with different plies.
- Knit swatches from yarn with different numbers of plies and observe the differences.
- Make swatches using yarn made with different spinning techniques.
- Unravel several different yarns to see how they were twisted together.
- Read about how Goethe and/ or Johannes Itten described color theory.
- Buy a color wheel and use it to help you plan your next project.
- Learn the intarsia technique.

- Refer to a color wheel, and use three colors adjacent to one another (analogous) as the main colors in a Fair Isle pattern, then choose one more color "across the wheel" (complementary) as the "oddball" color to give your palette a kick.
- Choose one of your favorite colors and find out what it symbolizes to people in different cultures.
- Learn to wind a center-pull ball of yarn by hand.
- Use a homemade nøstepinde to wind a ball of yarn.

GO

- Visit a fiber festival or agricultural fair and "meet" the animals.
- Visit a fiber farm.
- Visit New England's fiber hot spots, including Green Mountain Spinnery, Harrisville Designs, Quince & Co., and Still River Mill.
- Plan a trip to a faraway place and schedule fiber-related activities.
- Attend a "sheep-to-shawl" demonstration.
- Watch herding dogs in action.
- Search for commercial spinning operations where you live.

EXPERIENCE

- Don't resist buying cashmere — buy just one skein, at least.
- Treat yourself to luxury: knit with bison.
- Treat yourself to even more luxury: qiviut.
- Experience the unique qualities of yak.
- Knit something with baby camel hair.
- Find a possum blend and try it out.
- Swatch yarns from different breeds and blends to compare.
- Knit with a silk-alpaca or silk-Merino blend.
- Choose fiber from your favorite designers' yarn lines.
- Be inspired by images and colors you experience when you travel.
- Pay attention to the colors and textures of the seasons and base knitting projects on them.
- Pick three yarn colors you love and two you aren't usually drawn to when planning a project.
- Photograph patterns and colors on a city street that catch your eye and use them in a project.
- Select colors you don't usually gravitate toward, and make a striped scarf with them.

KNIT WITH

- Wool from at least ten different breeds of sheep.
- Angora
- Cashmere
- Mohair
- Qiviut
- Bison
- Yak
- Alpaca
- Camel
- Guanaco
- Llama
- Vicuña
- Bombyx silk
- Tussah silk
- Cotton
- Hemp
- Linen
- Bamboo
- Banana-fiber yarn
- Corn-fiber yarn
- Metal-wrapped yarn
- Milk-fiber yarn
- Paper yarn
- Pineapple-fiber yarn
- Ramie
- SeaCell
- Soy silk
- Sugarcane-fiber yarn
- Tencel
- Take a tip from Clara Parkes's step-by-step approach to analyzing yarn, and try it with a yarn you're not familiar with.
- Color Planning, Day 1: Lay out several skeins of different colors. Color Planning, Day 2: Decide if you still like them.

EXTRA CREDIT

- What fiber is lighter than, yet warmer than, wool?
- What animal gives us cashmere?
- What is Japanese *washi*?
- Who was one of the earliest promoters of using soy for making fabric?
- Where was the first mechanized textile factory in the United States?

MORE FOR MY YARN LIST

We All Need Protein

All yarns that come from animals, whether fleece or hair, consist of protein fibers. The fleece or hair is shorn, combed, or in some other way collected from the animal, then cleaned and carded or combed (or both) before being spun into yarn. The price of the yarn is often determined by not only the quality or rarity of the fiber but also by how easy or difficult it is to get it off the animal and prepare it for use. Both quality and availability are dependent on the conditions necessary for successfully raising healthy animals. Some of the most luxurious (translation, "expensive") fibers come from animals that are difficult to domesticate or that grow small amounts of fiber very slowly.

Knit a Cloud: Angora

Angora fiber comes from several angora rabbit breeds, including English, French, German, Giant, and Satin, each with different characteristics. Although no one really knows where these long-haired rabbits originated, their name links them to what is now the Ankara region of Turkey. The soft, silky, white or colored hairs are removed from the animal by shearing, combing, or plucking. At a fiber festival you may even see a skilled spinner spinning the fiber straight from rabbit to wheel, which doesn't seem to bother the rabbit at all. Angora is often blended with another fiber, such as wool, both to make it go further and to give the yarn greater elasticity, as angora has almost no springiness of its own.

Softer than soft. This bright-white angora yarn *(left)*, handspun by Gail Callahan, begs to be gently cuddled every bit as much as does the wise-looking angora rabbit *(right)*.

Cover Yourself in Luxury: Cashmere

This fiber deserves its standing as a luxury fiber. This is clear the minute cashmere insinuates itself into your shopping bag, but even more so as you feel the stitches take shape under your fingers. If you've ever worn cashmere, you know that it keeps you comfortable over a wide range of temperatures without being hot or itchy. This quality of its fiber was first recognized in the fifteenth century in the Kashmir province of northern India. Cashmere is grown by goats, and the finest fibers come from goats raised in cold, harsh climates, such as Mongolia; China is currently the world's largest producer. The goats may be combed or shorn in order to gather the soft down undercoat that is mixed with stiff fibers called guard hairs. The guard hairs must be separated from the soft fiber in order to produce high-quality cashmere yarn.

LEARN CASHMERE ISN'T *JUST* CASHMERE

Linda Cortright points cashmere lovers to the Boston, Massachusetts–based Cashmere and Camel Hair Manufacturers Institute, which offers information to consumers and retailers and which she calls the "Ralph Nader of the cashmere and camel hair industry" (see appendix for website). "If you buy something that says it's 100 percent cashmere and it feels a little scratchy," she advises, "it has probably been blended with wool." (For more about Linda Cortright, see page 30.)

Luxurious curls. Visit the New York Sheep and Wool Festival ("Rhinebeck" for short) or any other wool festival and you'll be privileged to meet fiber beauties like this angora goat.

Get Your Goat: Mohair

Favored for its characteristic halo, sheen, and silkiness, as well as how beautifully it takes dyes, mohair is great alone or blended with other fibers. It's hard to believe that mohair, like cashmere, comes from goats, in this case angora, or mohair, goats. Like the angora rabbit, the name of angora goats (and also angora cats, as a matter of fact) is associated with the Ankara region of Turkey, but most of the commercial mohair produced today comes from South Africa and the southwestern United States. Adult goats are usually sheared twice a year, when their fiber is 4 to 6 inches long; an adult produces anywhere from 8 to 16 pounds of fiber a year. The mohair from the first, or "kid," shearing is finer and silkier than that of the fiber from an adult; it should be 4 inches when shorn and that first shearing

generally weighs in at 3 to 5 pounds. Mohair takes dye beautifully, but naturally gray-to-black- and "red-"coated goats are highly prized. (The so-called red is more copper- or apricot-colored than true red.)

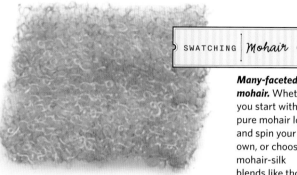

SWATCHING | *Mohair*

Many-faceted mohair. Whether you start with pure mohair locks and spin your own, or choose mohair-silk blends like those shown here, it's hard to resist the textural possibilities this fiber offers.

So Many Wools, So Little Time

Possibilities without end. Only four skeins of wool, but because of the way they've been dyed and/or plied, each suggests dozens of different projects for your needles.

If yarn is your passion, and wool is at the top of your list, now's the time to challenge yourself to discover the myriad kinds of wool. Get your hands on yarns from as many breeds as possible and discover the very different characteristics and possibilities of each. Two recent books, Clara Parkes's *The Knitter's Book of Wool* and Deborah Robson and Carol Ekarius's *The Fleece and Fiber Sourcebook* describe the most popular wool fleeces and the sheep that grow them. Both books encourage knitters, spinners, and other fiber crafters to distinguish among the fibers from different sheep breeds, recognizing, for instance, that the qualities of one breed's fleece might be appropriate for a baby sweater, while another's would be just the thing for a heavy outdoor jacket.

In her lively introduction to *The Knitter's Book of Wool*, Clara notes that blending all different kinds of wools together is just as bland, uninteresting, and inappropriate as dumping all kinds of wine into one vat, thus losing the characteristics that make each kind special.

(For more about Clara, see page 26.) Deb and Carol's book includes information and photos of raw and clean fleece, spun yarn, and knitted and woven swatches from more than 150 sheep breeds, as well as from goats, rabbits, camelids (such as alpaca, llama, and vicuña), and even dogs, yaks, and possum — more than 200 animals in all.

Most wool fleece is obtained from sheep by shearing once (or, for a few breeds, twice) a year. Depending on the breed, the fibers may be long, silky, and wavy (Romney and Bluefaced Leicester, for instance) or shorter and soft with a great deal of crimp (Merino is a familiar example). The fineness of the fibers is one of the primary ways by which wools are classified. Yarn stores are beginning to carry breed-specific yarns, and you're likely to find even more selection (and temptation) if you can schedule a trip to a fiber festival into your year. There, not only can you enjoy the animals, chat with their owners and breeders, and take in all the joys of a fair, but you can also purchase some very special yarns or, if you're a spinner, fleeces direct from the farms where the animals were raised (see Fiber Festivals, page 42).

MEET DEBORAH ROBSON

It wasn't so long ago, Deborah Robson reminds us, that all the fibers used for sweaters, socks, ropes, and rugs were natural. But in the last 150 years, synthetics have worked their way into our knitting bags and everywhere else. And many traditional plant and animal fibers are now obscure.

"If we don't keep our eyes open and take care of these resources, we're not going to have them," warns Deborah.

Deborah, who lives in Fort Collins, Colorado, was thinking about diverse plant and animal fibers even before her days as editor at *Spin-off* magazine, a job she held for 12 years until leaving in 2000. While she was there, she worked on the Save the Sheep Project and edited *Handspun Treasures from Rare Wools: Collected Works from the Save the Sheep Exhibit.* More recently, this author, editor, and expert knitter and spinner immersed herself in another project involving rare wools: a wide-ranging survey of animal fibers and their potential uses. Working with writer and natural resource enthusiast Carol Ekarius, Deborah rounded up samples of fleece and fiber from scores of animals around the world, washed and spun them, and assessed their qualities and best uses. The effort resulted in *The Fleece and Fiber Sourcebook,* which she hopes will bring awareness and broader consumer demand for some lesser-known fibers.

"I want to stretch people's conception of the materials they can work with and what they can do with them," she says, going on to explain that the various fibers reveal characteristics that are perfectly suited for certain projects and ill suited for others. For instance, the musk-ox fiber qiviut is much lighter yet much warmer than sheep's wool. Thus, she says, it makes a wonderful scarf or neck gaiter — soft and easy to breathe through when you wrap it around your face. Meanwhile, Rough Fell, a hardy, long-haired breed of English sheep whose origins date back to the Middle Ages, produces fiber with no crimp or elasticity, making it a candidate for projects like sturdy rugs, knitted or woven chair seats, and perhaps even dog collars and leashes — items that so often are made with nylon fiber. Each fiber Deborah works with is full of discoveries and surprises, she says. "Each opens a door into a new castle."

EXPLORE GOING RIGHT TO THE SOURCE

As you develop your yarn preferences, you're very likely to become increasingly perceptive about the different characteristics of not only, say, bamboo and cotton or wool and alpaca, but specific breeds of sheep as well. Some local yarn stores have begun to offer these yarns, especially from nearby farms.

Fiber festivals are another place to find breed-specific yarns, and some online research will also help you discover businesses that specialize in one breed or another. A few of the very many excellent examples include Marr Haven Wool Farm in Michigan, Mostly Merino in Vermont, Good Karma Farm and Spinning Co. in Maine, Botanical Shades in Massachusetts, and Morehouse Farm in New York's Hudson River Valley. (At Morehouse, Margrit Lohrer and Albrecht Pichler raise prize-winning Merino sheep and market not only the sheep, but a large line of their sheep's natural and dyed yarns, as well as unique, fun-to-knit patterns, knitting kits, and finished items.)

Happily, new specialty operations such as these are popping up in many areas across the continent. In addition, some commercial yarn manufacturers identify their yarns by breed, most notably Merino and Bluefaced Leicester. You may also discover shops that specialize in providing fleece from a variety of breeds. (See The Spinning Loft, page 271, and Stitchuary, website in the appendix.)

Meet Gretchen Frederick at Solitude Wool

If you're looking for almost one-stop shopping, discover Solitude Wool, a small farm in western Loudoun County, Virginia. Working with her neighbor at Red Gate Farm, Gretchen Frederick creates breed-specific, artisanal yarns made from wool from their own and other small farms in the Chesapeake watershed. The yarns are designed to match the character of the wool, custom-spun off-site, then hand-dyed at the farm. Among the wools and blends they offer are Clun Forest, Dorset, Suffolk/Dorset, Shropshire, Leicester, Romney, Tunis/Alpaca, Icelandic, Karakul, and Corriedale. They plan to continue to add varieties to their offerings.

CHOOSING THE BEST. Gretchen explains that, when choosing fleece, "We look first for lively fleeces with a good hand that match the breed characteristics. We then give them a sniff (no mildew odor wanted!)" and check for breaks in the fibers. Dry, weathered areas that came from the "top line" (center back), "cotting" (felting), and excessive vegetative matter all make them put a fleece aside. They love getting both white and natural-color fleece.

JUST LIKE COOKING. When it comes to blending different fleeces, Gretchen says, "It's a little bit like cooking — working with what we have in our fiber pantry and seeing what might be complementary flavors. We usually look for fibers that have similar staple length and that bring different fiber characteristics to a particular yarn. For example, we blend Clun Forest wool, which is fairly fine and has incredible elasticity, with alpaca, which adds softness but has no 'memory' (elasticity)." The attributes of each combine to create a yarn that works beautifully for hats, baby wear, and scarves.

RIGHT YARN, RIGHT USE. Gretchen encourages knitters to explore the qualities of each type of fleece in order to take advantage of their appropriateness for the project. For instance, she likes Romney fleece to be spun semiworsted style, then loosely plied. "This is appropriate for a longwool breed like Romney, which has a long staple and is lustrous and strong," says Gretchen. "The yarn is then great for scarves, slouchy hats,

a cape, throw, or sweater. If not knit too tightly, the finished project will drape and flow." This is in contrast to a Suffolk/Dorset blend that works beautifully as sock yarn. "This wool is a down type, shorter and very springy, with a matte appearance." Spun woolen and made three-ply, it results in a strong, round yarn. Socks knit with it are cushiony and comfortable, and the elasticity of the yarn provides memory, which means the socks hug your feet nicely.

Gretchen adds that it means a lot to her to have "the opportunity to knit with yarn made from wool of a sheep (or a flock) that I've had a chance to meet . . . it really adds to the enjoyment. Even more so if you got to spin it yourself!"

Jack Frost is a Karakul lamb from Red Gate Farm in Leesburg, Virginia. He won the competition for best fleece in the Karakul breed show at the Maryland Sheep and Wool Festival.

Twenty-first-century mills carry the banner of New England's textile heritage: Green Mountain Spinnery, Harrisville Designs, Quince & Co., and Still River Mill.

The face of early nineteenth-century New England was quite different from what it looks like today. Places such as Williamstown, Massachusetts, and other towns in the Berkshire Hills of western Massachusetts were green and denuded of trees to make way for the thousands of sheep that grazed on the rocky hillsides; sheep raising was a much more practical way of making a living than trying to plow such unfriendly soil. The first two Merinos in New England arrived in Pittsfield, Massachusetts, from Europe in 1807.

All this wool was needed for the nation's young textile industry blossoming toward the coast, where the many waterways supplied abundant power for the mills. Although the first textile machinery was in operation in England in the late eighteenth century, Samuel Slater brought the technology back to Pawtucket, Rhode Island, and built his yarn-spinning mill in 1792, the first mechanized textile factory in the United States. Mills sprang up on the Charles and Merrimack rivers in the early nineteenth century, with those in the city of Lowell, Massachusetts, becoming among the most successful. Later in the century, these mills converted to steam and eventually electricity for their power.

GREEN MOUNTAIN SPINNERY is located in rural Putney, Vermont, where the small worker-owned cooperative manufactures a line of high-quality yarns from natural fibers. The Spinnery is committed to promoting regional sheep farming by purchasing from individual fiber growers (with a focus on New England) and to developing environmentally responsible spinning processes. They use vintage mill equipment to create yarns that retain the natural characteristics of the fibers. No chemicals are used to bleach, mothproof, or shrinkproof the yarns, and a number of their yarns are Certified Organic. All the fibers they use (alpaca, mohair, wool, and organic cotton) are grown in the United States.

The Spinnery also custom spins for a number of farms that in turn offer their yarns in stores, at farmers' markets and festivals, and online. Some of these include Eugene Wyatt, Catskill Merino Sheep Farm in Goshen, New York; Barbara Parry, Foxfire Fiber & Design at Springdelle Farm in Shelburne, Massachusetts; Margaret Wilson, Mostly Merino in Putney, Vermont; Debbie Hayward and Maxine Bronstine, Island Fibers on Lopez Island, Washington; Full Belly Farm in Guinda, California; and Holy Myrrhbearers Monastery in Otego, New York. In addition to their specialty yarns and fleece (often hand-dyed), each of these farms offers other vibrant sheep- or fiber-related items, including knitting kits, knitted and hand-woven pieces, animals, fresh lamb, and other farm products.

HARRISVILLE DESIGNS. When the Lowell mills converted to steam and then electricity, one New England mill town didn't abandon water as its power source. In the small village of Harrisville, New Hampshire, woolen yarn was spun in the water-powered brick mills from 1794 until the 1930s; and although the operation is no longer water powered, yarn has been spun in Harrisville every year since its early beginning. For that reason the village has been designated a National Historic Landmark. It is the only industrial community of early nineteenth-century America whose buildings still survive in their original form. The town is completely charming, with its brick buildings reflected in the millponds. If you visit, you'll see at once that the enthusiastic staff is proud of the yarn, as well as the handweaving looms and other equipment that they manufacture. Harrisville Designs offers a series of on-site weaving, spinning, knitting, felting, and dyeing workshops year-round. Harrisville also custom spins yarns for individuals, and is now spinning Jared

A haven for fiber people. Set in the most picturesque of small New England towns, Harrisville Designs is a memorable destination for any knitter, weaver, or spinner.

Flood's Brooklyln Tweed Shelter, a yarn spun of a Targhee-Columbia blend.

Pat Colony, who with her husband, Chick, operates the business, expresses their pleasure in their work this way: "We feel so privileged to be part of and carry on the textile tradition of this region."

QUINCE & CO. Located in Biddeford, Maine, Quince & Co. is the newest New England mill to pick up the baton. The brainchild of designers Pam Allen and Carrie Bostick Hoge, with mill operator Bob Rice, Quince & Co. is dedicated to making high-quality basic yarns in Maine. The wool is sourced from Merino, Rambouillet, and Columbia-based sheep from Montana and Wyoming. Bird names (Chickadee, Lark, Osprey, and Puffin) are the theme for Quince & Co.'s first lines of yarn, which range in weight from sport to bulky and come in 37 clear, cheerful, solid colors. (For more about Quince and Pam Allen, see page 77.)

STILL RIVER MILL, in Eastford, Connecticut, is a family-run business owned by Greg Driscoll and Dierdre Bushnell. They raise their own sheep and also offer processing services for small farms nationwide. They process not only wool, but also qiviut, bison, cashmere, yak, alpaca, llama, angora, mohair, and pet fibers. Using a specialized lace-weight spinner, they are able to spin very fine yarns. They use environmentally friendly, low-impact, and organic detergents for scouring, organic processing oils, water-soluble grease and oil to lubricate the machines, and appropriate treatment of wastewater. They also offer specialty yarns and roving through their online store. The adjacent river served mills, including a woolen mill on the same property as their current mill, in the early nineteenth century.

MEET CLARA PARKES

At one wool festival Clara Parkes found what she described as "the Tiffany of buttons": miniature, handmade works of art with hidden compartments. Another time, she happened upon a Midwestern woodworker who hand-turns needles of rare woods.

As Clara travels through the vast world of knitting yarn and fleece, needles and gauges, patterns and books, driven by her abundant curiosity, she takes the time to look and looks very closely. Each week she bundles up her observations and descriptions for Knitter's Review, *the e-mail newsletter and website she began in 2000. It now has tens of thousands of subscribers.*

"I love the discoveries," says Clara. "That's why I keep doing it. There are hundreds of thousands of people in the world who are putting their hearts and souls into objects we might otherwise not even notice."

Also the author of two books on yarns (*The Knitter's Book of Yarn* and *The Knitter's Book of Wool*), Clara lives in Maine near the coastal town of Blue Hill. Each morning she reaches for a hand-knit sweater to stay warm in the damp coastal air. But her latest favorite garment is a lacy shawl, knit in a hand-dyed cashmere-and-silk yarn that was spun in a water-powered mill in Switzerland.

"It's extraordinarily soft, it melts in your fingers," Clara says, with the thoughtful assessment she gives the products she reviews. She chose this project as a "carrot" for herself as she labored to finish her second book. "I had not knit for myself in years," she recalls. "I still remember the casting on, and the first few rows, and it feeling so good to be knitting something out of such beautiful yarn." She keeps the 4-by-4-inch swatch for that project in her bag; touching it, she says, brings back all the satisfaction of knitting that shawl.

Clara calls herself an experiential knitter, preferring to savor her projects rather than knitting for deadlines, and suspects this relates to her work as a "serial swatcher." Swatches are key to *Knitter's Review*. Each week she knits them, washes them repeatedly, and notes everything from how the yarn acts on her needles to the texture and halo of the finished fabric.

"Variations in thickness — with thin spots and occasional excess gobs of fiber — gave my swatches a decidedly handspun look," she reported about one alpaca yarn. And working with another product, she observed, "My swatches dried quickly into nicely formed flat squares without any significant need for blocking."

When she began *Knitter's Review*, Clara remembers that the conversation among knitters tended to focus on a yarn's length, color, and gauge, but not about the characteristics of the fiber. Now, she says, "I'm proud of having brought a greater awareness to what the yarn can bring to the table."

Big, but Beautiful: Qiviut, Bison, and Yak

It may come as a surprise, but this trio of fibers comes from a group of animals that at first glance are just *really* big and hairy. But these animals share the characteristic of bearing an impressively soft undercoat of down, which, to produce desirable fiber, must be separated from the other coarse and stiff hairs that make up the animals' coats. This down helps them withstand the harshly cold winters of their native environments. Both the processing and the fact that some of these animals are difficult or impossible to domesticate explain the high cost of the yarns made from their down. But their down fibers also share the qualities of being incomparably soft and lightweight, yet warm and truly luxurious.

The fiber known as *qiviut* is a product of the musk ox (up to 800 pounds), native to the tundra of North America and Greenland. This down must be collected during the animals' once-a-year shedding period. As you can imagine, the processing, which includes separating out the hairs that are mingled with the down, is painstaking and time-consuming.

Like qiviut, *bison* fiber is a soft down, mixed with those guard hairs that must be removed before the lovely lightweight (but very warm), lanolin-free, and soft yarn is produced.

The desirable *yak* down must also be separated from coarse guard hairs before being spun into yarn. Both 100-percent yak yarn and wool blends are commercially available. Incredibly soft, warm, and springy — great for hats!

High in the Himalayas. The Nimaling Plateau in India is a beautiful valley where thousands of sheep, goats, and yaks graze in summer. This yak herder uses a handspindle while on watch over his animals.

An Unlikely Source: Possum

Early nineteenth-century New Zealanders had what seemed like a bright idea at the time: import possums to their country to initiate a fur industry. Unfortunately, possums subsequently have become true nuisances in New Zealand. Their numbers have increased because they have no natural predators, and their voracious eating habits threaten native plants and birds. Inventive twenty-first-century New Zealanders have found a practical use for these creatures, however: blend possum fur with wool in varying percentages to create a very soft, warm yarn that usually doesn't irritate skin.

International Stars: The Camelid Family

Alpacas, camels, guanacos, llamas, and vicuñas are all members of the camelid family and although originating from different hemispheres as well as different sides of the equator, they have some features in common. Their fiber does not contain lanolin, and because once the stiff hairs are removed, it is smooth and silky, it usually doesn't bother people who mind the itchiness of some wool. It is also very warm (some people feel it's even warmer than wool) and wears well.

Alpacas and llamas are sheared annually, and their fiber is processed in much the same way as wool is. Because neither llama nor alpaca fiber has the elasticity of wool, it's extra important to swatch before knitting. Too-small needles are likely to result in a dense, stiff fabric, whereas too large may work up as a fabric that at first feels good but that continues to stretch with use, rather than return to its original size, as wool does. This characteristic is called lack of yarn "memory."

Descended from vicuña and long raised in the Andes, *alpacas* are quite a bit smaller than llamas. Unlike their larger relatives, which have been bred as pack animals as well as for fiber, alpacas are exclusively bred for their fiber; you can find natural alpaca fiber in more than a dozen natural colors, ranging from white through brown to black and many shades in between. There are two kinds of alpaca: huacaya and suri. Huacaya alpaca fiber is dense and has some crimp, whereas suri alpaca is silky, straighter, and lustrous.

Most of the *llama* yarn on the market today comes from Peru. Llamas have bigger heads and

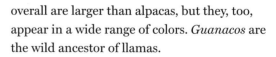

"Where'd ya get those eyes?" Walk into a shed full of llamas and alpacas and you can't help but love the friendly, curious faces. This alpaca was photographed at the Rhinebeck fiber festival.

overall are larger than alpacas, but they, too, appear in a wide range of colors. *Guanacos* are the wild ancestor of llamas.

Native to the high Andes and an ancestor of the alpaca, the *vicuña* offers a fiber that is in a class by itself. It has been recognized as the epitome of luxury for centuries: Incan law prohibited anyone but royalty from wearing garments made from vicuña, with death as the punishment for doing so. Although the fiber *is* to die for, the animals themselves were once endangered. Currently, their numbers have increased from near extinction in the 1970s to nearly 350,000 now. They run semiwild in their high Andean mountain habitats of Argentina, Bolivia, Chile, Ecuador, and Peru. They're herded for their once-every-three-years shearing before being again released. Like guanaco, vicuña fiber is very expensive.

Camel may be the unsung hero of this quintet. The soft inner coat of the baby camel is known as the "female" hair, whether it comes from a male or female camel, and may be as soft (or nearly so) as cashmere. Most of the camel hair that is made into yarn (sometimes blended with wool) comes from the Bactrian camels of Mongolia. Unfortunately, their numbers have drastically declined in the past 50 years, largely because they are frequently slaughtered for food, and little effort has been put into raising them for fiber.

DID YOU KNOW CAMEL HAIR YARN ON THE GO

Owen Lattimore, an author and China expert who traveled with camel caravans in Mongolia and China in the 1920s, reported seeing camel drivers knitting as they jogged along. When they ran out of yarn, they'd reach around to grab a handful of neck hair from the next camel in line, and roll it in their palms until it formed a short length of fiber, which they weighted so they could spin the additional yarn needed and keep right on knitting.

> SWATCHING | *Alpaca*

Seductively soft. Knitting with a 100% alpaca yarn is pure pleasure, and alpaca qualifies as one of the next-to-the-skin favorite fibers.

MEET LINDA CORTRIGHT

In Linda Cortright's living room, the African mud cloth draped on the back of the sofa and traditional masks from Zambia on the walls reveal something of her life as a worldwide fiber adventurer.

But the roots of Linda's story can be found right outside the door of her home in Union, Maine, where a dozen or so cashmere goats while away the days on 30 rural acres between the mountains and the sea.

"Cashmere comes from a goat?" she remembers exclaiming, as she pored over a friend's travel photos from a visit with the Dalai Lama. It was the mid-1990s, and Linda, a documentary producer who was feeling that her career had lost its luster, was on the cusp of a major change. "The fact that wool came from sheep didn't really blow my skirt up," she says with a laugh. "The fact that cashmere came from goats had just the right amount of exotic appeal for me."

Linda wasn't as much of an adventurer then; she was raised in a traditional way. "The idea that I could do anything I wanted in this world was something you could say, but it didn't have much meaning." But something about those goats spoke to her. "There was a real process of realizing if you want to make something happen, you have to be willing to take the steps, and be willing to leave your comfort zone," she says.

And so, not long after, she felt compelled to trade one kind of life for another: first, it was setting herself up in a rural farmhouse and learning how to trim hooves and comb cashmere; later, driven by a growing fascination with

fiber animals, she began making the forays to far reaches of the planet that she documents in her magazine, *Wild Fibers*. The magazine debuted in 2004.

From the heart of Namibia's Kalahari Desert, Linda brought back stories of Karakul sheep and talented handweavers; in New Zealand she went along on a helicopter rescue of four runaway sheep (only to discover later that they were not the sheep they were seeking); her story and stunning photos from the Tibetan Plateau introduces us to yaks, cashmere goats, and the nomadic people who live there.

"My goal is to hang out with the nomads," she says. Along with exploring all aspects of the industry — from the history of Polish shepherding dogs to ancient weaving traditions in Peru — she gets to spend hands-on time with animals. Her favorite fiber is qiviut, which comes from the musk ox. Linda says it's the softest fiber she knows, it is lightweight, and it has a beautiful blossom.

She devotes magazine space to plant fibers, too, although she admits, "I'm never going to dash out of bed and get all moony over a sisal plant."

Silk: In a Class by Itself

A fiber with an ancient history, silk is spun from the filaments of the silkworm's cocoon. Although silk is a protein fiber (it is made from animal protein), it is often separated from other animal fibers and placed in its own category because it doesn't come from a mammal (as does wool or alpaca, for instance). The two kinds of silk you are likely to encounter are tussah, most of which comes from a giant silk moth called *Antherea pernyi*, and bombyx, produced by the silkworms of the *Bombyx mori* moth.

Many of us take silk for granted, but for centuries China guarded the secrets of silk making, and only royalty were allowed to wear silk garments. The secret got out around 200 BCE, although Europeans didn't learn the methods until the mid-fourth century. Although lightweight, silk is surprisingly warm and strong, and it's hard to resist the luster and drapability of bombyx silk, as well as the vibrancy of its colors when dyed.

Although *tussah silk* is often referred to as "wild" silk, Michael Cook, a recognized authority on silk making, describes this silk as anything but wild. In fact, he says, the silkworms that produce tussah silk are "treated much like pasture-raised sheep, carefully watched and tended on hillside plantations of specially trimmed oak trees." The tan fibers are cut to lengths set by machine, in order to achieve fibers of consistent size for specific uses.

Bombyx silk, or mulberry silk, is produced by the silkworms of the *Bombyx mori* moth. These silkworms are hand-fed exclusively on mulberry leaves for about a month, after which

SWATCHING | *silk*

Nothing lowly about this worm! White and dyed-green cocoons of the *Bombyx mori* silkworm and gold-colored curricula cocoons from Habu Textiles may all be hand-processed to make yarn. The swatch is 100% silk.

time they spin their cocoons. The cocoons are boiled or steamed so the softened filaments can be unwound; each filament can be as long as 1,500 yards. To create a stronger thread, several filaments are reeled off together, spun to incorporate twist, then boiled to remove any remaining gum. The threads are white and, well, silky!

In addition to knitting with silk and silk blends, you might like to try dyeing some silk yarn. Silk absorbs dyes beautifully, and commercially dyed silks are available in a wide range of vibrant colors. Michael recommends dyeing silk fibers with the same acid dyes used for other protein fibers, rather than with fiber-reactive dyes used for plant fibers, as the sodium carbonate used in the latter process can dull silk's sheen. (Michael adds that it's possible to use a fiber-reactive dye with silk if you process it in the same way you work with acid dyes.) Silk also blends well with a variety of other fibers, adding sheen as well as strength to whatever it is blended with.

DID YOU KNOW THERE'S SOMETHING FISHY GOING ON

Michael Cook, an expert on silk and silkworms, as well as a talented silk weaver and embroiderer, says that the single most common question he gets about silk is why it sometimes has an odd, even fishy smell. He explains that this odor is most likely an issue of "industrial hygiene" rather than the silk itself. Waste that results from reeling the silk from cocoons is stored in containers, later to be processed as spun silk. If these containers aren't frequently emptied and kept clean, moisture and bits of dead bugs begin to ferment and create a smell that not only permeates the fiber but is also hard to remove. If, on the other hand, the silk smells more like kerosene or paint, the likely source is the dyeing or printing process, rather than unclean conditions.

Nothing to fear. If you can knit with laceweight or only slightly heavier yarns, you needn't be timid about tackling amazingly strong silk. Silk roving, both 100% silk and silk blends, is readily available for spinners.

Get to Know the Fiber Lover's Plants

Plant fibers, such as cotton and flax, require processing before becoming yarn. The methods for preparing both are ancient and can be done by hand, although flax requires a number of steps and waiting periods. Yarns based on plants like sugarcane and soy require commercial processing (see pages 36–38).

Move Over to Cotton

Spun from the *boll* of the cotton plant, cotton is graded by its color and the length and strength of its fiber (staple). High-quality *Egyptian cotton* is grown in Egypt, Sudan, and the Sea Islands off South Carolina and Georgia; the light brown cotton fibers are 1½ to 1¾ inches long. *Pima cotton* has a slightly shorter staple length, but it is also lustrous and strong. *Peruvian cotton*, naturally colored in a range of browns from beige to chocolate, as well as rust, mauve, and avocado, has been produced for more than 5,000 years. Fragments of cotton dating back to 3100 BCE were found at Huaca Prieta, an archeological excavation site near today's cotton-growing region in Peru.

Because cotton lacks the elasticity of wool, some knitters shy away from it. But cotton has many assets, including washability, lightweight comfort, and sometimes even silkiness. It is available from many yarn manufacturers dyed in a wide range of colors. If blended with wool, the resulting yarn has some of the elasticity lacking in 100 percent cotton. Mercerized cotton has been processed with caustic soda to increase its strength, luster, and ability to take dye.

Cotton candy? Pods, called bolls, form as the cotton plants' flowers mature and develop their seeds. Inside the bolls, fibers grow from the seeds, eventually splitting the bolls and spilling out as cotton.

SWATCHING | Cotton

Do you "cotton to" cotton? Knit with 100% mercerized Egyptian cotton, this swatch features the clear stitch definition and pure colors possible with cotton yarns.

Hemp: Not *that* Cannabis

Hemp is a *bast* fiber, meaning that it comes from a plant's stalk. Like linen (also a bast fiber), it is stiff when first knit or woven, but it softens with use and laundering. It is harvested and processed in much the same way as flax.

Dressing the distaff. The distaff (a long pole attached to the spinning wheel) holds flax fibers, which are fanned out, wound around it, and ready to be drawn off for spinning into linen yarn.

For centuries it was used to make strong cords and "canvas" sails. The hemp plant is *Cannabis sativa*, which is also the source of marijuana. Although the fiber plant is not the same type as the plant used for marijuana, growing hemp has been illegal in the United States since the 1970s. Several states have recently lifted the ban on growing industrial hemp, and advocates consider it an environmentally friendly and profitable crop, as well as a useful fiber.

Living with Linens

Although on your needles linen yarn may feel somewhat unyielding, linen fabric, whether knit or woven, softens with washing and use. Linen items are extremely sturdy and long-lasting, and because the linen absorbs moisture readily, it's a wonderfully comfortable choice for summer clothes. You'll find both 100 percent linen yarns, and linen blended with another fiber, such as cotton, wool, or alpaca.

Produced from the flax plant, linen has an ancient history in the textile world. Traditional linen processing is time-consuming, as it involves pulling the plant stems, then soaking them (known as "retting") for a period of weeks to break down the material holding the fibers around the central woody core of the stem. These fibers are then beaten ("scutched") to crush the inner core and combed ("rippled") to remove flax seeds and other unwanted plant material and align the fibers for spinning. Since the late-nineteenth century, these steps have been carried out by machine, shortening the time and lessening the manpower energy taken to produce linen thread and yarn (albeit at a cost to the environment and a decrease in the quality of the fiber).

Not just for pandas! Bamboo yarn, whether 100% or blended, tends to have a sheen and drape similar to silk.

Panda's Favorite: Bamboo

If you're looking for drape and luster, consider bamboo. Unlike the plant fibers just described, the processing required to make bamboo yarn must be done commercially. Because bamboo is biodegradable and the plant from which the fiber is processed grows rapidly, however, the yarn is considered sustainable and environmentally friendly. (Some environmentalists have raised concerns about the processes used for converting bamboo fiber into yarn, but manufacturers are working to find more ecologically responsible ways to do this.) Natural bamboo fiber is cellulose that is crushed, boiled or steamed, and treated with chemicals to break down the fibers. The solution that results is extruded through spinnerettes into another chemical to harden the fibers, which are then spun to produce yarn. Fabrics made from bamboo drape beautifully and have the luster of silk, and the yarn takes dye very well. A 100 percent bamboo yarn tends to stretch, so a wool-bamboo blend may be a better choice for knitting than bamboo alone.

Nothing *Really* New Under the Sun

The raw materials that go into the following yarns aren't new at all, of course, but many have only recently been processed in such a way that they can be spun into yarn. Whether appearing 100 percent or used in blends, they all deserve attention, as many are biodegradable, recycled, and sustainable. Admittedly, too, many also make great conversation pieces. Who would ever have thought of wearing fabrics made of yarn spun from milk, soy, or sugarcane?

BANANA. The decaying outer bark of the banana plant is harvested and soaked to create a pulp that is extruded and spun into soft, silklike yarn that can be dyed in vibrant colors. In look and feel it bears a resemblance to rayon.

CORN. This yarn is created through a chemical process that breaks down starches into sugars, which are then fermented to achieve a pasty substance that can be extruded into strands and spun into a tube. The resulting yarn is a lighter weight than either bamboo or cotton.

METAL. Silk– and wool–stainless steel yarns are created by wrapping fine silk or wool threads around a core of very fine stainless steel thread. The knitted (or woven) fabric can be twisted or curved into graceful forms that retain their shape. This lovely, unique attribute can be an especially effective design feature on collars, lapels, and the bottoms of flared jackets, for example. A copper-bamboo yarn has a reverse structure: the core is bamboo and the wrapping yarn is fine copper wire. Habu Textiles makes a specialty of importing these kinds of yarns.

A far cry from armor. A very fine silk-wrapped stainless steel yarn is used alone at the end of this scarf, then knit together with fine merino.

MILK. This yarn is made from milk protein extracted from skimmed, dehydrated milk; the fibers extruded from the protein paste are blended with cotton to make a soft, durable yarn. The milk fiber wicks moisture away especially well, so the yarn is ideal for items for babies and children.

PAPER. The yarn often termed "paper" is actually very thin linen or linen blended with another fiber, such as cotton or silk. These yarns are another specialty from Habu Textiles. Since the Middle Ages, the Japanese have treated "washi" (Japanese rice paper) with a plant-based starch, then crumpled it and cut it into thin strips that can be twisted to make a yarn called "shifu." This yarn is typically used in weaving as the weft, with silk, cotton, or hemp as warp to create fabrics that can be used for clothing as well as rugs.

PINEAPPLE. Derived from the veins of pineapple leaves, this fiber is sometimes blended with ramie to add strength.

RAMIE. *Boehmeria nivea*, the plant from which ramie is made, is a member of the nettle family. The fiber is similar to linen and comes from the plant stalk. (Nettle itself may also be used to make yarn.)

SEACELL (LYOCELL). A cellulose fiber made from seaweed, SeaCell is blended with silk, bamboo, or wool to create yarns that drape and dye beautifully.

SUGARCANE. This lustrous, soft, silky yarn is processed from the fibers in the stem of sugarcane.

TENCEL. Tencel is made of cellulose spun into yarn through a process using a nontoxic solvent that is reputedly almost completely recoverable and recyclable, making Tencel quite environmentally responsible. It drapes and takes color much like silk but is usually less expensive than silk. Tencel also blends well with wool.

DID YOU KNOW YARN WITH SOUL

Habu Textiles describes yarn as "the soul of fabrics," pointing out that unless the yarns themselves were made with care, the fabrics made from them "will not live long." Habu's specialty is to import high-quality, unusual yarns from Japan. The appeal of these yarns to knitters, crocheters, and weavers is clear if you've ever seen the Habu booth at a fiber festival — it's always jammed with curious shoppers admiring and handling the fascinating array of silks, linens, silver, cashmere, and other luxury and unique yarns that they offer. Some local yarn stores carry Habu Textiles; they are also available at many festivals and online.

Paper Ring is a lightweight yarn that features linen spun around a cotton core. It makes an airy but sturdy woven fabric: excellent for knitting, too!

SOY. Back in the 1930s Henry Ford was one of the first to promote the use of a soy yarn that could be woven for automobile seat covers and clothing. It took another 70 years or so, and a public committed to environmental responsibility, before soy yarn became widely available and piqued the interest of knitters and weavers. Produced from waste created in the manufacture of tofu, 100 percent soy yarn (often called soysilk) is soft and cottonlike. You can also find blends of soy-cotton, soy-wool (which can be felted), and even soy-milk.

Ahead of his time. An early advocate of the usefulness of soybeans, Henry Ford wears a suit made of 25% soybean "wool" and 75% sheep's wool in this photo from the early 1940s.

SWATCHING *Soy Silk*

It took a few decades, but soy fibers are now part of every knitters' yarn toolkit; this swatch is a 70% wool/30% soybean fiber blend called Tapestry from Rowan Yarns.

Yarns with a Conscience

Many of us have a renewed commitment to sustainability and to knowing where what we wear, as well as what we eat, comes from. We care, too, about the conditions that exist where those products originate. Sharing these concerns, a growing number of yarn manufacturers and distributors now offer organic, recycled, and/or fair-trade yarns. Here are some tips that can help you sort all of this out.

RECYCLED. Both commercial and small-scale yarn producers make recycled yarns. You can even make your own! (For how to do this, see Do-It-Yourself Recycling, page 49.) From commercial suppliers you'll find recycled cotton yarn made of scraps from T-shirt manufacturers. Recycled silk yarns from India and Nepal are spun from either silk sari remnants or "thrums" (lengths of yarn left at the back of the loom when weaving); some include rayon or cotton fibers. On a smaller scale, New Hampshire designer Ellen Jacobs offers Ellie's Reclaimed Cashmere yarns. The 100 percent cashmere, 100 percent recycled yarn comes from sweaters Ellen "rediscovers" in thrift stores, washes in eco-friendly soap, then unravels, and plies together with yarns from different sweaters to create new colorways. (For more on Ellen's yarn, see the appendix.)

ORGANIC. For animal-based yarn to be classified as organic, the animals must have received only certified organic feed and forage, and they must have been raised without the use of synthetic hormones, genetic engineering, or synthetic pesticides, internally, externally, or on their pasture.

In addition, the producers must encourage livestock health through good cultural and management practices. The fiber for plant-based yarns must also have been raised without the use of synthetic pesticides or fertilizers, and the seed must not have been genetically engineered. Both animal- and plant-based yarns must have been processed using environmentally sound washing and dyeing methods.

Recycling in full color. Based in Vermont, Anni Kristensen's Himalayan Yarns are imported from Nepal and India, and spun from recycled silk sari fabric.

FAIR TRADE. Yarns bearing this designation come from sources that treat their employees with respect (including fair pay and opportunities to advance); empower women; do not hire children; provide equal opportunities for all; use environmentally sustainable practices; are accountable; ensure safe, healthy working conditions; support employees both financially and technically when possible; and in other ways exhibit ethical practices.

COOPERATIVES. Communities, often composed mainly of women, in a number of developing countries are engaged in much-needed income-producing yarn businesses, including dyeing and spinning yarns.

EXPLORE LINDA CORTRIGHT URGES US TO ASK QUESTIONS

In the produce aisle of the grocery store these days, it's getting easier to find out where and how the beets and spinach and cantaloupes were grown. Finding out about the origins of your yarn can be a little trickier, although some companies are beginning to offer sourcing information.

"You need to be willing to ask questions," says Linda Cortright, editor and publisher of *Wild Fibers* magazine. "Hopefully, there will come a time when there is standardized labeling."

If you want to support a Third World yarn cooperative or be sure your yarn was spun in a factory with fair labor practices, one option, suggests Linda, is to shop at a festival. There, you can meet vendors and farmers and learn about the animals and fiber-processing methods.

Dyepot endeavors. This dyer works in Nyéléni village in Sélingué, Mali, a region active in fostering food independence and women's rights.

MEET MELANIE FALICK

You can see one of Melanie Falick's favorite moments in her book Knitting in America *(re-released in paperback as* America Knits*). She's standing in a golden field in Cushing, Maine, dressed in a lacy wedding gown knit of white plastic trash bags, the thick, fringy hemline fluttering at her knees and a matching wreath in her hair (shown here below).*

"I'm normally not one to jump up to have my picture taken," says Melanie, as she recalled her journey around the country in the mid-1990s, seeking out the stories and wisdom and artistry of leading knitters like Katharine Cobey, who crafted this garment. "But this was fun and easy and we laughed. . . ."

This moment and many others — a trip with a Montana couple raising musk oxen, her visit with knitting expert and designer Meg Swansen — helped give her groundbreaking book an all-important quality she herself looks for in books: heart. Melanie, also the author of several other knitting books, is editorial director for STC Craft, an imprint of Stewart, Tabori & Chang publishers, which is a division of Abrams. She spends long days immersed in knitting, craft, and art book projects. The books she responds to most, she reflects, exude warmth and passion. "I love books that are substantive, beautiful . . . not derivative, not just another book of 20 patterns that all seem like something else you've seen," she said.

Just as she enjoys the pleasure and peace of curling up with a great book, Melanie relishes the time she spends with her knitting needles in hand. She's an accomplished knitter but doesn't need a complex pattern to engage her. ("Stockinette stitch in the round is just fine for me.") As this book was under way, Melanie was knitting her son a sweater of undyed, organic Merino, loving the feeling of fiber passing through her fingers. "I love that knitting is quiet. It creates a peaceful place in my mind," she reflects. The hours it takes to knit a garment are "hours of pleasure," she notes. In an era of high-speed multitasking, Melanie finds that knitting balances other elements in her life. "We just whiz through the day, trying to keep all the balls up in the air," she observes. "When you make something by hand, it has great meaning, and it feels really good to have meaning in my life."

TRAVEL FIBER FESTIVALS

Not that we knitters are proud, but where better to show off our favorite handknits than at a fabulous fiber festival?

Finding treasures. This hall at the New York Sheep and Wool Festival is only a fraction of the space devoted to vendors with all sorts of products eagerly sought by knitters, crocheters, spinners, weavers, and felters.

It's one of those events where perfect strangers don't hesitate to walk right up to you to compliment you on your elegant lace shawl or intricately patterned intarsia sweater, with the excuse, "Did you make that?" (And it's perfectly fine to reply, "No, but I could have.")

Visiting fiber and livestock festivals could keep you occupied for more than a lifetime, not only in the United States, where nearly every state has one, but also internationally. And think of all the knitting you get to do while traveling to and from! This is just a sampling of festivals in North America, as well as the United Kingdom and Australia. Some have a decades-long tradition; others are relatively new. Search out smaller fairs and festivals in your area. State, county, and local agricultural fairs often feature fibers and fiber animals, as well.

Festival events vary, often including fleece sales and competitions; shearing, spinning, weaving, knitting, crochet, and felting competitions and demonstrations; workshops and classes; fashion shows; live music; herding dog trials and shepherds' workshops; animal exhibitions and auctions; all kinds of fiber animals, from rabbits to goats, alpacas, llamas, and, of course, sheep. Vendors are an important feature, giving you an opportunity to find unusual fleece and yarn; handcrafted knitting, weaving, and spinning supplies and equipment; books and

magazines; handcrafted garments; dyes and baskets — the list is endless, and inevitable surprises make attending even more fun.

Grab the chance to meet the animal raisers, often young 4-Hers, who are more than eager to talk about the breeds they're raising, or to discover a local craftsperson with unusual hand-dyed yarns. And then there's the food, from grilled lamb treats of all kinds, to local wines, cheeses, and other specialties, not to mention lots of things fried, from dough to artichokes (even ice cream). Fairs take on the interests and aesthetics of the region, so the colors and breeds you'll find in Taos, New Mexico, are very different from those in Rhinebeck, New York — and each one has its own very special appeal. (For website addresses, see the appendix.)

Check off the festivals listed here to add them to your life list, and as you keep track of the festivals you attend, keep a list of your favorite vendors (and what you bought from them). You may bump into the same folks again and again or find their products at local shops or online.

United States

ARIZONA
Amado // October
◇ Southwest Fiber Festival

CALIFORNIA
Boonville // May
◇ California Wool & Fiber Festival

Dixon // October
◇ Lambtown Fiber Fair

COLORADO
Estes Park // June
◇ Estes Park Wool Market

CONNECTICUT
Vernon–Rockville // April
◇ Sheep, Wool & Fiber Festival

IDAHO
Idaho Falls // May
◇ Snake River Fiber Fair

ILLINOIS
Grayslake // July
◇ Midwest Fiber & Folk Art Fair

INDIANA
Franklin // June
◇ Hoosier Hills Fiberarts Festival

Corydon // October
◇ Southern Indiana Fiber-Arts Festival

IOWA
Adel // June
◇ Iowa Sheep & Wool Festival

KENTUCKY
Lexington // May
◇ The Kentucky Sheep and Fiber Festival

MAINE
Unity // September
◇ Common Ground Country Fair

Denmark // April
◇ Denmark Sheepfest

Windsor // June
◇ Maine Fiber Frolic

MARYLAND
West Friendship // May
◇ Maryland Sheep and Wool Festival

MASSACHUSETTS
Cummington // May
◇ Massachusetts Sheep and Woolcraft Fair

MICHIGAN
Allegan // August
◇ Michigan Fiber Festival

MINNESOTA
Lake Elmo // May
◇ Shepherd's Harvest Sheep and Wool Festival

MISSOURI
Bethel // September
◇ World Sheep & Fiber Arts Festival

MONTANA
Hamilton // June
◇ Big Sky Fiber Arts Festival

NEW HAMPSHIRE
Contoocook // May
◇ New Hampshire Sheep and Wool Festival

NEW JERSEY
Hunterdon County // September
◇ Sheep & Fiber Festival

NEW MEXICO

Albuquerque // June
🔹 Fiber Arts Fiesta

Tsailé, NM, Navajo Nation // June
🔹 Sheep Is Life

Taos // October
🔹 Wool Festival at Taos

Farmington // November
🔹 Best of the Southwest Fiber Arts Festival

NEW YORK

Hemlock // September
🔹 Finger Lakes Fiber Arts Festival

Rhinebeck // October
🔹 New York State Sheep and Wool Festival

NORTH CAROLINA

Fletcher // October
🔹 Southeastern Animal Fiber Fair

NORTH DAKOTA

West Fargo // July
🔹 Fiber Arts Festival at Bonanzaville

OHIO

Wooster // May
🔹 Great Lakes Fiber Show

OREGON

Eugene // June
🔹 Black Sheep Gathering

Canby // September Oregon
🔹 Flock & Fiber Festival

PENNSYLVANIA

Waynesburg // May
🔹 Waynesburg Sheep and Fiber Festival

SOUTH DAKOTA

Watertown // September
🔹 North Country Fiber Fair

TENNESSEE

Dickson // May
🔹 Middle Tennessee Sheep, Wool & Fiber Festival

TEXAS

Dallas–Fort Worth // April
🔹 DFW Fiber Fest

UTAH

South Jordan // September
🔹 Great Basin Fiber Arts Fair

Primping for show. A joy of fiber festivals is the chance to chat with animal raisers as they wash and clip their animals, preparing them for show and/or sale.

LEARN KAY GARDINER ON RHINEBECK (NEW YORK SHEEP AND WOOL FESTIVAL)

Ann Shayne and I are regulars at the New York Sheep and Wool Festival in Rhinebeck. It's in October, which is a perfect time of the year to spend two days outdoors among sheep, wool, sheepdogs, and spinning wheels. It's an amazing festival and a wonderful annual tradition. You come home smelling like garlic and chlorine (the first because of that foodie favorite, Artichoke French, and the second thanks to the Kingston motel where we always stay), but it's worth it.

My dream festival destination is the Tokyo International Quilt Festival, always held in January. I pore over the pictures every year. The pictures alone totally overstimulate my imagination and give inspiration to both my quilting and my knitting; my brain might explode if I ever actually get there in person.

VERMONT

Tunbridge // October
- Vermont Sheep & Wool Festival

VIRGINIA

Charlottesville // March
- Blue Ridge Llama & Alpaca Show

Montpelier Station // October
- Fall Fiber Festival of Virginia & Montpelier Sheep Dog Trials

WASHINGTON

western Washington // April
- Alpacapalooza

Puyallup // April
- Shepherds' Extravaganza

WEST VIRGINIA

Lewisburg // June
- Eastern Angora Goat and Mohair Association

WISCONSIN

Jefferson // September
- Wisconsin Sheep & Wool Festival

Australia

Bendigo, Victoria // July
- Australian Sheep and Wool Show

Canada

Alberta // June
- Olds College Fibre Week

Victoria, British Columbia // June
- Victoria Fibre Fest

United Kingdom

Builth Wells, Powys // April
- WonderWool Wales

Cockermouth, Cumbria, England // June
- Woolfest

A feast of color. Bins of stunning hand-dyed fleece and yarns fill every aisle, waiting to be admired, touched, and added to your shopping bag.

Checking Out Designer Yarns

Many knitters enjoy making their work unique by choosing their yarns from the wide palette of fibers, textures, and colors available (or even by spinning their own), rather than using the yarns specified by a pattern. On the other hand, many yarn companies and fiber farms offer patterns that are especially developed for their yarns, and many well-known designers have created their own lines of yarn. Using the combinations they suggest takes you a step closer to satisfying results, and at the same time, even experienced knitters can learn from the way skilled and talented designers use yarns and colors in combinations they may not have thought of.

Yarn in the making. Designer and photographer Jared Flood's Shelter yarn is spun at Harrisville Designs in New Hampshire.

The following designers are just a few whose patterns and yarns are uniquely intended for each other. Have fun discovering other happy marriages of yarns and designs that especially appeal to your own taste and needs.

PAM ALLEN. Yarns from Quince & Co. are spun from American wool or sourced from overseas suppliers who grow plants, raise animals, or manufacture a yarn in as earth- and labor-friendly a way as possible. Available in several weights, the 37 solid colors mix and match together in infinite variety.

DEBBIE BLISS. Debbie's patterns and yarns reflect her love of classic colors and styles and soft, practical fibers, including an Aran-weight cotton yarn and a lighter weight of the same yarn for baby knits. Debbie explains that these yarns are 100 percent fair trade, organic cotton, dyed with nontoxic dyes.

LEARN MARIANNE ISAGER ON FINDING INSPIRATION

Marianne found inspiration for her first book in the seasons of the year — the changing weather and festivals year-round in her native Denmark — and continued that theme in her *Japanese-Inspired Knits*. She says, "I never really think about where the inspiration is coming from: it just comes as I travel and experience other cultures. And then it is always fun to work with a theme and to have one idea be followed by a new one." Marianne's travels and teaching have taken her to Peru, Nepal, and Japan, where she lives for much of the year.

JIL EATON chose 25 colors for a single-ply, worsted-weight Merino yarn for her MinnowKnit line of patterns for babies and children.

VIVIAN HØXBRO, whose books on "domino" knitting (a modular technique) and shadow knitting have intrigued and influenced many knitters, offers her patterns and yarns in kit form, available in many yarn stores and online as Vivian Høxbro Design Collection. She recently worked with Pat Colony at Harrisville Designs to develop their new line of colors. (For Vivian's ideas about color, see page 54.)

MARIANNE ISAGER. This Danish designer's stylish designs feature meticulous detailing. She selects her yarns from mills where she's assured of high quality and a stable selection of colors over time. "I don't change my colors very often," she says, "and have used them for 30 years now. Based on the hues of natural plant dyes, the colors fit together in a nice way. To me, it's very important to work with good yarns, as it takes a long time to knit a sweater, and then I know that it will be used for years and get old in a nice way. I enjoy seeing my customers wear a sweater for years and still love it." Marianne usually works with lace- or fingering-weight yarns, sometimes holding two strands together for interesting texture and color effects.

KRISTIN NICHOLAS. A distinctive color palette and joyful approach to combining knitting with embroidery are Kristin's trademarks. Her two lines of yarn, Julia and Best Foot Forward, feature the colors and textures she loves to design and knit with. (For more about Kristin, see page 289.)

Distinctively Kristin. The range of colors in Kristin Nicholas's Julia and Best Foot Forward yarns (from Nashua Handknits) is inspired by nature and her ethnic and historical research into beautiful fabrics worldwide.

Why the Ply?

When we start a new project and are thinking about what it ought to look and feel like, the yarn's fiber content is probably one of our first considerations. But the way a yarn was spun, as well as the number of plies it has, creates significant impact as well ("ply" refers to the separate spun strands that make up the yarn). Exploring the various ways fiber can be — and is — spun leads to all kinds of discoveries that impact texture, drape, durability, and many other features of a fabric, even including the way you perceive its color.

Resolution: Read the Band

Making a habit of reading the yarn band may seem awfully mundane advice compared to fun ideas like going to yarn festivals. But following a few practical "knitters' rules" can make a real difference in the success of your projects. (Swatching is another failure-busting habit; see Watch That Swatch! on page 69 for advice on ensuring the right gauge.)

Reading the small print. A yarn band contains an enormous amount of useful information, bound to get you off to the right start.

YARN WEIGHT. If you need to substitute a yarn for the one called for in a pattern, check the weight category and make your new choice within that classification. The most common weights in current use in the United States are fingering, sport, DK, worsted, and bulky. (The Craft Yarn Council has a chart giving typical stitch counts, needle sizes, and yardage for these yarns; see the appendix for their website address.)

AFTERCARE. Take note of the care instructions for whatever yarn you're considering, and remember who's going to be carrying out that care. Does it matter to the user if the item is machine washable? Machine dryable? Hand washable in cold water only?

COLOR CONSISTENCY. Ignore dye lot numbers at your peril: when yarn is in skeins, the colors from different skeins may appear to be exactly alike, but they might turn out to be noticeably

different side by side in the knitting. Many yarns are coded by both dye lot and color number. Be sure to distinguish between the two: skeins can have the same color number but if they were not dyed at the same time can have different dye lot numbers. Buy as much yarn as you need — don't skimp! Many yarn shops accept returns (usually for store credit) of unused skeins, if you take them back within a reasonable time period. In a pinch, you can "cheat" the problem by alternating the dye lots row by row as you knit, or by using the odd color for just the ribbing or other isolated areas.

Shades of difference. One line of color, but two different shades from two different dye lots (note the numbers on the purple tags cut from the yarn band).

LEARN DO-IT-YOURSELF RECYCLING

To make your own recycled yarn, unravel a sweater, winding the yarn into skeins using a niddy-noddy (see page 267), the back of a chair, or two dowels clamped about 2 feet apart on a solid base. Once your skein is wound, use short lengths of string or yarn to make loose figure-8 ties in three or four spots evenly spaced around the skein and then remove the kinks in the yarn by washing it in warm water. Use a mild (pH neutral) detergent, such as Dawn; rinse thoroughly. Take care not to agitate the yarn or to run water directly on it. Hang the skeins until dry.

If the yarn is a lighter weight than you typically knit with and you're a spinner, you can ply two or more strands together to get a yarn more to your liking. If you don't have a spinning wheel, simply hold two strands together or "chain ply" the yarn as you knit. Here's how: Make a loop in the yarn near the needle, then reach through the loop and pull through an arm's-length loop (just like crocheting). You now have three strands to knit with. When you get near the end of the loop, pull another large loop through. Continue this way throughout.

Tying a figure-8. Divide your skein roughly in half widthwise and trace a figure-8 with string or a different-color sturdy yarn through the middle and around the outsides.

EXPLORE TWISTING AND PLYING WITH SARAH ANDERSON

Anyone lucky enough to take one of Sarah Anderson's spinning workshops comes away both inspired and fortified with a curiosity and knowledge about the effect a yarn's structure has on whatever you use it for. Even if you're not a spinner, Sarah's insights, born of years of study and spinning, will bring you a new appreciation of what yarns are best for projects you have in mind, and why.

Here's Sarah speaking: "The perfect project is the one that has the right combination of design and yarn. So how do you choose the perfect yarn? Knitters have a plethora of yarn choices these days. When I was a child knitting in the 1960s, it seemed the only available yarn was the kind with a heart on the label. Today just walking into a yarn shop can cause sensory overload. As a spinner, I feel a yarn shop isn't only a place for knitting inspiration, it is also a place to look for interesting yarn constructions. Understanding a little bit about yarn construction and how those yarns perform in different situations will help you choose the right yarn for your project. Some yarns have nerves of steel wool and can hold up under severe abrasion, but these yarns may give up their softness in exchange for strength. Other very delicate yarns frazzle out with just a little rubbing. Fortunately, most yarns fall somewhere between these extremes. As a spinner, I can choose fiber, color, and construction to create the yarn that is perfect for the project at hand. I *love* that! The following is a brief introduction to a few yarn constructions from a spinner's point of view.

Twist

"The first thing to understand about yarn is the direction in which the fiber is twisted. This is easy to remember because there are only two options: S and Z. Notice that the center lines in these letters lean in opposite directions. If the angle of the fiber in a single ply of yarn ("singles") leans to the left, then it has an S twist. If it leans to the right, it has a Z twist. If a singles is spun with a Z twist and you want to ply it with another Z-twist single, you ply them together with an S twist. This removes the original twist and locks together the plies. The result is a balanced (that is, it won't bias your knitting), stronger, and more elastic yarn than a single-ply.

Ply

"So why would you choose one type of yarn — singles, plied, or cabled over another? Your choice depends on the intended use.

SINGLES (one group of fibers spun together) can be very attractive. If your fiber content or color is varied, the colors and textures won't get so blended together or diluted by spinning finer and plying. You can also get an earthy, textured appearance when knitting with a singles that has an irregular diameter, such as a slub yarn. If you are knitting with many colors and therefore have many ends to weave in, singles come apart with a simple untwisting of the fiber and a pull. This leaves a nicely tapered end that blends into the fabric when you weave it in. On the other hand, handspun singles may not wear as well as plied yarns (commercial mills often felt singles or treat them in a some other way to stabilize them). Very softly spun singles can start to pill and abrade before it is even knitted. Although singles are great, if they haven't been felted or otherwise treated, twist energy remains in the yarn. This can cause the knitted fabric to bias (move into a diagonal, rather than staying squared up). To avoid this tendency when knitting with a singles, choose a "balanced" stitch, such as seed, basket weave, or garter — in other words, any stitch pattern with an equal amount of knit and purl stitches, thus, balanced.

2-PLY. "For a lace scarf or shawl, you will most likely use a 2-ply yarn, because when knitted in a lacy pattern, the holes tend to open up more than with a rounder yarn, such as singles or a 3-ply. This makes your lace more airy and delicate.

3 OR MORE PLIES. "A yarn with 3 or more plies is very round, which gives you better stitch definition than a 2-ply yarn. Multiple plies add strength and durability. Spinners rarely go past three plies because of the extra labor involved, but commercial yarns often have many plies. I once purchased a very large man's sweater (3-plus pounds) for about six dollars with the intention of reusing the yarn. Its fiber was an extremely soft ecru wool, and when I unraveled and examined a piece of the yarn, it had 24 very fine plies, all spun with a Z twist, plied into twelve 2-ply yarns, also with a Z twist; these were then all plied together with an S twist. This type of yarn, called hawser, is elastic and durable."

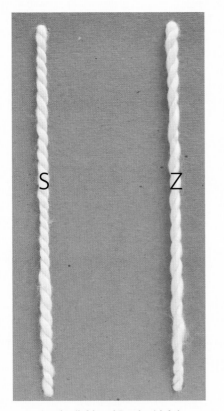

S-twist (left) and Z-twist (right)

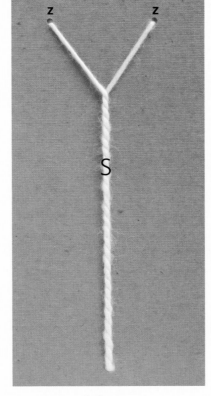

2-ply yarn

3-ply yarn

Cabled Yarn

Cables are one of Sarah's favorite yarns: "They can take many forms, but the most common one that spinners make is 4-ply. I generally start with four singles spun with an S twist. From these I spin two 2-ply yarns with a Z twist, which I purposely overtwist. I then ply the resulting two yarns together with an S twist until they are balanced and they 'pop' into the cable structure. Cabled yarns are beautiful, durable, and great for high-wear garments such as socks. Because the spinning process hardens the hand of the yarn, I like to start with very soft fibers to avoid producing twine.

"This discussion only scratches the surface of yarn construction," Sarah reminds us, "but even a little knowledge can help you when choosing from the wealth of available yarns. Knit with joy!"

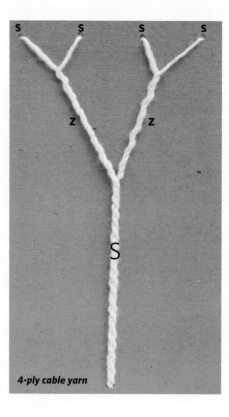

4-ply cable yarn

TRAVEL CLASS ACTS

Opportunities to learn more abound, no matter what your knitting level. The events listed below are sponsored by two major book and magazine publishers, XRX and Vogue Knitting. For additional classes, workshops, and retreats see Fiber Festivals, pages 42–45; Back to School, page 88; Restore Yourself at a Retreat, page 123; and The Joy of the Fiber Community, page 174.

Vogue Knitting Live

Featuring workshops, a marketplace, fashion shows, and competitions, and sponsored by *Vogue Knitting* magazine, this event took place for the first time in January 2011 in New York, with plans to expand to other locations.

Stitches

XRX's Knitting Universe sponsors four events that offer excellent opportunities to explore both yarns and techniques. These events are open to the public and feature hundreds of vendors, as well as workshops led by top fiber teachers and designers. (See appendix for website address.)

STITCHES WEST
Santa Clara, California // February
STITCHES EAST
Hartford, Connecticut // October
STITCHES SOUTH
Atlanta, Georgia // April
STITCHES MIDWEST
Schaumburg, Illinois // August

The Power of Color

"What's your favorite color?" This seems to be a favorite question of an eight-year-old, and I confess that it used to drive me crazy when one of my own young kids would insist on an answer. I just don't have a favorite color. I know that, like many people, I gravitate to certain color combinations, but even those preferences shift with the time of year and evolve as my taste and what's in fashion change over time. I find color endlessly absorbing, however, and as much as I love color, I know that I'll always be a learner. It's one of those things that only increases in complexity, as well as fascination, the more you think you know. Here are some thoughts from fiber artists whose work sings with color.

Knitting Extemporaneously

Brandon Mably is a purist when it comes to yarns. He explains: "Since I wear only natural fibers, I use only 100 percent natural yarn in my knitting. I prefer to knit with fine-gauge yarns, which gives me the option of running two strands of color together, making my own tweeds and other color variations. I knit to put colors together. The rhythm of 'rubbing two sticks together' is an added bonus, creating a meditative rhythm — just like listening to the ticking of a grandfather clock. When I begin working with a palette of colors, I look at what I have available, then start playing, watching what I'm doing all the time. I don't think, 'Oh, this is going to be a waistcoat or a bedcover' until my swatch starts to talk to me. The colors dictate how much or how little I need for the scale of pattern and intensity of the colors. I approach knitting just like I do cooking: If I'm making carrot soup, for instance, I add a small amount of fresh ginger and a squeeze of lemon to give the flavors a lift. If I were to add a lot, it would overpower the subtle flavor!"

Ingredients ready to go. Maybe a neutral analogous scheme sparked by one of those blues? Nice!

MEET VIVIAN HØXBRO

When it comes to choosing colors, Vivian Høxbro says she follows her own rules but always has the color wheel and the theories of the German writer Goethe and early twentieth-century painter Johannes Itten (who was associated with the Bauhaus movement in Germany) in mind.

"I always begin with neighbor (analogous) colors, and then I give them a punch." For instance, she explains, with a palette of yellow, golden green, and grassy green, she might use magenta as the "wake-up color for maybe just a stitch or two." (Her Navajo Jacket shown here is one example.)

She advises that having a sense of the traditional color wheel doesn't hurt, because it's good to get the colors "organized," making it easier to understand what happens. But she adds that "one should be true to one's own feeling." She's never tested herself to see if she's a spring or summer person, for instance. Instead, "If I am in the mood for red, I use red. There is, after all, a red and green and blue for everybody"; it just depends on whether the red tends toward being warm or cool and how light or dark it is.

When Vivian teaches about color, she likes to help her students become surprised. She suggests that they pick three colors they really like and two colors that are very unusual for them — colors they would never use. When the knitters work with the unusual colors, they almost always end up exclaiming, "Had I not used the unusual colors, the sample would not have been so vibrant!" Vivian encourages everyone to try this technique. "Give yourself a surprise," she says. But then she admits, "To be honest, I always grab the lime green when I go shopping."

One of the enjoyments of getting older, according to Vivian, is that she no longer has to worry so much about what colors are fashionable. "Now I want to go by my own feelings and rules. I don't need to go with the flow. I can relax and do exactly what I really love to do, including when it comes to colors. What a privilege!"

Her inspiration for color comes from everywhere and anywhere. "It can be a politician's tie in the television news or a painting at an art museum. Nature is an endless source, but most of all it is playing with colors here in my studio that matters. I place colors next to each other and see what happens.

Leaving Your Color Comfort Zone

Gail Callahan, author of *Hand Dyeing Yarn and Fleece*, offers this challenge for your life list: "Venture outside your color comfort zone, and work with colors and color combinations that you aren't usually drawn to." Getting out of your comfort zone *can* make you uncomfortable. Gail suggests that one way of overcoming the indecision that that can involve is to choose a painting or even another piece of fabric that you admire and try to match the colors in it as closely as possible in your next knitting project. For best results, don't just match the colors: try to maintain the same proportions of each color that the artist used as well.

> "I try to apply colors like words that shape poems, like notes that shape music."
>
> JOAN MIRÓ

EXPLORE "GROWING" PALETTES OVERNIGHT

Vivan Høxbro likes to let her color combinations simmer — or "grow" overnight. Here's one of her methods, which all knitters might like to try: "I 'grow' colors (yarn) in flat baskets. What looks great when I go to bed may look bad in the morning, so I have to switch one or two colors or replace one or two colors with new colors and see what happens. Then I knit, and what may look really great as yarn butterflies (small pull-skeins; see page 255) may look really bad when knitted. So color is constant work, but that does not matter because I love colors so much. I never get tired of them. Colors really make me happy."

Building Your Color Confidence

Pat Colony, co-owner of Harrisville Designs, suggests another way to build your color confidence: collect yarns that especially call to you whenever you happen upon them. This isn't just a rationalization for going on a yarn-buying binge, even though it is a pretty convincing excuse for buying what you love. In consultation with Vivian Høxbro, Harrisville Designs recently introduced an entirely new line of colors and yarns. Pat describes how she and Vivian spread out their collections of favorite yarns in order to analyze what made each one special and determine whether that particular color deserved a place on the color wheel of hues that they were developing.

For more about working with color, see Margaret Radcliffe on Color in the Round, page 182.

MY COLOR LIFE LIST

◇ _____

◇ _____

◇ _____

◇ _____

◇ _____

Get Out of Your Color Rut

Sometimes we need help in freeing ourselves from our color ruts. Resolve to make a habit of being a better observer of colors and combinations all around you, whether in the city, on a beach, or in the forest. Capture your inspirations with photographs. Let yourself be influenced by colors that you don't usually choose. Collect photos, magazine clippings, postcards, and fabrics that could serve as the color palette for your next project. Field guides (wildflowers, butterflies, birds, fish) offer a lifetime's worth of color ideas!

Sourcing your inspiration. Make a habit of collecting museum postcards, clippings from magazines and catalogs, photographs, even nature guides whenever you see colors and color combinations that make you catch your breath.

DID YOU KNOW — WHAT'S BEHIND A COLOR?

It's not always been personal taste that has dictated color, and even today many colors, as well as color combinations, evoke strong emotional responses. Historically, in part because of the steep expense of certain dyes, restrictions were often placed on specific colors, allowing only people of certain ranks to wear them.

Color symbolism is a fascinating study. Two cultures may assign entirely opposite meanings or have diametrically opposed reactions to the same color. Because of this, some meanings are obvious to us, but others may come as surprises. At the right is just a small sampling. Depending on where you live and your cultural traditions, colors may have any of these connotations. For a fascinating book with a chapter on each of the major colors, see Victoria Finlay's *Color: A Natural History of the Palette*.

RED	passion, power, danger
PINK	love, happiness
YELLOW	joy, jealousy, deceit
BLUE	peace, cold, sadness
PURPLE	royalty, wisdom, mourning
ORANGE	warmth, energy, balance
GREEN	nature, sustainability, envy
WHITE	purity, innocence, cold
BLACK	death, anger, sexuality

MEET KAFFE FASSETT

LEAFING THROUGH ONE OF KAFFE FASSETT'S BOOKS is like stepping inside a kaleidoscope or sitting among stacks of shimmering antique saris or studying, close up, a peacock's iridescent fan of plumage. Usually, it's all of these and more, with his wildly varying color combinations and patterns leaping out from every page, evoking everything from cottage gardens to Persian carpets, from Japanese quilts to a heap of autumn leaves. Kaffe, a world-renowned designer whose work has been commissioned by the British monarchy, the Royal Shakespeare Company, and Oxfam, seems to find inspiration everywhere he looks, both for color and pattern.

"I like industrial things. I love stuff on the edges of things, old rusty bridges, good structures of that nature," he said during one recent book tour, ambling along a stretch of Illinois highway in a van loaded with books and quilts and yarn. As Kaffe travels, he grabs his sketchbook to experiment with a motif inspired by, for example, acres of tractors or a series of containers at a plant nursery. Other times, he uses a camera to capture the detail in an antique patchwork quilt or an intricately decorated tile. Eventually, the drawings, scribbled notes, and photos may make their way into fabric patterns, mosaics, quilts, knitwear, and needlepoint designs.

An American-born artist now living in London, Kaffe (whose name rhymes with "safe asset") began his career as a painter. But he began to apply his color sense and design skills to knitting after visiting a Scottish woolen mill and, as he returned home that day, learning to knit from a fellow train passenger. He can't get enough of color, whether in his scarf or on his teacups.

In his home his favorite room, colorwise, is his bathroom, where the floor is covered in "reject tiles" from his friend Rupert Spira, the potter, in rich shades of forest green, pinky rust, and cobalt blue. Spira also made him a red-and-green pottery sink. "The walls are deep ochre, the ceiling is a periwinkle blue . . . it makes me happy, every time I walk into the room."

In his knitted work, which uses Fair Isle and intarsia techniques, he often uses dozens of colors to achieve both subtle shading and bold contrasts, and he touts a "more is more" approach to designing with color. (His Carpet Coat, shown here, is just one example.)

Despite his passion for intricate design — he'll spend hours painstakingly working out a new colorway or pattern — he has no patience for cables and bobbles. "I can never understand those bloody instructions!" he complains, laughing.

Winding Up

Before you even begin to knit with that yarn you couldn't resist, you may have to prepare it so it will feed smoothly and without tangling. Some yarn comes packaged ready to knit from. Just pull out an end and begin. It's worth poking around in the middle of the ball to find the inside end, rather than starting with the outside end. You'll find that the ball holds together better and the yarn is less likely to become tangled as you use it up.

Often yarns are packaged in skeins (also called hanks), and these must be wound into balls before you begin. Don't even think of trying to knit directly from the skein. It won't be very long at all before it collapses and results in one very big tangle. Ask a patient, willing friend to hold the skein taut between outstretched arms or slip the skein over the back of a straight chair or over your knees while you wind the yarn into a ball. If you use a lot of skeined yarn, consider buying an umbrella swift, a terrific tool that clamps onto a table and expands umbrella-fashion to hold any-diameter skein; the swift turns as you reel off the yarn. Combine this with a ball winder (or, for real luxury, an electric ball winder), and you'll be all set.

One of the advantages of a ball winder is that it creates a center-pull ball, which feeds your yarn in much the same way as a commercially wound ball. Not only is the yarn less likely to tangle when drawn out this way, but the ball doesn't roll across the room (or down the theater aisle) as you knit. Center-pull balls are also useful for methods of knitting (twined, for instance) that use two strands of yarn, one coming from each end of the same ball.

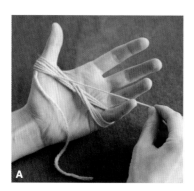

Winding a perfect center-pull ball.
Wind a butterfly of 15–20 strands (A).

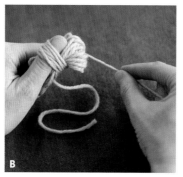

Fold the butterfly in half, and, being sure to keep a 10" tail free, hold it against your thumb and wrap the yarn to begin forming a ball (B).

Rotate the ball in quarter-turn increments, building it up by wrapping the yarn diagonally across the ball's "shoulders" (C).

Even without a ball winder, however, you can create a center-pull ball of yarn by hand, following the photos on the facing page. Or, if you're interested in a more traditional approach, learn to use a nøstepinde. Like many fiber tools and methods with a long history, this clever item goes by many names, including nøstepinde (the plural of which is nøstepinder), nöstapinna, nostepinne, yarn winder, winding pin, and winding stick.

According to Robin Hansen, most nøstepinder are homemade, often from dowels or discarded broom handles; more elegant ones are made of walnut, cherry, or cocobolo turned by a woodworker. You can use any ½- to ¾-inch diameter stick 6 to 8 inches long, sanded smooth and possibly rubbed with beeswax.

Here's how Robin describes the method: Secure the yarn end to the nøstepinde using a clove hitch. Slide this loop down toward your hand. Begin winding, at first crosswise around the stick, then, after you've made a dozen or so turns, diagonally across these turns.

Rotate the stick slightly away from you with each turn of the yarn, so each length of yarn lies neatly beside the length from the last turn. The ball will soon begin to fatten and take on the regularity of a machine-wound ball of yarn. Allow the ball to develop a shoulder by keeping each new wrap on top of the previously wound yarn, rather than letting it touch the wood.

When you are almost out of yarn, take a couple of turns crosswise around the ball and tuck the end under these turns. Remove the ball from the nøstepinde, tuck all but a short end into the hole in the center of the ball and give it a little squeeze to collapse the center and relax the yarn. You now have a ball with both ends readily accessible.

EXPLORE TRACKING YOUR NIDDY-NODDIES AND NØSTEPINDE WITH YOUR APP

People who work in the fiber arts in the twenty-first century must be among the most agile of any people on earth at balancing — and benefitting from — the ancient and the contemporary. The age-old textures and rhythms of knitting restore our sense of well-being and link us to the past, while the Internet and other electronic technology put us in immediate touch with information, inspiration, and a whole community of knitters worldwide who share our passion. Who but a knitter could casually mention their niddy-noddy and their apps in the same breath?

Although Ravelry, along with many excellent blogs, podcasts, e-magazines, and e-newsletters, is a lively resource for fiber folk, knitting, spinning, and weaving apps may be less widely known. When you toss your nøstepinde into your knitting bag, toss your PDA or your iPad right in next to it. Among other resources, you'll find apps that review knitting techniques as well as some that allow you to inventory your needles, hooks, and stash, or help spinners keep track of angle of spin, wraps per inch, and much more.

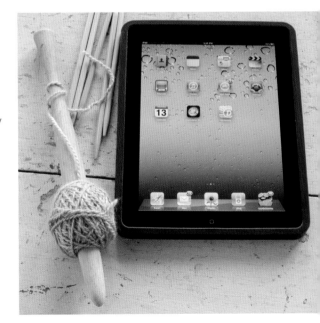

Chapter 2

THE Know-How LIFE LIST

Lori Gayle, a very savvy technical knitting editor, has this advice: "Try to learn a new trick every month." It's hard to believe that anyone could ever run out of new things to try!

In fact, Diana Foster, master knitter and owner of Lowell Mountain Wools in northern Vermont, relishes the fact that no matter how much she learns about knitting — and she admits that she's always learning — there are still so many techniques to try, projects to knit, and stash to dissolve that her only fear is not living long enough to do it all. So as she grows older, she just knits more, and knits faster, to compensate.

Discovering how to do something new or, equally important, how to do something in a new way can not only make you a better knitter, but it can also make you feel the way you do on a beautiful April day after a particularly cold and gloomy March: energized. Since this book isn't intended to provide an encyclopedia of techniques, it covers only a few tricks to help you shine up your knitting skills. In addition to those included in this chapter, you might also want to check out the following:

KNOW-HOW

MEET
- Pam Allen
- Lily Chin
- Kate Gilbert
- Margaret Radcliffe

DISCOVER
- If you see other knitters when you're traveling, observe how they hold and manage their yarn and needles.
- Invent ways of using your swatches.
- Look for DVDs that feature techniques to explore.
- Search for paintings, photographs, drawings, and sculptures that include interesting textiles or craftspeople whenever you visit a museum.
- Browse museum websites to learn about their collections.
- Collect museum postcards (or posters) of your favorite textile-related art and use them for inspiration.

DO/TRY
- Swatch, just for the fun of it!
- Block your swatches before measuring gauge.
- Start a notebook with your swatches, and jot down what you knit with each one.
- Treat your needles to a swipe of moisturizer or liquid soap.
- Choose unconventional colors for traditional styles.

- Use nontraditional yarns for classic styles.
- Knit something designed by Lily Chin.
- Take part in a Knit Along.
- Knit a simple, classic stockinette sweater.
- Knit a sweater from the top down.
- Knit one of Pam Allen's designs.
- Block your swatches following the advice in All Buttoned Up.
- Make something Edie Eckman designed.
- Decide how to handle edge stitches depending on how the edges will be used in the finished project.
- Knit a Margaret Radcliffe design.
- Research and use appropriate blocking techniques.
- Don't be shy about pulling out your knitting wherever you are.
- Keep your knitting handy for use in waiting rooms, traffic jams, and boring meetings.

GIFTS TO MAKE
- Knit a baby hat.
- Create a hand-knit toy.
- Knit a baby blanket.
- Make some baby booties.
- Felt a knitted Möbius basket.
- Make a Christmas stocking for everyone in your family.
- Knit a pillow cover — with beads.

- Knit a hat from the top down.
- Make felted knit slippers.
- Base a hand-knit blanket on a quilt design.
- Choose a style and yarn colors by picturing the finished sweater on the wearer.
- Make a hand-knit cowl.
- Give yarn — handspun, if you're a spinner.
- Use leftover yarns to knit doll clothes.
- Knit with handspun yarn for a very special gift.
- Knit socks — and more socks!

LEARN
- Learn a new knitting trick or technique every month.
- Read up on nalbinding.
- Examine the way your stitches are mounted on the needle: no twists, unless you're working a twisted-stitch pattern.
- Find someone to teach you other knitting variations, including "pit," sheath, and Norwegian purl.
- Invent new stitch patterns and knit one unique swatch each day.
- Knit a pattern from a stitch dictionary every day.
- Choose five yarns from your stash, swatch each, and follow Clara Parkes's method for evaluating each one.

- Swatch the same yarn with 3 different-sized needles, and notice the differences.
- Concentrate on keeping your hands still while knitting.
- Try to keep your stitches close to the needle tips.
- Tension your yarn so that it moves smoothly.
- Avoid rearranging your yarn when you turn to work back across a row.
- Practice some of the techniques speed-knitting record holders use.
- Purposely drop a stitch on a stockinette-stitch swatch, let it unravel two or three rows, then pick it up again.
- Purposely drop a stitch on a garter-stitch swatch, unravel it and pick it up again.
- Sign up for a knitting class.
- Buy (or check out of the library) a knitting book featuring a technique you've never tried and try it.
- Search YouTube for a technique you're not familiar with: watch three or more examples.
- Swatch in stockinette stitch, starting each row with a slip stitch, then pick up stitches along the edge.
- Swatch in garter stitch, then practice picking up stitches along the edge.

- Unravel a row or two of knitting and observe how the stitches work together.
- Learn to block ("dress") a lace shawl or scarf.
- Experiment with different ways of weaving in.
- Learn the "spit method" of splicing yarn ends.

GO

- Locate the yarn shops within a 50-miles radius of your home, and explore each one.
- Sign up for a class, workshop, or course at a craft center or school.
- Sign up for a class in one of the "sister" crafts to knitting.
- Put at least three museums on your list of must-visit places.

EXPERIENCE

- À la Cat Bordhi, sketch stitches in stockinette, garter, and ribbing — without looking at your knitting.
- Knit English style, "throwing" your yarn with your right hand.
- Knit continental style, holding the yarn in your left hand and "picking" it through the stitch.
- Knit in the Portuguese style, tensioning your yarn by running it behind your neck.
- Knit with one needle tucked under your arm.

- Knit something for yourself with yarn that you especially love.

EXTRA CREDIT

- Where were the earliest known examples of knitted socks found?
- What is a knitting shield?

MORE FOR MY "KNOW-HOW" LIST

What Style Knitter Are You?

No matter what you may have been told, there's no one "right" way to knit or even to hold your yarn. Knitting has a long and very far-flung history. Some archeologists haven't distinguished the method used to create the cloth fragments they discover. For instance, a technique known as "nalbinding" as well as single-needle methods have sometimes been incorrectly identified as knitting. No one therefore yet knows for sure when and where the first knitting was done, although some scholars believe the oldest knitted examples to be cotton socks from 1000 to 1300 CE found in what is now Egypt.

Not surprisingly, given its widespread origins, knitting methods vary depending on where in the world you live. Learning how people in other times and other places knit provides connections to other cultures that can enrich your life, as well as your knitting. There are practical reasons to explore other techniques, as well. For instance, if you can master both "throwing" the yarn with your right hand and "picking" (that is, knitting the "continental" way) with your left, you'll find stranded knitting goes a lot faster. ("Stranding" is when you carry more than one color along a single row or round.) Alternating between knitting styles may also help you avoid repetitive stress injury.

A pit knitter in action. This Japanese woman secures one needle under her arm, freeing both hands to work the stitches.

Socks for flip-flops. These third- to fifth-century Egyptian socks for wearing with sandals were made using one needle and 3-ply wool. The resulting stocking stitch looks a lot like a knit stockinette stitch, though the technique was more like sewing.

The continental, English, combined, and Portuguese methods described here are probably the ones you'll most likely encounter, but within these knitting styles is endless variety in the way knitters manage their yarn tension, as well as how they hold their needles. For instance, many Portuguese knitters hold the working needle much like a pencil. Traditional gansey and Fair Isle knitters often anchored a long steel needle either under one arm (now sometimes graphically referred to as "pit knitting") or in a knitting sheath or knitting stick held against their body by tucking it into a belt. Proponents of these methods say they're fast and easy on the hands, since the stationary needle supports the weight of the fabric.

LEARN FRESH EYES MAKE THE OLD NEW

One of Cat Bordhi's obsessions is taking familiar things apart to identify and examine the smallest parts, then rearranging them to make something new. She reports putting knitting itself to this test as she works on a new book of tricks for generating original stitch patterns. Cat suggests this good warm-up: "Try drawing stockinette, garter, and ribbing, front and back, from memory. When these drawings are compared to actual swatches, most knitters are astonished at how little they have so far observed, and they are inspired to begin playing with new ways of manipulating the stitches that have lain nearly invisible before them for years."

Knitting on the go. These decorative knitting sheaths were worn at the waist so that the left-hand knitting needle could be inserted, leaving the right hand free to knit, even while walking or pursuing other tasks.

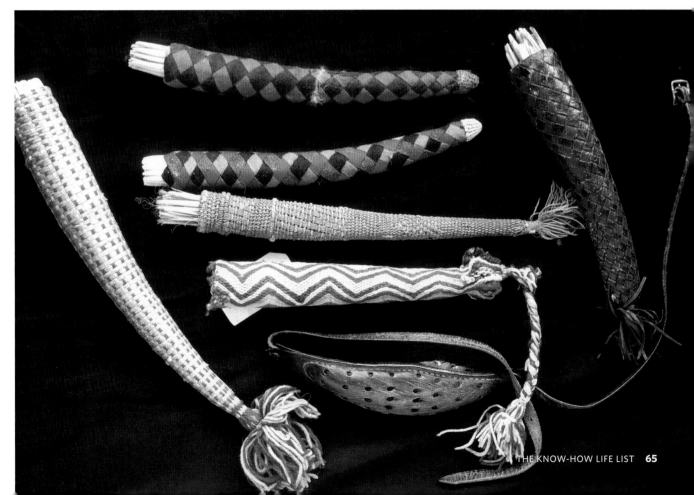

ENGLISH, AMERICAN, THROWING, RIGHT-HANDED.
Sometimes described as "throwing the yarn," using this method you hold and tension your yarn in your right hand. Insert your needle through the first stitch on the left-hand needle from left to right, then wrap the yarn around the needle counterclockwise. Draw the loop back out through the stitch, and move it to the right-hand needle. You can speed up this approach by learning to wrap the yarn around your right index finger in such a way that you don't have to drop the right-hand needle as you complete the stitch.

CONTINENTAL, GERMAN, EUROPEAN, LEFT-HANDED.
Many knitters feel this approach (sometimes called "picking") is faster, especially when working knit stitches. This is particularly true when working seed, rib, or other stitch patterns that alternate between knit and purl stitches. The motions are somewhat similar to crochet, so people who have learned to crochet before

they've learned to knit may find it easier to adopt this style. (Conversely, people who knit this way may be able to learn to crochet with less trouble.) Some lefties also find this a more natural method.

In continental knitting you hold and tension your yarn in your left hand. To make a knit stitch, insert the right-hand needle through the front "leg" of the stitch on the left-hand needle from left to right, and scoop up the working yarn by dipping your needle over the yarn and pulling a loop through to create the first new stitch on the right-hand needle, as you drop the original stitch. To purl, bring your working yarn to the front, insert your right-hand needle into the next stitch from right to left, then wrap the yarn counterclockwise around the needle, and pull the loop through.

The truth is that the stitches are pretty much the same no matter which of these two methods you use: The difference is in the way you handle the yarn. Since some knitters use less motion

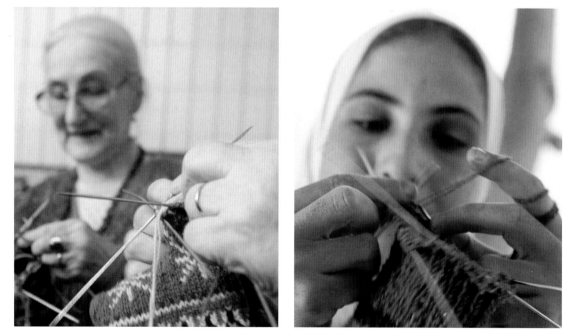

Sock knitters of many ages, from many countries. The Latvian knitters (*left*) use four needles and a different-color yarn in each hand; the Bedouin woman (*right*) knits at a community cooperative about 300 miles southwest of Cairo.

when picking than when they throw the working yarn, many find the continental style not only more efficient but also less tiring. When you're tensioning your yarn, it's important to wrap it around your finger counterclockwise so your needle doesn't push the yarn off your finger when you're catching it to draw a loop through.

One action that you may find a bit fussier when you use the continental method is working a knit 2 together: the needle isn't naturally angled quite conveniently for this maneuver, and depending on the yarn, you may have to first use the needle to open the stitches from the right, before knitting them together from the left. It helps, too, to give the working yarn a little push with one of your left-hand fingers to encourage it to follow the proper path through the stitch loop.

Some Norwegian knitters practice a variation on purling when using the continental method that allows them to keep the yarn at the back of their work, rather than moving it forward. They feel this makes it easier and quicker to work ribbing or seed stitch or other pattern stitches that require switching back and forth between knit and purl stitches in the same row.

COMBINED. After being unfairly intimidated by being told she didn't knit "right," author and designer Annie Modesitt came to realize that there's more than one way to arrive at a knit or purl stitch and that the only thing there is *not* is a right way. Bringing your attention to the way stitches sit on the needle, and how they must therefore be approached so they don't twist, is the first step in successful combined, or combination, knitting. And no matter how you knit, it pays to observe how the stitches are mounted on the needle. The way you insert your needle into your stitches is determined by whether the forward "leg" of the stitch sits in front of or behind the needle.

When working stockinette, many knitters make a purl stitch in such a way that the forward leg is in front of the needle after their work is turned to begin the next row. To knit, they insert their needle into that forward leg from left to right. Some ways of making a purl stitch, however, result in the forward leg being behind the needle. In this case, in order to avoid twisting the stitch on the knit row, you insert your needle into the back leg from left to right. Annie describes this and other nonconventional techniques (as well as her journey toward confidence) in her 2004 book *Confessions of a Knitting Heretic*. There's more than one way to skin a cat — or knit!

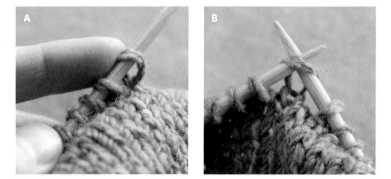

Right foot forward. The most common position for a knit stitch is for the "leg" of the stitch that lies in front of the needle to be slightly forward of the leg at the back (A). When the stitch is positioned this way, the right needle tip goes into the stitch from left to right at the front of the left needle (B).

EXPLORE TRY SOMETHING NEW

Be on the lookout for knitters who hold their yarn or needles differently from the way you do. If you're a picker and you notice someone throwing her yarn (or vice versa), ask her to teach you "her" way. You'll make a new friend, and you may also find a knitting style that suits you better or works more successfully for certain projects. The Internet (including YouTube) is another great source for observing different styles of knitting.

PORTUGUESE. This traditional technique is used in Bulgaria, Greece, Turkey, Egypt, Peru, and parts of Brazil, as well as in Portugal. (Knitting wasn't known in South America before the Europeans arrived on that continent, and it's believed that missionaries and explorers taught indigenous people what we call the "Portuguese" technique, which Peruvians, in particular, still use today.) In Portuguese knitting the yarn is tensioned by letting it run around the back of your neck or through a knitting pin on your left shoulder. This keeps the working yarn readily available, ensures uniform tension, and requires fewer movements.

LEARN — ANDREA WONG ON PORTUGUESE KNITTING

Brazilian-born Andrea Wong, who teaches the Portuguese style of knitting (and also has published a book and DVDs on it), has found that, like continental knitting, the method is often preferred by people with arthritis, carpal tunnel problems, or other joint issues. Andrea says she enjoys Portuguese knitting in part because of the pleasant rhythm of stitch patterns that alternate knit and purl stitches in the same row. She feels that the purl stitch is easier to learn than the knit stitch in this style of knitting, which may be one reason why Peruvians hold their piece inside out when working in the round, allowing them to purl continuously.

The "jewel in the crown." Monsaraz is a walled hilltop town in the Alentejo region of Portugal that boasts a thirteenth-century castle and steep, ancient streets lined with beautifully maintained old homes. In this hand-painted tile, a young woman sits in the sun, clearly knitting in the "Portuguese style," with the strand of yarn tensioned behind her neck, and her small cat nearby.

Watch That Swatch!

Some knitters love to swatch; others can't imagine doing it. Unless you've used the same yarn on the same needle for the same purpose in the past, however, swatching may be the one essential that determines the success or failure of your project. Even using the yarn and needles recommended by the pattern directions isn't enough: your gauge may be quite different from the designer's. Sure, you can be lucky and have everything turn out just fine even if you don't take the time to swatch, but how much of a gambler with your time (and money) are you?

A 6-by-6-inch swatch is usually just fine, so note how many stitches you should be getting per inch, then cast on six times that. Notice also whether the indicated gauge for your pattern is done in stockinette stitch or pattern stitch, and be sure to knit the center of the swatch in that pattern. So that your swatch doesn't curl at the

DID YOU KNOW ALPHABET SOUP

When you first start reading blogs and joining online groups, you may be thrown by the number of acronyms the knitting world has dreamed up (in addition, of course, to those the general public uses). Here's a knitter's glossary to help you sort out some of these terms. (For more knitting short-cut vocabulary, see the appendix.)

EPS. Elizabeth's Percentage System (see page 120)

EZ. Elizabeth Zimmermann

FO. Finished Object

FROG. "Rip it, rip it, rip it"

KAL. Knit Along

KIP. Knit in Public

LYS. Local Yarn Store

SABLE. Stash Acquisition Beyond Life Expectancy

SNB. Stitch 'n Bitch

TINK. Unknit (knit spelled backwards)

UFO. Unfinished Object

A pile of possibility. Swatching is not only necessary, but it also lands you with a treasury of colorful knitted squares just asking to be used as pockets, potholders, afghans, iPod cases — use your own imagination for the options.

edges, work two or three rows of garter or seed stitch at the top and bottom and garter or seed stitch at each edge for about ½ inch.

Wash and block the swatch the way you plan to finish whatever you're knitting. (For blocking, see page 83.) Lay the piece flat, place a ruler along a row, and count the stitches that fall within 4 inches. (It's risky to count the stitches in just 1 inch, because you're likely not to account for partial stitches, which can make quite a difference in the finished item.)

If you are getting fewer stitches than you're aiming for, knit another swatch using a smaller-size needle. If you have more stitches than the pattern calls for, knit another swatch with a larger needle. Usually, one size increment does the trick, but you may have to go further.

Some patterns give guidance for rows as well as stitches, per inch. If you can't get gauge for both stitches and rows, it's often okay to stick with the correct stitches per inch, and follow pattern measurements for length.

A Feeling for Fabric

As important as getting gauge is, you need to apply some subjective thinking to your evaluation as well. Even if you get the correct gauge, if you're substituting the *yarn* (especially a different fiber), you may not get the fabric you want — the proper "hand." You may get four stitches to an inch with a fingering-weight yarn as well as with a worsted-weight one, even using the same size needles. But the item made with fingering weight is likely to be light, airy and fluid, whereas one knit with worsted may be dense and rather stiff. Neither is wrong — unless it's unsuited for your purpose.

It's also a good habit to stop every so often and spread out your work and take a good look at it. First, admire it! Then, look more critically so that you can catch any stitch pattern errors or dropped stitches. You don't want to get so lost in the rhythm of your knitting that you overlook a problem that can be quickly addressed if you notice it soon enough, but that could be a huge disappointment if you don't find it until many rows later.

LEARN JIL EATON ON GAUGE

Gauge, gauge, gauge! My students hear this mantra over and over. If you simply take the time to make your gauge swatch, and actually get the gauge, your garments will fit properly and will have the drape and shape the designer intended. Just do it; you'll be a better knitter for life!

Measure by measure. To check your gauge, knit a swatch 5 or 6 inches square, wash it as you plan to wash the finished project, then lay a ruler across a row and count the stitches within 4 inches. The gauge for this swatch is 16.5 stitches for 4 inches.

MEET LILY CHIN

LILY CHIN, THE KNIT AND CROCHET WHIZ who once finished a sweater for David Letterman in 40 minutes and has held the title of world's fastest crocheter, got her start in needlework around age eight with finger knitting and a fascination with yarn. (For an explanation of finger knitting, see pages 234–35.) Many decades later she still loves to hold yarn in her hands.

"The craft is sensual. I'm taken by the colors and textures and feel of the yarns. I adore being able to manipulate something almost one-dimensional (string) in a sculptural and often seamless way," says Lily. "Knitting and crocheting are cerebral yet physical. It's satisfying to have my 'vision' realized in a material way."

Lily, a New Yorker who has designed knitwear for magazines and yarn companies for 25 years and works with such fashion designers as Ralph Lauren and Vera Wang, is also a prolific author of books on knitting, crocheting, and beadwork. She is a well-known teacher and spokeswoman for the yarn industry.

While her designs are wide-ranging, her work retains certain consistent elements. In every garment she designs, for instance, she works to give it an interesting construction or stitch or detail. As she explains, "My design philosophy has always been to reinvent or refresh an approach. Why bother going through the trouble of making something that you can easily get in a store?" For instance, if she is asked to create a Fair Isle sweater, she may opt to choose neon bright colors rather than traditional ones, or she may use an unconventional yarn, such as a metallic bouclé or chenille with mohair.

Lily's work tends to be project driven, whether she's putting together a book or consulting on a designer knitwear collection or creating her own patterns. But when she has free time, she likes to simply work up some swatches, with no particular goal in mind. Experimenting leads her to new ideas and discoveries.

"We live in such a goal-oriented society that we sometimes forget to just play," Lily observes. "If you remember kindergarten, playtime was very important in early childhood development. Well, I say that as adults we should not give that up. Swatching, one of my favorite activities, is when you practice things, and it's also a time of revelation. It doesn't have to *be* anything ultimately; just let your mind and your needles and hooks wander. That way, it's a journey."

Straight Talk on Circulars — and Straights

They're just a pair of sticks, right? Wrong! Knitting needles come in a surprisingly wide variety of materials and styles, and choosing which to buy is not quite as straightforward as you might think it would be. Although knitters usually develop strong preferences for certain types or even brands of needles, the truth is that not every needle brand or material is always just right for every project. Pattern directions often dictate what needle type is appropriate for the project. For example, to knit in the round, you use double-point needles and/or circular needles. For knitting a relatively small-diameter tube, such as mittens or socks, you usually work with double-points. In hat knitting you need double-point needles when you're decreasing at the crown to finish the hat and you have too few stitches to stretch around a circular needle.

DOUBLE-POINT NEEDLES have points at both ends, so you can knit across one, then move right on to the next as you work around the tube. They come in sets of four or five and are available in several different lengths. (It's possible to use one or two circulars for knitting tubular items as well, if you master the "magic loop" technique or other special techniques; see Five Ways with Needles on page 129 and The Magic Loop on page 141.)

CIRCULAR NEEDLES consist of two needles joined with a flexible, usually nylon cable. It's not only important to select the right needle size (see page 70), but it's critical that the cable length be appropriate for the project you're making. A relatively short cable is perfect for hats but won't hold an entire sweater. Be guided by your pattern's suggestions. You'll notice that the length of the needles also changes as the cable length changes, with generally shorter needles attached to a short cable. Unfortunately, some knitters, especially if they have arthritis or other joint issues, find the shorter needles uncomfortable.

Many knitters like to use circular needles even when working back and forth "flat." Large items, such as afghans and some sweaters, get heavy as they grow, and bearing the weight on the needles can quickly tire you out. With most of the weight distributed on the cable, on the other hand, you don't have to support it as you work. Circulars are also more convenient when you're knitting in close quarters, such as on planes and trains, and want to avoid continually bumping your neighbors. With everything all in one compact unit, you're also less likely to drop or lose a needle.

A number of companies offer interchangeable circular needle sets, which contain several different cable lengths and an assortment of needles that you attach to the cables. You can also buy cables and the needles designed for them separately, if you don't want to purchase a whole set.

Needle Material Matters

This is where the choices get even wider and opinions even stronger. The following descriptions ignore the fact that needle tips differ in how sharp they are, in part, but not entirely, depending on the material they're made of. If you're knitting lace or other stitch patterns that require many "knit 2 together" or similar stitches, you may prefer distinctly sharp tips. On the other hand, it may be easier to manage a yarn that tends to split if the needle tips aren't so very sharp.

BAMBOO. These needles have a naturally organic feel that appeals to many knitters. Yarn doesn't slide quite as easily along them as it does on metal needles, so they're often a good choice when working with slippery yarns; the stitches are less likely to slip off them. New knitters may also find them easier to work with. On the downside, smaller-size bamboos tend to bend, and may even break, with use.

WOOD. Like bamboo, the feel of wooden needles is pleasing to many knitters. They have many of the same advantages and disadvantages of bamboo, although some handcrafted or high-quality rosewood needles can be as silkily smooth as metal, and warmer than metal to boot.

NICKEL-PLATED BRASS. Sturdy and dependable, these needles are adaptable to a wide variety of yarns and stitch patterns.

ALUMINUM AND STEEL. Often a less-expensive choice, aluminum needles are widely available. They can feel cold, and they do usually noticeably "click," but maybe neither of these characteristics bothers you.

PLASTIC AND CELLULOSE ACETATE. These materials share the actual warmth that's characteristic of wood and bamboo, and like these materials, they may hang onto the yarn and slow you down, especially if your hands tend to sweat in warm weather. They often come in an assortment of cheerful colors and so can be a fun tool for kids.

OTHER. You may easily be tempted by the beautiful handcrafted glass needles that you can find at wool festivals and craft shows.

DID YOU KNOW HAVE NEEDLES, WILL TRAVEL

Traveling by air with knitting needles can be confusing and frustrating, especially if you're traveling abroad, as each country has its own rules about what's allowable in carry ons. You may find that you breeze through security outbound, only to have your needles taken from you on your return. Deb Robson has found that Bryspun needles are usually acceptable, because the points bend (although she isn't sure whether long circulars will always pass muster). "When in doubt," she advises, "even though I'm a dedicated circular-needle knitter, I plan ahead for airplane travel and set up a project that can be done on short (10-inch), single-point, flexible needles, such as those from Bryspun."

Explore Your LYS

It would obviously take an entire book to describe all the many exceptional local yarn stores (LYS) in communities around the world, each with its own special character and offerings. Many are much more than places to stop in for a quick purchase; they've become an oasis for support (and often not just technical knitting support!), meeting new and old friends, feasting on color and texture, classes, and personal attention for learning new skills — the list goes on and on. For just a tantalizing taste, here are two shops, one "back East," the other "out West." Discover the shop near you that offers a similar haven of friendship and community.

THE HILLSBOROUGH YARN SHOP IN HILLSBOROUGH, NORTH CAROLINA. A lifelong knitter, Anne Derby had a dream that carried her through various life stresses, including a high-powered job in corporate America. When their youngest child was about to graduate from college, she and her husband decided it was time to put that dream into action: open a yarn shop. Not only has fulfilling her dream lowered her own dangerously high blood pressure, but as she explains, "it has created a community of knitters in our area, and we all seem to be thriving."

Anne's small shop literally bursts with an impressive selection of yarns, and in addition, she generously takes the time to fulfill special orders for yarns she doesn't have on hand. Located in a lovely, picturesque town just north of Chapel Hill, the shop is what customers describe as the perfect "hangout place" (and it's no small matter that there's an amazing chocolate shop nearby). Anne carries only natural fibers and makes an effort to offer local and fair-trade yarns whenever possible. The shop has come to serve as a refuge and meeting place for people from many different backgrounds, and according to one loyal, enthusiastic customer, through her wise, warm manner, Anne offers more emotional, as well as practical, support in a single day than many professional therapists.

YORKSHIRE YARNS IN LAKEWOOD, WASHINGTON. Described as a "place for yarn solace," Yorkshire Yarns provides homey, comfortable areas for relaxing, sharing triumphs, and getting answers to problems. The shop hosts the "Lunch Bunch" a couple of days a week, as well as an evening each week as a time for "social" knitting and crochet. Before starting her yarn shop, Sonya Acord

"Painting is easy when you don't know how, but very difficult when you do."

Edgar Degas

sang gospel, R&B, blues, and soul, and she traveled the world (including Greece, Uganda, France, England, and Australia) as a music missionary. When her youngest child was in middle school, she decided to go into the yarn business, but she says, "I still do a bit of music at local music festivals on the side when and if I have time." She now generally sticks to festivals that feature R&B and Motown. The vivacious warmth that illuminated her musical career certainly spills over into the welcoming environment she has created for her fiber customers.

EXPLORE YOU'RE NOT ALONE

The acronym KAL (Knit Along) has inspired a book that describes the history of this phenomenon, including the online events that attract tens of thousands of knitters around the world. For information about Knit Alongs, search the Internet for your own special interests — a specific sweater pattern, for example — to learn about Knit Alongs you can take part in. You'll also find dozens of KALs on Ravelry. (For more about the online knitting community, and Ravelry in particular, see Tapping into Knitting Online, page 211.)

EXPLORE SPEEDSTERS

Mademoiselle Thuillier knit "at such a pace that she might have been a machine driven by steam."

HONORÉ DE BALZAC
Les petits bourgeois (The Middle Classes)

THE SLOW FOOD MOVEMENT has picked up many advocates in recent years, with its emphasis on buying locally, slowing down to appreciate not only our food but friends, family, and life in general. While the movement's principles surely resonate with many knitters, sometimes a gremlin inside us just wants to speed things up — perhaps even compete — even if we'd never want to admit it. And so there are indeed world records made and broken and reported in The *Guinness Book of World Records* of knitters surpassing 115 stitches per minute.

Speed is probably not why most of us pick up our knitting (except for those times when we're desperately trying to finish a last-minute gift or you're afraid you're about to run out of yarn, and with the same illogic that takes over when you fear running out of gas, you speed up to somehow make the yarn — or gas — go further). Some of the techniques that speed-knitting competitors use are less tiring, however, and may actually help us in other ways to become better slow knitters. It may be revealing, for instance, that most speed knitters advocate using the continental method (working yarn held in your left hand). Here are a few other tips from the speedsters for smoother, if not faster, knitting:

HAND POSITION. Keep your hands as still as possible as you knit.

STITCH POSITION. Try to keep the stitches you are working on close to the tips of your needles, until the moment when you let the new stitch slip onto your right-hand needle. At that point, you need to push it onto the widest part of the needle, so your stitches don't become too tight.

YARN TENSION. Experiment to find the best way to tension your working yarn so it flows smoothly and easily and, if possible, so you don't have to rearrange it around your fingers every time you turn to work back across a row.

LEARN PUT SOME GREASE INTO IT

If you want a little more speed in your needlework, expert Lily Chin suggests greasing up your hooks or your needles. Take a little moisturizer, or even liquid soap, and smear it on a crochet hook or needle tips, then wipe it off with tissue.

"It leaves a nice slick finish, and your work glides more easily," she says. "This is what I did in competition when I won the Fastest Crocheter titles."

MEET PAM ALLEN

IN HER LIFETIME OF KNITTING, Pam Allen has been known to spend a whole year on a single sweater, playing with the colorwork, proportion of motifs, shaping. But these days, in a stitching scene that's saturated with trendy shapes and intricate patterns, this leading designer is pointing her needles toward simpler garments.

"There's a lot to be said for stockinette stitch," says Pam. "At this point, a part of me hungers for something that's very minimal." And yet, she also hungers for something very big.

Pam, whose 25-plus years in the knitting industry include a stint as editor of *Interweave Knits* and more recently as creative director for Classic Elite Yarns, has taken stock of the international yarn industry and the economics of her home state of Maine, as well as her own thirst for satisfying work, and has reinvented her own world of knitting — starting with the yarn. Quince & Co., her new yarn company and ultimate DIY project, reaches for her ideals: sustainable production, rich and inspiring colors, and designs that produce great-feeling garments, to name a few. "I'm a control freak," she admits in a quiet, thoughtful voice. "I wanted to finally do something I wanted to do and not make compromises."

Pam, who lives in Portland, Maine, surrounded by old, abandoned mills, finds it heartbreaking to watch fiber production go overseas. Quince is staying right in Maine, spinning its yarns in a reclaimed mill in Biddeford owned by business partner Bob Rice. Each of their yarn lines showcases fiber from American sheep farms, some blended with other carefully sourced, organic fibers (see yarn card below).

With design partner Carrie Hoge, Pam luxuriates in creating patterns featuring their yarns, spending countless hours playing with just a few tools: knit, purl, and top-down construction. Each piece follows Pam's trademark aesthetic: simple and well fitting, with a few special details. "We want to go after the thing people will feel good wearing," she says. "I love easy knitting. You don't need to be a virtuoso to knit these patterns."

Pam finds herself relishing the other work involved in making this dream come true, as well. "To invent the yarn, choose the colors, take the pictures — it's thrilling," reflects Pam. "It's exploring what knitting is."

How to Be a Problem Solver

Learning to "read" your knitting and solve problems can be the most empowering thing you'll ever do as a knitter. When you realize it's not the end of the world to drop a stitch, or to cast on one or two more stitches than your pattern calls for, you'll enjoy the whole process so much more. Usually, as knitters gain experience they can distinguish between absolutely needing to rip out a row (or two, or more) to correct an error that will always haunt them or finding a way to fudge that compensates for the mistake so "no one will ever know."

Since a dropped stitch seems to be the most paralyzing fear of most new knitters, here's some advice for how to make it right. You can repair the mistake from either the right or the wrong side of the fabric, but let's look first at a stitch dropped when working stockinette and make the repair on the right side. Here are two ways to make the fix. In both cases these fixes assume that the dropped stitch is only one row back.

It's often possible to use either of the methods described in Fixer Uppers on the facing page for multiple dropped stitches, either down the columns or adjacent to one another. Sometimes there's not enough length to the strands to make the new stitches, with the result that they are tight and the fix becomes noticeable. This is not usually a problem if you discover the dropped stitch soon enough. If your dropped stitch is only one or two rows back, you can usually disguise any unevenness by simply stretching the fabric gently to distribute the discrepancy along the row. If this doesn't work, you may have to rip out to the place where you dropped the stitch.

DROPPED PURL STITCHES. If the dropped stitch should have been purled on the right side and knit on the wrong side, or if you are working garter stitch or reverse stockinette stitch (where the "smooth" side of the stitches is on the wrong side of the fabric), you'll need to pick up the dropped stitch or stitches in such a way that you maintain the characteristic "bumps" of the purl stitches in pattern on the fabric surface. When working stockinette stitch, you may find it easier to work this repair with the knit side of the stitch facing you. With garter stitch you'll have to alternate between the right and wrong sides of the fabric if you're picking up stitches from more than one row back.

MORE TECHNIQUES FOR MY LIFE LIST

Fix Method #1

Find the offending loop, and capture it with another needle the same size as those you are working with. Run this repair needle through the stitch so that it lies on the right side of the fabric (A).

Examine the wrong side of the fabric, and find the strand that joins the stitches adjacent to the dropped stitch. Make the new (missing) stitch with this strand by dipping the tip of the repair needle under it (B).

Lift the loop of the dropped stitch over the strand and let it drop off the needle. Voilà — a new stitch! Place the restored stitch on the left-hand needle, adjust its "legs" as necessary, and knit the stitch as usual (C).

Once you master this technique, it's easy to use the right-hand needle for the repair, making it my preferred technique — no extra tools to bother with!

Fix Method #2

Find the dropped stitch, capture it with a crochet hook, and draw it toward you to the right side of the fabric.

Examine the wrong side of the fabric, and find the strand that joins the stitches adjacent to the dropped stitch.

Insert the hook into this strand, and draw it through the dropped stitch to make your new stitch. Place the restored stitch on the left-hand needle, and knit it as usual.

Be Fearless!

Every one of us sometimes needs a cheerleader, whether it's to try a tricky new technique or to explore a daring colorway. If you know you may hit one of those roadblocks, flag this page for some wise words from the experts. Gardeners have a saying: "You don't know a plant until you've killed it." Knitting is nowhere nearly that life-threatening. When something goes wrong, we knitters can say, simply, "It's just knitting!"

KATE GILBERT has these words for new and long-time knitters alike: "Don't be scared of your knitting." In workshops and classes Kate notices that many knitters seem terrified of dropping a stitch or misreading a pattern or needing to rip out a row.

"Making mistakes is awesome, and you figure out how to fix it," says Kate, a self-taught knitter. She urges knitters to see an error as a chance to experiment and learn. Knitters can benefit enormously by taking the time to understand the structure of their knitting, she says, noting how the stitches sit on the needle, observing that the knitting consists of one continuous piece of yarn, and realizing that the stitches are merely rows of interlocking loops. Rip out a few rows and see!

EDIE ECKMAN advises, "I'm a firm believer in encouraging knitters and crocheters to attempt anything they want to stitch. Just because a project or technique may be beyond your current skill level, that's no reason not to do it! Indeed, that may be just the encouragement you need to gain new skills. The more you know, the more you want to learn. Unless you do some research, you don't even know what you don't know! Take a class, go to your local yarn shop, ask a more experienced friend, buy books (or check them out from your library), and, of course, search the Internet. There are so many ways to pick up new skills, there's really no excuse not to be learning new things all the time. Knitting and crocheting are supposed to be fun. There's no room for fear!

CAT BORDHI has this to say about getting lost in a knitting pattern: "Misinterpretation is your best friend, because it takes you places you never intended to go."

LEARN — MARGARET RADCLIFFE ON PLANNING AHEAD

Margaret advises that one of the key factors in successfully finishing a garment is something you do all the while you're knitting: decide how to handle the edge stitches. You have several options: (1) always slip the first stitch, (2) maintain the pattern at both ends, (3) keep the edge stitches in garter, or (4) keep them in stockinette. None of these is wrong, but there are reasons for choosing each one. For instance, if you later will have to pick up stitches along an edge (such as a heel flap), they will be easiest to see and knit into if you slip the first stitch of each row knitwise and purl the last stitch of each row. When working decreases along the edge of a garment knit in a garter or other pattern stitch, keep two or three edge stitches in stockinette and work the decreases one stitch away from the first and last stitches in a row (for example, K1, ssk, knit to last 3 stitches, K2tog, K1).

"Knit on, with hope and confidence, through all crises."

ELIZABETH ZIMMERMANN

MUSEUM HOPPING

Do you experience a chill when you come across a shred of fabric dated 1500 BCE in a museum, or when you notice that the Virgin Mary depicted in a medieval painting is, yes, knitting? (One of the most famous of these knitting madonnas is part of an altar piece in Buxtehude, Germany, painted around 1400 CE by Master Bertram of Munich, and referred to as The Visit of the Angels.) If discovering this connection with centuries-old knitters gives you a thrill, this is the list for you.

When it comes to places to go and things to see, museums are full of rich experiences for fiber-arts lovers. If you need an excuse to travel, here are some destinations to add to your itinerary and justify your trip. And even if Norway or Sweden or the Shetland Islands isn't in your immediate future, it's a treat simply to visit these websites. Many have beautiful examples of their collections and interesting information about the textile culture they preserve. For depictions of the fiber arts in paintings, see Art Spotting, page 215, and It's Greek to Me!, pages 276–77. (For website addresses, see the appendix.)

American Textile History Museum

Lowell, Massachusetts

The mission statement for the American Textile History Museum is to "tell America's story through the art, history, and science of textiles." Affiliated with the Smithsonian Institution, the museum is located, very appropriately, in a former textile mill in historic Lowell, a center of the nineteenth-century textile industry in the United States.

Bohus Museum

Uddevalla, Sweden

An exhibition of garments made by women in the Swedish cottage industry begun in the 1930s by Emma Jacobsson (for information about Bohus knits, see page 115). The museum also retails Bohus sweater kits.

Museum of Norwegian Knitting Industry

Salhus, Norway

This museum, housed in an original 1859 factory, focuses on the impact industrialization had on people who moved from a traditional agrarian society to an industrial town.

Shetland Museum

Lerwick, Shetland, United Kingdom

Featuring the story of the Shetland Islands from prehistoric times, the Shetland Museum includes a textile exhibit that traces the development of that industry from a barter system through the nineteenth century when textiles became an important commercial force in Shetland, allowing women to support family incomes. The museum's collection goes on to showcase changes in style to the present time. Textiles have always been an integral part of the Shetland economy, and although the weaving industry has not survived, knitting guilds still promote the craft. You can have fun here experimenting with an interactive display that allows you to design a Fair Isle sweater.

Texas Museum of Fiber Arts

Austin

The Texas Museum of Fiber Arts was created to foster education and creativity in fiber art expression, experience, and appreciation. You won't find this museum in a building in the city of Austin, however: it is a "museum without walls" that arranges exhibits to tour throughout the state.

Textile Museum

Washington, D.C.

The mission of the Textile Museum in Washington is to expand "public knowledge and appreciation — locally, nationally and internationally — of the artistic merits and cultural importance of the world's textiles."

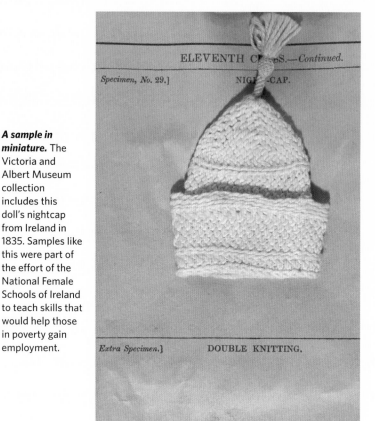

A sample in miniature. The Victoria and Albert Museum collection includes this doll's nightcap from Ireland in 1835. Samples like this were part of the effort of the National Female Schools of Ireland to teach skills that would help those in poverty gain employment.

Textile Museum of Canada

Toronto, Ontario

The Textile Museum of Canada includes objects (12,000, in fact) from more than two hundred countries and regions. Their permanent collection "celebrates cultural diversity and includes traditional fabrics, garments, carpets and related artifacts such as beadwork and basketry." Special themed exhibitions include items from their permanent collection, as well as the work of Canadian and international artists.

Versterheim Norwegian-American Museum

Decorah, Iowa

The Versterheim Museum includes 16 historic buildings and is thought to be "the largest, most comprehensive museum in the United States dedicated to a single immigrant group." It has large samplings from the fine arts, the decorative arts, and folk arts, including a collection of Norwegian textiles and traditional dress.

Victoria and Albert Museum

London

This is the mecca for fiber-arts lovers! A vast collection in different media from all parts of the world, particularly Europe, offers days of browsing and study, no matter your interest. Their website is rich with details and photos of all of the fiber arts. Search on "knitting" for articles on styles and techniques, as well as for historical patterns. The museum's textile collection covers a period of more than 2,000 years. Most techniques are represented, including woven, printed, and embroidered textiles, lace, tapestries, and carpets.

All Buttoned Up...and Other Finishing Tips

"It ain't over 'til . . ." **you block it,** weave in the ends, and sew on any buttons or other fasteners it needs. Finishing can make an amazing difference in any project, and even though this book avoids knitting "musts," blocking is right up there with reading the yarn band and swatching as one of the three most significant steps you can take to ensure that you'll be happy with your work.

The Final Touch: Blocking

When you're talking about knitting, "blocking" is a finishing technique, but no one technique works for every project, every fiber, or every stitch pattern. When your fine lace project is still on needles, for instance, it may look a bit like a dishrag, but moisten it and stretch it to its potential size and shape with lace pins (in lace knitting, this is known as "dressing"), and like the ugly duckling, it "matures" to a thing of true beauty, with the lovely lace pattern wholly revealed. Sweaters, hats, socks, and similar items knit in wool or a wool blend are less dramatically transformed. If you dampen them, however, lay them flat (or simply lay them out and moisten them by laying a damp towel over them), then pat and gently pull them into shape, you'll find that the stitches relax, settle in, and become more integrated; lumps and bumps disappear; and the whole item transforms itself into a more professional-looking piece. Blocking Fair Isle and other stranded knits, as well as intarsia, is especially satisfying. Note that some patterns (and some experts) suggest blocking sweaters and other items before assembling them. Here are some tips on how to proceed.

* Run a basin of room-temperature water, and settle your knitting into the water until it's thoroughly wet. Be sure to wait until you've filled the basin with water before adding the knitted item. (You can use a small amount of detergent at this stage. The detergent helps the yarn completely absorb the water, and of course, it also serves to clean your project, a benefit if you've been working on it for quite some time in all sorts of places. It also removes spinning oils and other residue that

LEARN BABY THEM FOREVER

To wash hand-knit items after they've been used, it's wise to use pretty much the same technique described here for blocking newly knit items. Meta Nesbitt, owner of Metaphor Yarns in Shelburne, Massachusetts, advises washing wool knits with the same care you use when washing a newborn baby.

might be left from the manufacturing process. If you use detergent, rinse in the same gentle way before proceeding to the next step.)

✻ When blocking wool, mohair, cashmere, or other "feltable" fabrics, be vigilant about not letting water run directly on it, agitating it, or exposing it alternately to water of different temperatures, all of which can begin the felting process. Equally important, take care not to allow the fabric to stretch when you're handling it when it's wet.

✻ Remove some of the water by rolling it in a thick terry cloth towel. To do this, lay the item on the towel, fold the towel over it, then roll the whole thing up and apply pressure so that the water is absorbed by the towel.

A perfect finish. To block wool items, gently soak them in lukewarm water, then roll in a terry cloth towel to remove excess water. Lay them out on a dry towel, pat them gently to shape, and pin as necessary to maintain the shape until dry.

Alternatively, you can put the item in your top-loading washing machine and use the final spin cycle to remove the water. If you follow the latter method, take care to set the machine so that it no longer sprays water on the fiber, or the spray may start a felting process.

✻ Lay the item on a clean terry cloth towel. This helps absorb remaining moisture allowing your project to dry more quickly. If possible, elevate the towel on a drying rack or screen (commercial purpose-built screens are available). This, too, helps speed drying.

✻ Use the pattern's finished measurements or schematic to guide you in shaping the pieces into their proper dimensions. As you do this, avoid stretching areas, such as ribbing, that are intended to be elastic and draw in when worn.

✻ Although some knitters like to steam their completed items, take care never to let your iron rest on the fabric: this can distort and crush the fibers, eliminating the characteristic (and desirable) loft of the knitting and distorting the stitches. This is especially important if there are any synthetic fibers in your project. To further protect the fibers, you can lay a light cotton fabric (dampened, if the knitting is dry) over the piece as you hover the steam iron over it.

✻ The best way to block items knit with cotton or acrylic yarn is to lay them out flat, then place a damp terry cloth towel over them for an hour or so until they are damp enough that you can shape them as needed. Then allow them to lie flat until dry.

EXPLORE GO AHEAD AND KNIT IN PUBLIC

First celebrated in 2005, World Wide Knit in Public (WWKIP) Day has now grown to more than 200 local events. It is held worldwide in mid-June each year, with events promoted in every continent except possibly Antarctica. Its motto is, "Better living through stitching together."

KIP aims to connect knitters and show non-knitters just how diverse and social the craft can be. Events feature snacks, signing each other's WWKIP gear, and a feeling of being part of "the largest knitter-run event in the world." The KIP website has suggestions for how to organize a KIP in your community, along with publicity ideas and materials. (See appendix for more information.)

Even when you're not part of an organized KIP event, however, there's no shame in knitting in public.

* Tanya Murphy, who knits in Washington State, likes to remember the many interesting conversations that have sprung up with perfect strangers when she's knit in public places.
* A favorite knitting memory of Michelle Carter, from Illinois, is knitting a sock on a park bench near the Eiffel Tower.
* California knitter Linda Price loves to knit and knits everywhere. She says, "My children accuse me of knitting while I drive, but that isn't true. I only knit at stoplights."

Have you ever knit in, at, or on any of the following places?

- Subway
- Bus
- Train
- Plane
- Taxi
- Car
- Motorcycle
- Restaurant
- Movies
- Opera
- Concert

- Theater
- Sports stadium
- Your kids' games
- Dentist
- Class
- Meetings at work
- Public park
- At the gym
- Walking
- Traffic jam
- Other

Parisian party. In a "flash mob" event, French knitters organized a knitting party in the Paris Métro.

Weaving in Ends

I have to admit that weaving in ends isn't my favorite part of a project, especially if there are a lot of them, and I know I'm not alone. Because I find it satisfying for my knitting to look neat while I'm working on it (and also because I dread not being truly finished when the actual knitting is finished), I often weave in the tails as I go. As with cast ons and bind offs, there's no one right way to handle joins, so it pays to have a variety of methods to choose from, depending on the yarn and the stitch pattern you're working with. Here are three approaches.

new yarn (working)

new yarn (tail)

old yarn (tail)

METHOD 1 (SEEN ON WRONG SIDE)

METHOD 1. When you need to start a new yarn, leave a 2- or 3-inch tail on both the old and the new yarns. As you begin knitting with the new yarn, catch in the tail of the old yarn by taking it under and over the working yarn at the back of the piece for the first four or five stitches. When you come back to the spot where you started the new yarn, weave in that tail in the same manner.

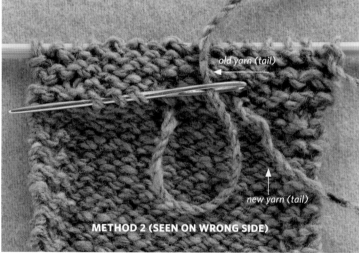

old yarn (tail)

new yarn (tail)

METHOD 2 (SEEN ON WRONG SIDE)

METHOD 2. You need slightly longer tails for this method: about 6 inches. Tie the two tails together just once so the knot lies against the fabric. (This is a temporary knot only. You're going to undo it later, and you want it to be easy to untie. See Jil Eaton: No Knots in

"We might knit that knot with our tongues that we shall never undoe with our teeth."

JOHN LYLY, *Euphues* (1579)

LEARN **JIL EATON: NO KNOTS IN KNITTING — EVER!**

Always leave a 6-inch tail when starting a new ball of yarn, and always weave ends in when finishing. Knots can come undone, either when your garment is being worn or when it's washed, leaving you with a hole that is impossible to fix.

Knitting — Ever!, below) Work a few stitches, then pull gently on both tails so the stitches at both sides of the join are neither too tight nor too loose: they should look just like the surrounding stitches. After you've knit two or three rows (or rounds) beyond the switch, undo the temporary tie; thread each yarn tail separately in a large-eyed, blunt-tip needle; and weave the ends along the back through several stitches in the same row, taking the old yarn forward along the row and the new yarn backward. Take care not to let the tails show on the right side. *Note:* Making the temporary knot is especially helpful with slippery yarns or very open patterns, but you may not need to tie off "toothier" yarns; simply knit subsequent rows, then gently tug the tails to even up the stitches, and weave them in as just described.

METHOD 3. A traditional, almost invisible method for joining wool yarn tails is by splicing, sometimes colorfully referred to as the "spit method." It is particularly useful in lace knitting, where it's often difficult to disguise woven-in ends. Spread out the fibers at the ends of each tail until you have enough length (1 or 2 inches) to allow you to break off about half the diameter of each end. (It's quite simple to do this if you're working with two-ply yarn: just remove 1 or 2 inches of one of the plies on both the new and the old yarns.) Next, overlap the ends where you've split them off so their combined thickness is about the same as that of the original yarn. Moisten the area of this splice (spit is not only the preferred moistener, but it's always at hand, after all), and rub the area rapidly between your palms to create heat and friction until the two ends are firmly joined.

LEARN BRANDON MABLY ON WEAVING IN

Brandon knits in the tail ends at the back of his work as he goes along, so he doesn't have to deal with them all at once when he's finished. (Weaving all those ends in with a tapestry needle is to be strongly avoided, he advises with a smile, "unless you have a maid to do it for you.") Since the two knitting techniques he favors are intarsia, for working blocks of color, and Fair Isle, repeating small areas of a color across the row, he works with both hands: with one hand he carries the yarn he's knitting with and controls its tension; with the other hand he holds the yarn that he's carrying at the back of the knitting. "When I'm working Fair Isle, I continue to carry the yarn across the row. When I'm working intarsia and will not be using the carried yarn again, I break it off after I've caught it with the working yarn along the back after I knit about four stitches. This way it is knitted in nice and tidy in the back, and on you go. It's what we call 'angst-free knitting!'" (Brandon describes and illustrates his method in his books; see the appendix for information.)

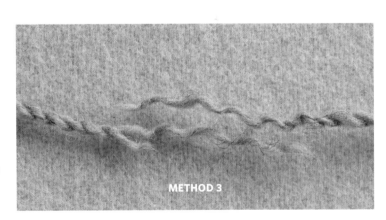

METHOD 3

TRAVEL BACK TO SCHOOL

School isn't just for kids. Knitters who are just as eager to learn new techniques as they are hungry for more time to knit have a wealth of opportunities to choose from.

Signing up for a weekend or weeklong workshop is also a terrific way to get an introduction to those sister crafts of dyeing, spinning, weaving, or any other fiber craft. (For retreats, see page 123; for websites for the following schools and events, see the appendix.)

CALIFORNIA

Golden Gate Fiber Institute

Bonita Point, San Francisco // August
Mendocino Art Center, Mendocino // throughout the year
Workshops on a variety of fiber arts, including surface design, spinning, and weaving

MINNESOTA

North House Folk School

Grand Marais // textile workshops in February and May
Traditional northern crafts such as timber framing, wooden boat building, basketry, woodworking, and various fiber crafts

Split Rock Arts Program

Minneapolis or Cloquet Forestry Center
The University of Minnesota's series of summer workshops and seasonal retreats

MISSOURI

Ozark School of Creative Arts

Joplin
Founded in the belief that everyone can be creative if given the time and space to grow artistically and spiritually; offers a variety of classes on knitting, as well as sewing, basketry, weaving, and other crafts.

NEW JERSEY

Peters Valley Craft Center

Layton // textile workshops May through September
Skills and core values of traditional craftsmanship and creative expression

NEW HAMPSHIRE

Harrisville Designs

Harrisville
Day- and week-long classes on a variety of fiber-related topics, including knitting, weaving, and dyeing year-round; students can stay in the nineteenth-century boarding house that is part of the historic mill complex.

NORTH CAROLINA

John C. Campbell Folk School

Brasstown
Founded in 1925; year-round classes in crafts, art, music, dance, cooking, gardening, nature studies, photography, and writing. Modeled after the Danish *folkehojskole* (folk school), founded by Nicholas Grundtvig in 1844, to preserve traditional crafts and emphasize "civic virtues, the ideas of the enlightenment, and lifelong learning." Knitting workshops include knitting socks and lace knitting, as well as creating a project from concept through dyeing to carrying out the design.

88 THE KNOW-HOW LIFE LIST

Penland School of Crafts

Blue Ridge Mountains

One-, two-, and eight-week workshops on books and paper, clay, drawing, glass, iron, metals, photography, printmaking and letterpress, textiles, and wood.

TENNESSEE

Arrowmont School of Arts and Crafts

Gatlinburg // May through October

Weekend, as well as one- and two-week sessions; areas of study include ceramics, fibers, metals/jewelry, painting, woodworking, and book and paper arts.

WASHINGTON

Nordic Knitting Conference

Seattle // time varies

Traditional Nordic designs and techniques are taught by Scandinavian and U.S. knitting experts in a three-day conference.

VANCOUVER, BRITISH COLUMBIA, CANADA

Jean Wong Course

Based on the Nihon Amimono Culture Association's program in Japan; offers five levels of instruction, which include classes on how to adapt or create your own patterns using yarns of your choice; upon completion of a four-year certified NAC course, the student is equipped to teach these unique techniques.

MY TRAVEL WISH LIST

LEARN FAVORITE GIFTS

A hand-knit gift often becomes a treasured belonging, and the process of knitting the gift and seeing the pleasure it gives the recipient can bring as much joy to the knitter as to the person who receives it.

Here are some thoughts and suggestions from a variety of designers, teachers, yarn-store owners, and knitters. (For more about most of these contributors, see Who's Who in This Community of Knitting Experts, page 290.) As they share what they most enjoy making for friends and family, you may get ideas and inspiration for your own next hand-knit gift. When you give someone a hand-knit present, be sure to include a note that describes the fiber content of the item and how to care for it.

SUSAN ANDERSON. There is no better gift out there for a newborn baby than a hand-knit item. Whatever it is will be treasured as an heirloom, saved, displayed, and hopefully passed on for generations to come. Some of my favorite knitted gift items for a newborn will come as no surprise. If you show up at a baby shower with one of these hand-knitted items, I guarantee your gift (and you) will be the hit of the day! Here are my top three hand-knit baby gift recommendations: (1) baby hat, (2) toy, (3) blanket.

DEBBIE BLISS. Even though I know they hardly ever stay on the foot, there's something so appealing about bootees, particularly if they have rabbit ears on them, too!

SANDY BLUE. I like to give handknits to shop owners who can use the item as a model for one of the yarns I represent. (Sandy is a yarn sales rep.) I particularly like to choose something that I've already made when an opportunity comes up to give it to a special friend — that takes the stress out of worrying about not finishing in time!

CAT BORDHI. For nearly all occasions my favorite gift is one of my felted Möbius baskets, for they mesmerize everyone from young children to the most jaded adult. (For more about Cat's Möbius creations, see page 159.)

GAIL CALLAHAN. Make a Christmas stocking for every new member of the family. This is the beginning of an important family tradition. I also recommend making toys, because they're small (therefore easily carried along), relatively inexpensive, and usually quick. But equally important, they allow you to practice so many techniques, including increases, decreases, and short rows.

JUDITH DURANT. I love to gift my knitting and beadwork.

For baby gifts, if I have enough advance notice, I almost always knit a receiving or christening blanket out of lace-weight yarn. I find many possibilities for the ground, including lace, textured, or slip stitches, and I always knit a decorative border. If I don't have enough time for a lace-weight blanket, I go with a thicker yarn and knit a mat that's meant to go between the baby and the floor. For heavier-weight yarns, I use domino, entrelac, intarsia — anything goes here!

For wedding gifts, if I'm familiar with the tastes and chosen décor of a bride and groom, knitted couch blankets and pillows are my gift of

choice. I especially enjoy it when a couple goes for shiny bright objects, such as beads, in their textiles. Pillows with beads look great, and if the beads are large enough, they can offer a little massage.

EDIE ECKMAN. I love to make hats for gifts. I'm a bit ADHD when it comes to knitting and crochet; I have to find something that keeps my attention long enough to finish it. With hats I can use up small amounts of beautiful yarn and experiment with color and stitch patterns without too much of a time commitment. Even better, if I start at the top of the crown and work in the round, I can increase just to the point where the hat circumference is big enough — without having to worry about a gauge swatch.

BEV GALESKAS. For a new baby I knit a blanket if there's time. It's a gift that is often passed on from one generation to the next. When I'm in a hurry, I go for a pair of my Felt Baby Shoes. For holiday gifts I like to give my Felt Clogs or other felt slippers.

KAY GARDINER. Although I dabble in almost every kind of knitting, when whimsy strikes,

I am always drawn back to knitting log cabin blankets — for gifts, for myself, and for when I just feel like knitting. I like the freeform way they are constructed, and I find that log cabin is such an open-ended, adaptable technique for graphic design. Since my blankets are often inspired by quilts and modern art, the straight lines of log cabin strips or blocks are not a hindrance, but an advantage. Recipients seem to love the blankets; they look new or "modern." I'm not sure that every new parent or bride is interested in knowing that their blanket was inspired by a Gee's Bend quilt or a Sean Scully painting, but I need to tell them anyway! Sometimes I even include a postcard of the inspiration textile or painting.

A recurring fantasy is that one of my blankets will appear on *Antiques Roadshow* in 2070, and the 2070 version of the Keno brothers will *freak out* when they recognize it for the priceless, one-of-a-kind textile that it will be by then. (Leigh Keno of 2070: "It seems to have some slight condition problems." Lesley Keno of 2070, "No, I think Kay did that with a bleach pen back in 2009. She was crazy for the bleach pen. That actually adds to the pricelessness. She was so awesome!")

VIVIAN HØXBRO. Because of time constraints, my gift knitting is pretty much limited to my grandchildren. When I was traveling, I knitted a special sweater for each grandchild using Koigu yarn in fun colors. Those sweaters were used until they were worn out. When I buy things for friends, I of course always think of the person I buy for. As all knitters know, when you put a lot of time and effort into a hand-knit gift, it's disappointing if the one who gets it doesn't use it. I like to talk to the person about it before I choose the project and yarn and then knit something

EXPLORE MEASURE FOR MEASURE

Gather the sizes and measurements of all your family members and friends who may be lucky enough to receive a handknit from you one of these days. Keep these measurements with your knitting supplies so they're easy to find when you discover the perfect yarn and just the right pattern for that special person. Stick to one form of measurement, however. Holly Abery-Wetstone, a knitter in Connecticut, shares a memory with a moral: she once measured a sweater she was knitting in inches, but the pattern was written in centimeters. The result, she said, was "sleeves down to my knees."

that my friend or relative will be proud of and love to wear.

When I design a gift, I think of different friends or persons I like. I then try to design something different depending on what will be best for each person: one idea for those who look great in naturals, another for those who love colors, and another for those who are "jeans people." In order to get the colors just right, I picture each person and imagine what would look great on her or him.

MARY MCGURN. I generally choose projects that require no specific measurements, which means that my husband is the only one who gets a sweater. For babies I opt for blankets; for adults, scarves and shawls. Now that cowls are popular and stylish, I've added them to my list of gifts to knit or crochet. Knitted soft, stuffed toys are also gaining favor with me. The patterns for knitted toys are so unique and captivating that they appeal to young and old. Adults who walk into our shop (Colorful Stitches, in Lenox, Massachusetts) often break into smiles when they pick up and hug our toy samples, so why not give toys, since the purpose of a gift is to bring joy?

MELISSA MORGAN-OAKES. My hand-knit gifts tend to be small things, like socks, scarves, hats, and mittens. I don't generally knit whole sweaters as gifts, except for babies.

MARGARET RADCLIFFE. I like to give yarn, frequently hand-spun, and needles, and sometimes copies of my patterns.

JULIE REED. Julie knits in Deer Isle, Maine. One of her best knitting memories is having an old friend tell her that socks she had given him so long ago that she'd forgotten she had knitted them were still his favorite thing in the world!

CHARLENE SCHURCH. I generally knit socks. Although this may seem like a somewhat pedestrian gift — we do walk on them — they tend to get used rather than saved.

KATHLEEN TAYLOR. Socks are my default project. I always have a pair (or three pairs) on the needles. I work on them during odd moments, or on trips, since socks are small and portable. No matter what pattern or yarn I am using, I can always count on them fitting someone on my recipient list. I also do a lot of knitting for my granddaughters' 18-inch dolls, which is a good way to use up leftover bits and pieces of sock yarn.

SANDI WISEHEART. I love to knit with hand-spun wool but use it for baby gifts only if I'm sure the gift will be appreciated for what it is.

MY GIFT LIST

◇ _____

_____

◇ _____

_____

◇ _____

_____

◇ _____

_____

Chapter 3

THE

Sweaters

LIFE LIST

If you're an experienced knitter with many sweaters already off your needles, I hope you'll enjoy the following brief trip through time and space that describes some of the most classic sweater styles and knitting techniques. Some of these you may already have tried, but others might still challenge you. If you're a new knitter, however, please do read on. There's quite a bit here for you as well.

When you're just learning to knit and still addicted to scarves, you might think knitting a sweater is far off in your future, but many experts think a sweater is the ideal first project for beginners. After all, reduced to its essentials — a back, a front, and two sleeves — a sweater is simply four different-size rectangles (what Meta Nesbitt, owner of Metaphor Yarns in Shelburne, Massachusetts, describes as "a bunch of scarves"). Sew these four pieces together, and you've got a very presentable sweater.

Once you have the basics under your belt, the sweater design menu is endless, from big, baggy, and comfortable to the latest fashion statement with an elegant fit. You can stitch your sweater in plain-but-reliable old garter stitch or in a lovely delicate lace. If you're in love with color, you can go for multiple-color patterns or, if complex texture is more your thing, a rhythmic dance of cables and bobbles. And those possibilities are just the tip of the iceberg.

Whether you prefer traditional or contemporary styles, plain and practical, or pure romance, it's clear that the inventiveness of knitters reaches one of its peaks in sweater design. A whole lot of creativity has gone into the construction and stitch combinations used for sweaters over time and places. Long-ago sweater knitters may have started out driven by the need to keep warm, but evolution being what it is, aesthetics insistently elbowed in, and pattern and color design took over in folk knitting everywhere.

No matter where you are in your knitting journey, with all these possibilities a sweater can be the perfect knitting "school," the place where you can practice and master all sorts of stitches and techniques. In fact, if you never knit anything but sweaters (not that I'm suggesting that!), you'd have a lifetime's worth of ideas to discover and explore. This chapter describes some traditional and contemporary sweater styles and designs to get you started.

"As for me, although I seem to be busy knitting this blue sweater, what I'm really doing is composing poems in my head, while my hands are occupied."

Kai Sijie, *Balzac and the Little Chinese Seamstress*

LEARN KRISTIN NICHOLAS ON LEARNING TO KNIT

Kristin suggests that knitting a yoke-style sweater in the round from the bottom up with chunky yarn is a great first project. Her reasoning: sweater knitting gives you a chance to accomplish many basic techniques, including ribbing and increases. Importantly, you also learn not to pull the yarn too tight when you're casting off the stitches that form the neckline! Then, when you're finished, you say, "Whoa, I made that myself," and you feel great! (For more about Kristin, see page 289.)

Sisters' sweaters. These colorful sweaters designed by Kristin Nicholas show off her palette as well as her signature embroidery. The sweater on the left features set-in sleeves; the one on the right is a yoke-style sweater.

MEET

- Beth Brown-Reinsel
- Alice Starmore
- Meg Swansen

DISCOVER

- Read "The Charge of the Light Brigade" and think "cardigan"!
- Read J. M. Synge's play *Riders to the Sea*
- Listen to the Clancy Brothers sing "The Work of the Weavers" (on *The Best of the Clancy Brothers and Tommy Makem*).
- Watch the film *The Quiet Man.*
- Read about Bohus knitting in Wendy Keele's *Poems of Color.*
- Read at least one of Elizabeth Zimmermann's books (and laugh and learn).
- Watch a DVD from Zimmermann's PBS television series.
- Discover Mary Thomas's work.
- Find a copy of June Hiatt's book.
- Meet James Norbury through his book.
- Explore French and German stitch pattern sources.
- Discover Japanese stitch patterns and designs.
- Learn about Herbert Niebling's lace work.

DO/TRY

- Knit a sweater with a yoke.
- Knit a pullover.
- Knit a cardigan.
- Knit a sweater with set-in sleeves.
- Knit a sweater with raglan sleeves.
- Knit a sweater with saddle shoulders.
- Knit a sweater with a scoop or jewel neck.
- Knit a sweater with a turtleneck.
- Knit a sweater with a crew neck.
- Knit a sweater with a V-neck.
- Knit a sweater with long sleeves.
- Knit a vest.
- Knit a "hoodie."
- Knit a kimono-style sweater.
- Knit a sweater with a shawl collar.
- Make a knitted coat.
- Knit a tailored jacket.
- Knit a tank top.
- Choose indigo yarn and knit a gansey.
- Knit an Austrian twisted-stitch sweater.
- Knit an Alice Starmore sweater featuring a classic Fair Isle design.
- Knit an Aran sweater using naturally cream-colored wool.
- Work a stranded Scandinavian pattern in red and white.
- Knit one of Beth Brown-Reinsel's traditional patterns.
- Work a Bohus pattern.
- Use a classic Icelandic wool yarn to work a typical sweater design.
- Work an Icelandic sweater in the round from the bottom up.
- Make an Icelandic cardigan using the steeking method.
- Knit the Baby Surprise Jacket.
- Use I-cords whenever you can.
- Work a typical Kaffe Fassett intarsia design.
- Design colorful button bands for a sweater.
- Contribute to the online Walker Treasury Project.

LEARN

- Learn to cast off loosely.
- Discover the meaning of gansey stitches.
- Design more complicated cables, with groups of stitches traveling under and over one another in a variety of paths.
- Learn to work reversible cables.
- Cable without using a cable needle.
- Make a 4-stitch-wide cable.
- Work a 2-stitch mock cable.
- Explore the differences among Swedish, Norwegian, and Danish patterns.
- Knit a sweater in the round, and then cut a steek to make a cardigan.

- Cut steeks for armholes in a sweater.
- Cut a steek for a sweater neckline.
- Work an afghan in the round and then steek it.
- Experiment with machine-stitched steeks.
- Try a crochet-style steek.
- Add a zipper to a steeked cardigan.
- Work a button band on a steeked cardigan.
- Work ribbing around a steeked armhole or neckline.
- Choose a retreat to learn a new technique.
- Use Elizabeth Zimmermann's percentages system (EPS).
- Use arm's length yarn pieces instead of bobbins or butterflies when working intarsia.
- Learn to "read" your knitting.

GO

- Visit the United Kingdom, including the Shetland Museum, in Lerwick, Shetland.
- Also in the UK, visit the Victoria and Albert Museum in London.
- Visit Scotland.
- Visit Ireland.
- Visit Norway, including the Museum of Norwegian Knitting Industry in Salhus.
- Visit Sweden, including the Bohus Museum in Uddevalla.

- Treat yourself to a retreat once a year.
- Combine knitting with another favorite activity when you travel to your retreat.
- Make a retreat a special travel opportunity.
- Take your daughter/mother/best friend with you on your retreat.
- Sign up for Meg Swansen's Knitting Camp.

EXPERIENCE

- Knit in the round on circular needles.
- Design your own sweater pattern.
- Use a long-tail cast on to begin a project.
- Join shoulder (or other) seams with a three-needle bind off.
- Knit multicolor designs working with one (or more) colors in each hand.
- Add a band of Fair Isle patterning to a plain sweater design.
- Work a sweater from the top down.
- Work a sweater from the bottom up.
- Knit a sweater from side to side.
- Knit a sweater based on panels or modules.
- Knit sweater pieces (front, back, sleeves, for instance) on straight needles ("flat").

- Knit the whole sweater on circular needles ("in the round").
- For a top-down project, check your gauge after completing the neck.
- Adjust for size as you knit from the top down.
- Take photographs to inspire your color choices.
- Explore slip-stitch patterns for mosaic knitting.
- Don't be afraid to rip out.
- Swatch one pattern a week from a Barbara Walker stitch dictionary.
- Explore Meg Swansen's and Elizabeth Zimmermann's tricks and tips.

EXTRA CREDIT

- How did raglan and cardigan sweaters get their names?

MORE FOR MY SWEATERS LIFE LIST

- _____
- _____
- _____
- _____

The Journey Begins

Every time you consider a new project, whether it's a sweater, socks, a scarf, or a hat, you bump up against at least four important design decisions:

* Where to start — in other words, whether to knit from the top or the bottom, work from side to side, from the center out, or by turning corners as you knit
* Basic style and stylistic details
* Surface design and texture
* Yarn!

Although no one of these decisions necessarily comes first, they're obviously interrelated, so once you commit to a particular approach, yarn, or stitch pattern, that decision places limits on the other elements. If you fall in love with a yarn, its characteristics determine its use: you probably wouldn't work a lacy sweater in a fat, fuzzy yarn, for instance, unless you wanted to try for some special effects.

When it comes to deciding on the color (or colors) and stitch pattern of your sweater project, you face what is most addictive about knitting: yarn, the seductive Siren that keeps us coming back for more. Sometimes you fall for the color or feel of a yarn before you have any idea what you're going to make with it, but its characteristics will determine many of your stylistic decisions. On the other hand, if you need a cozy cabled sweater for the coldest days or a dressy sheer one for summer evenings, you'll go looking for yarns that work for the purpose you have in mind. For a rundown of fibers and yarns, see chapter 1, The Yarn Life List, beginning on page 13.

DID YOU KNOW — CARDIGANS AND RAGLANS: WHAT'S IN A NAME?

How strange that such "comfort clothing" as a cardigan sweater gets its name from a far-from-comforting source. James Brudenell, seventh Earl of Cardigan, was the British commander who led his troops into ill-fated combat with the Russians in the Crimean War. (The battle is the subject of Tennyson's poem "The Charge of the Light Brigade.") The button-down-the-front uniforms of the soldiers in his brigade inspired the name of the sweater.

Another sweater style was named for the earl's commanding officer, Fitzroy James Henry Somerset, Lord Raglan. After the loss of his arm in the Battle of Waterloo, Lord Raglan had his tailor design a jacket with a sleeve seam that ran diagonally from the neck to the underarm, making it easier for Raglan to put on his jacket without help.

Elements of Style

Do you need a pullover or a cardigan? Should it have set-in or raglan sleeves? Which works, a sleek look or a loosely casual fit? What about the neck: jewel, crew-, or turtleneck? Should the sweater be waist length or knee length? Are you going for a traditional style, or do you gravitate toward a contemporary take on classic design?

The choice is yours, of course, but don't get stuck in a rut when it comes to sweater styles. If you just finished knitting a pullover sweater, start a cardigan next. Look for an unusual neck treatment, or make a "hoodie." Here's a mix-and-match selection of those and other sweater elements to get you started. For advice on creating your own pattern, see Ann Budd's *The Knitter's Handy Book of Sweater Patterns*, which provides six templates for designing your own sweater.

PULLOVER WITH TURTLENECK
AND DROP SHOULDER

PULLOVER WITH CREW NECK
AND RAGLAN SLEEVES

PULLOVER WITH V-NECK

PULLOVER WITH SADDLE
SHOULDERS

SLEEVELESS
VEST

PULLOVER WITH SHAWL COLLAR

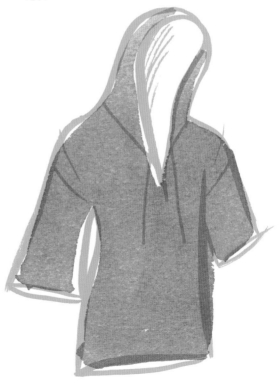

HOODIE

COAT WITH HOOD

PULLOVER WITH SCOOP
NECK

CARDIGAN JACKET

TANK TOP

KIMONO STYLE

ASYMMETRICAL CLOSURE

DOUBLE-BREASTED

WRAP FRONT

From the Top: Not Always!

You can knit sweaters from the top down, the bottom up, or, what's less conventional but can produce interesting results, from side to side. You can also build your fabric in modular units or panels that give you even more design freedom (see Modular Madness, page 249). You can knit the pieces for front, back, and sleeves separately on straight needles and sew them all together when you're finished, or you can use circular needles and knit the sweater "in the round," so you have very little stitching together to do at the end. Even cardigans can be knit in the round. The opening is created by cutting right up the front when you're finished, a process known as "steeking" (for how this is done, see No-Fear Steeking, page 118). The contemporary designers Norah Gaughan and Debbie New are particularly adept at devising new ways to approach sweater design.

You'll discover that many classic sweater styles, such as ganseys and Arans, are characterized not only by the direction the sweater is knit in, but also the style of the yoke or sleeves and so on. Modern sweater design isn't tied to these criteria, however, and even the early twentieth-century Bohus sweaters were sometimes knit from side to side.

LEARN SEAMLESSLY PERFECT SWEATERS

Blogger and shop owner Susan Sarabasha believes every knitter should make both a bottom-up and a top-down sweater, but she's especially enthusiastic about the top-down approach for several reasons. For one thing, you can make sure your gauge is correct while you're still at the neck, and adjust the pattern for fit as you work down, increasing, if necessary, as you go. When you get to the point where the sleeves begin, you put those stitches on holders until you finish the body, then complete the sleeves, too, on circulars. The only seams are relatively short ones under the arms. Perfect fit, nearly seamless construction!

Designer and publisher Bev Galeskas, too, finds the seamless approach the most intriguing knitting technique. As she explains, "Planning seamless shaping and construction with short rows, increases, decreases, and so on, is great brain exercise."

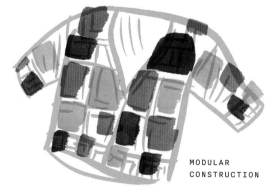

MODULAR CONSTRUCTION

KNIT SIDE TO SIDE

LEARN A GOOD BEGINNING AND A FINE ENDING

LONG-TAIL CAST ON. There are lots of ways to cast on, but for Pam Allen nothing beats the long-tail method. Also called, among other things, the continental cast on, the long tail provides a sturdy, even edge.

When you knit designs with simple edges, she explains, "You can't have a loose cast on. That little detail is really important."

THREE-NEEDLE BIND OFF. Pam is also a huge fan of the three-needle bind off at the shoulders. In this method you bind off front and back shoulder edges of a sweater or vest simultaneously, joining them as you go, so you don't need to stitch the seams together later.

Hold both needles in your left hand with the tips facing to the right and the two layers of fabric (back and front, for instance) with their right sides facing. (In most cases, the fabric is held this way, with right sides together, but some designers make a decorative element out of the shoulder seam by working this bind off with wrong sides held together. The seam in this case is on the outside.)

Insert the empty needle into the first stitch on the front needle, and go right on through to the first stitch on the back needle, as if to knit. Wrap the yarn as usual, draw the loop through both stitches, and let the stitches drop off the needles. Repeat for the next stitch on each needle, then take the first stitch knit on the right-hand needle over the second stitch (as in a normal bind off). Proceed across the row (or round) until one stitch remains, then fasten it off.

Tip: Be sure that any design features, such as cables or stripes, match perfectly before you proceed with this bind off.

Three-needle bind off. Here, the bind-off shows at the right, as a decorative feature of the garment. Hold the needles parallel, wrong sides of the knit fabric facing. (Here, several stitches have already been bound off, so there is one stitch on the right-hand needle as this step begins.) Insert a third needle into the first stitches on both the front and back left-hand needles (A).

Knit these two stitches together (B). Complete the bind off of these stitches by drawing the stitch already on the right-hand needle over the new stitch, just as you do in a "normal" bind off (B).

Folk Sweater Classics

Although sweater styles come and go, many classic designs always seem to be popular, perhaps tweaked a bit to suit current taste. Some contemporary designers have made specialties of traditional styles, often interpreting them for a twenty-first-century look. The reason a style developed in its distinctive way is often a fascinating story that can make knitting — and wearing — the garment extra special. In her book *Knitting in the Old Way,* Priscilla Gibson-Roberts provides a fascinating history of traditional sweater design. Not surprisingly, some of the most popular sweater styles have developed from folk designs characteristic of many cold-winter regions around the world. Those that have been particularly influential are sweaters from the British Isles and from Scandinavian countries. (See the appendix for the designers who have created patterns for sweaters in the styles discussed in this chapter, and for books and other resources that specialize in them.)

Ganseys of the Channel Islands

According to Beth Brown-Reinsel, who has studied, taught, and written about historical knitting traditions for more than 20 years, there was a knitting industry on Great Britain's Isle of Guernsey as early as the 1500s. Until the nineteenth century, however, most knitting was done for undergarments. In fact, according to a curator at the Bata Shoe Museum in Toronto, Ontario, once Queen Elizabeth experienced wearing luxurious Spanish silk socks, she swore off her linen hose. Another legend has it that Mary, Queen of Scots, wore a pair of white

SWATCHING | *gansey*

Mood indigo. Purled stitches on a stockinette-stitch background form a classic chevron design framed by typical seed-stitch borders. This swatch is knit with hand-dyed indigo yarn.

guernsey stockings to her execution. (The terms *guernsey* and *jersey* referred to the stockinette stitch fabric that was made at that time.) The earliest written record we have of a gansey sweater is 1832, most likely worked in plain stockinette stitch.

Gansey sweaters are knitted in the round, typically with indigo blue yarn, and characterized by their square shape and fitted wrists and waists. The tradition of making these "fisherman's" sweaters spread north to Scotland, where the stitch patterns became increasingly complex. The whole idea was to create sweaters that would keep the wearers warm and dry, and both the tightly spun worsted yarn and the cables and other stitch patterns that covered the surface did just that. The patterns were often symbols of the sea, fish, weather, or parts of a ship.

A trio of Ganseys. These three young fishermen from Burra, the collective name for two of the Shetland Islands off the northeast coast of Scotland, proudly wear their traditional gansey sweaters.

Fair Isle Stitch Patterns

Fair Isle sweaters get their name from the place where they originated, an island that is part of Shetland, but located about halfway between the biggest island of Shetland and the northernmost part of the Orkney Islands. (Both the Shetlands and the Orkneys are part of Scotland.) Fair Isle sweaters may owe their rise in popularity to Edward, Prince of Wales, who favored them in the 1920s.

Like ganseys, Fair Isle sweaters are worked in the round, but they are knit in multiple colors using a technique known as "stranded knitting," in which different-colored yarns are interchanged across a row to create intriguing graphic designs. The yarn not in use is carried loosely across the back of the fabric, then periodically caught up by the working yarn before again coming into use. Traditional Fair Isle patterns have a limited palette of five or so colors, but what distinguishes them from many other stranded knitting designs is that in Fair Isle no more than two colors are worked in any one row.

One of the best arguments for learning to knit holding the working yarn in either your left or your right hand is that you will be able to work a Fair Isle sweater more easily and quicker: you don't have to pause to pick up a different yarn each time you have to change colors. (For two-handed knitting, see What Style Knitter Are You? page 64.)

It's possible to knit Fair Isle flat, working back and forth on straight needles in stockinette stitch. For this method, you must follow the Fair Isle chart from right to left on right-side rows and left to right on wrong-side rows. It's much easier, however, to work on circular needles in the round, so that you're always working on the right side (reading the chart from right to left) and can therefore watch the pattern develop. If you want a cardigan, you cut the piece up the middle after the knitting is completed, a process called steeking. (See page 118.) Steeking is a technique that did not originate in the Shetlands, however, and knitters there do not favor it. In fact, when they use the term "steek," they are referring to something entirely different: the line of increases or decreases at the center back of a shawl.

SWATCHING | *Fair Isle*

Exploring colors with Fair Isle. Designing Fair Isle patterns is fertile ground for experimenting with color palettes and breaking out of your color comfort zone. It's also fun to make a break from tradition and explore more contemporary yarn weights and color combinations. Notice that although this swatch uses several colors, there are never more than two colors on any one row (or round) of stitching.

Sweater girl. Swedish-born actress Ingrid Bergman wears a Fair Isle sweater in this photo from about 1945.

Royal influence. Edward, Prince of Wales, seemed to love wearing V-neck, Fair Isle knitted vests, and so from his lead, the style caught on in the 1920s.

Twisted-Stitch Knitting of Austria

Garments knitted in the eighteenth century in the Enns River valley near Salzburg represent a distinctive folk style of knitting. The basic knit and purl stitches are purposely twisted by knitting into the backs of the stitches. The traveling stitches (stitches that cross over the background in infinite variety) have a twist that makes them stand out. Garments knit in this style, usually in 100 percent wool with a firm twist, are sturdy and long-wearing. *Twisted-Stitch Knitting: Traditional Patterns & Garments from the Styrian Enns Valley*, by Maria Erlbacher, is a collection of three booklets containing stitch patterns and patterns for garments. A cautionary note in the introduction warns that after they've been crossed by the traveling stitches, purl stitches sometimes become knit stitches, and vice versa, and therefore the knitter should "remain alert" — so true!

SWATCHING | *Twisted-Stitch*

Twisting for total texture. Garments made by Austrian knitters were composed of many different stitch patterns, resulting in extremely complex, beautifully textured fabrics. The stitch patterns bore wonderfully descriptive names, such as "Rooster Steps," "Forgotten Love," and "Ear of Wheat."

MEET ALICE STARMORE

RISING EACH MORNING ON THE ISLE OF LEWIS, Scotland, where she was born and still lives, Alice Starmore checks on her Highland cattle, a ritual she calls the "perfect way to start the day."

"Not only is it life affirming, but it also brings me close to nature, the land, the sea, the sky, and all the creatures thereon," says Alice. A little while later she's on to the tasks of the day, a list of which has recently included everything from working on knitting designs and teaching workshops to filming for a BBC program on natural dyeing and meetings involving her yarn and graphic design companies.

"With me, it is a case of design, design, design. It's a driving force. I love clothes, and I like to have something interesting to knit and something special to wear, so I regularly design for myself, for family, or for artistic purposes."

"It may seem that my various activities are disparate, but they are not at all," she explains. "Everything is closely related. When I am working on my croft [a small farm with a tradition of self-sufficiency and hospitality]; or taking photographs; or studying wildlife; or taking people on nature walks; or preparing classes for children; or walking hills, moors, and coastlines; or visiting London or the Louvre, I am doing what every creative person does — absorbing inspiration and allowing ideas to form. It is a crucial part of the process that ends up in a piece of art or design."

Alice is widely considered an authority on Fair Isle and Aran design and technique; she also broke new ground with her book *The Celtic Collection,* using Celtic art as a theme for knitting. Among her many books are the classics *Alice Starmore's Book of Fair Isle Knitting* and *Aran Knitting,* both of which have been recently reissued. She has her own yarn company, Virtual Yarns, and a graphic design company, Windfall Press. Her professional career also includes photography; she focuses on the natural world. She is also an expert on Scottish moorland habitats.

She began working with photography as a child, when she received a box Brownie camera. "I have never stopped since that day," says Alice, although she now uses digital photography extensively. "Photography is my third eye, and I use cameras in every area I work in. I use them constantly to take photographs of anything I may find visually inspirational, and that inspiration may well end up in part, or in whole, in a textile design form."

She finds much inspiration in nature. "Though a lot of my work in the natural world involves close and acute study, my approach when designing is quite different. I establish some kind of theme and allow the inspirations to soak in and percolate in my mind. I work from my own memories and impressions, and I really enjoy seeing what comes out in terms of shape, form, texture, and color when I draw up an idea."

Classic Irish Arans

Aran sweaters are associated with the Galway Bay islands off the west coast of the Irish mainland in the early twentieth century. Patterns were first published in England in the 1940s by the Patons yarn company. Elizabeth Zimmermann wrote an Aran sweater pattern for *Vogue Knitting* in 1958, the first time one was knitted and photographed for an American magazine. (Although Zimmermann provided the instructions for knitting the sweater in the round, as was traditional for Aran sweaters and was also her preferred way of knitting sweaters, the publisher revised the pattern so it could be knit back and forth on straight needles.)

Like ganseys, Arans have a square shape and are famous for their organic textures resulting from bobbles, cables, and other stitch combinations. Unlike the indigo blue ganseys from other parts of the British Isles, however, Arans are worked in cream-colored, undyed yarn called *bainin*. Much of the natural oil in this yarn is purposely left in the fleece during processing to make garments that are knit with it warmer and more water resistant.

Two imaginatively romantic notions about Aran stitch patterns, unfortunately, have to be exposed as untrue. Until recently, it was commonly believed that the stitch patterns were handed down from mother to daughter over generations, and symbolized various themes related to nature, the sea, and spirituality. One plaited cable pattern, for instance, was said to represent the complexity of family life and diamond-shaped patterns (like a fishing net) to symbolize success. The more likely truth, however, is that the names and their meanings were developed by Heinz Edgar Kiewe, a German visitor to Ireland in the 1930s, who published a book on his theories in the 1960s.

A tradition maintained. A woman knits an Aran sweater in her cottage on Inishmaan Island, one of the main Aran Islands in Galway Bay on the west coast of Ireland.

DID YOU KNOW CARRYING ON THE TRADITION

High-quality, authentic Aran sweaters are still being created and sold in Ireland. One source is ÓMáille's store, founded in 1938 in Galway. In 1951 the shop supplied the sweaters for the cast of the film *The Quiet Man,* starring John Wayne and Maureen O'Hara. The current generation of ÓMáille's employs 170 knitters from Connemara, west Clare, and north Mayo, who use the traditional yarns and designs to create sweaters and other items. One young American tourist was recently advised against buying a V-neck cardigan, because this was considered an old man's style; he was told that at his age he should wear only a pullover. Tradition is a serious matter in Ireland!

I love a parade!
This two-year-old Irish-American shows off her beautiful Irish sweater and beret, marching along in the annual St. Patrick's Day parade in New York City.

It's also true that although some legends hold that fishermen lost at sea and then found wearing a gansey or an Aran sweater could be identified by the stitch patterns typical of the village or even the specific knitter who made the sweater, this notion, too, is now considered myth. However, it was used by the playwright J. M. Synge as part of the plot in his 1904 play *Riders to the Sea*, in which the sister of a drowned man recognizes him by a dropped stitch in his knitted socks. Exploding these notions of historical tradition does nothing to detract from the well-deserved popularity of this lovely knitting style.

> SWATCHING | *Aran*

The look of the Irish. This small swatch demonstrates two commonly used Aran stitch patterns: in the center, Twisted Tree, a variation of Tree of Life, is sometimes said to represent stages of life. Honeycomb, which flanks Tree of Life, is often repeated side by side, creating the look of a lattice or net. Some knitters like to think of this pattern as a symbol of good luck. Although Aran stitch patterns can certainly be worked in colors other than white, the most traditional yarn is unbleached wool.

An Irish brand. The Clancy Brothers, who popularized Irish folk music in the United States in the 1960s, regularly wore their iconic Aran sweaters in concerts. Some of their recordings feature fiber-related activities, such as weaving and spinning.

LEARN CAPABLE WITH CABLES

Cables provide an impression of muscularity, and because of their density, they contribute actual warmth to a fabric as well. They are important features of both gansey and Aran knitting.

One of the simplest versions consists of four stitches that cross in pairs every six rows. If they always cross in the same direction, the effect is of a simple twist, much like cabled roping. The stitches that form the cable are usually set off from the rest of the pattern against a background of reverse stockinette, one or two stitches wide. But that simple version is only the beginning of the story. Multiple sets of stitches can be carried over and under one another in any direction, creating intricate swirls and knots in infinite variety. Designer and author Janet

Szabo has made cables, especially those in Aran knitting, a specialty. (For her books, see the appendix.)

CABLING WITHOUT A CABLE NEEDLE. If you dislike fiddling with a cable needle, take a deep breath and learn to cable without one. Don't try it (at least, at first) with cables of more than four stitches or with slippery yarn. And it's best to have had some experience with cabling the traditional way. Here's an example of one way to make a 4-stitch left-slanting cable:

Slip the first two stitches purlwise onto your right-hand needle, then knit the next two stitches. Working on the front, insert your left-hand needle into the two slipped stitches from left to right. As the slipped stitches become seated on the left-hand needle, allow the two just-knit stitches to drop off the right-hand needle. Then, moving your work and the needles as little as possible, quickly slip the dropped stitches back onto the right-hand needle. Finish the left-cross cable by knitting the two slipped stitches.

SWATCHING | *Cables*

Cabling potential. A robust 6-stitch cable is flanked by two 2-stitch mock cables. The mock cables are created by knitting first into the second stitch on the left-hand needle and then into the first, which draws the second stitch over the first. In a variation of this stitch, some knitters knit 2 stitches together, leave them on the needle, then knit the first stitch again before sliding both off the needle.

Let it snow! This swatch features both the traditional colors, red and white, and one of the classic design elements of Scandinavian knitting, the snowflake.

The Scandinavian Countries

The familiar bold graphic stars and snowflakes are just some of the motifs used in Scandinavian folk knits, which date from the mid-nineteenth century, probably originating in Selbu, Norway. Like Fair Isle designs, these patterns are created using the stranded knitting technique. Because the yarns not in use are carried along on the wrong side, the sweaters are thicker and warmer than fabrics knit with just one yarn would be.

Beth Brown-Reinsel, who has made traditional knitting a specialty, points out that Swedish knitters usually knit with only two or three colors, one of which is almost always red. Unlike the soft yarns worked on largish needles that many Americans favor, Scandinavian style calls for a yarn with a high twist, which gives greater definition to stitches — the better to see the lovely patterns of those stranded knits. As Beth notes, the garments firmly knit with these high-twist yarns are meant to last, so the knitter's valuable time has not been wasted.

Swedish hospitality. On a cold, dark Scandinavian afternoon, what could be more welcome than a hot cup of cocoa and some heart-shaped cinnamon cookies, all in a color palette of warm red and white.

MORE FOR MY CLASSIC SWEATERS LIFE LIST

◇ _____

◇ _____

Twentieth-Century Classics

Two popular styles that most people think of as classics were relatively new twentieth-century developments: Bohus and Icelandic knitting. Bohus *stickning* (knitting) was developed as a cottage industry in Sweden during the Great Depression. Icelandic can be recognized by the soft, loosely spun yarn with which the sweaters, hats, and mittens are knit; this style, too, originated in the early part of the last century.

Swedish Bohus Designs

Bohus Stickning was founded and operated by Emma Jacobsson in the 1930s and 1940s in southwestern Sweden. This cottage industry provided extra income for the local women during the Great Depression. At first the women produced practical socks and mittens, but as the business developed and the economy improved, they created sweaters and other garments for sale internationally in boutiques and other high-end outlets. The designs were not at first intended to be reproduced by hand knitters outside the cooperative, and in fact Mrs. Jacobsson stipulated that the patterns not be published until 50 years after her death. Wendy Keele's *Poems of Color: Knitting in the Bohus Tradition* provides the history of this remarkable woman and her commitment to her vision, along with instructions and charts for many of the most popular designs. Bohus Stickning sweaters are characterized by the fine angora-blend yarns worked in an array of carefully chosen colors, with as many as 15 shades in a garment and 5 colors carried along in a single row or round. In addition to the colorwork, purl stitches strategically placed on the right side of the mostly stockinette-stitch fabric provide striking accents in the patterning — and also add to the interesting challenge of knitting the sweater. The swatch below is a simplified adaptation of Bohus design and technique, using multiple, closely related colors and purl stitches accenting the stranded pattern work on the right side.

SWATCHING *Bohus*

Bohus inspired. Although classic Bohus knitting is done with very fine angora-blend yarns of multiple colors, this swatch captures the spirit with its soft blend of shades, textured with purl stitches spotted on the smooth stockinette. The purl "bumps" also bring two colors to the surface in one stitch, contributing to the blended effects.

Icelandic

Icelanders have a knitting tradition that goes back to at least the sixteenth century, although the characteristic Icelandic sweater we think of today is a twentieth-century development. These warm sweaters have circular yokes and patterned cuffs and borders, often worked in natural whites, grays, and browns, although dyed yarns are also available. Lopi yarn is unspun (roving) or very lightly spun, because the individual fibers (staple) of the fleece used for this yarn are so long that little twist is needed to ensure the yarn's strength. The hardy, long-haired sheep that bear this handsome fleece have been bred in Iceland for more than a thousand years. The sweater body and sleeves are generally knit in the round from the bottom up, then joined so the yoke can be knit circularly as well; cardigans are created by steeking.

Shades of difference. Many Icelandic designs use only the lovely range of natural colors of the fleece; here I've slipped in a couple of dyed yarns as well.

A fine marriage. The evolution that has led to the smooth, long-fibered fleece borne by Icelandic sheep is a perfect partner for the bold graphics of typical Icelandic knitwear.

MEET SANDI WISEHEART

SANDI WISEHEART DESCRIBES HERSELF AS an avid knitter, spinner, and beader who forays into crochet, weaving, sewing, quilting, and . . . In other words, she's totally passionate about the fiber arts, and she has generously shared her passion (what she calls being a "craft enabler") with very appreciative others through her writing and teaching. Founding editor of Interweave's online magazine Knitting Daily (KD), she now regularly contributes to KD with "What's on Sandi's Needles." She also blogs at Wiseheart Knits and is active on Ravelry.

Much of Sandi's professional life has been devoted to building community in the fiber world.

Although spinning may be her first true love (when she can't sleep at night, she gets up and spins), she admits that her knitting what's-next list is long and "probably more than I can knit in the next five years." With so many possibilities to try, she doesn't like to knit the same thing twice but remembers that one of her favorite projects was Evelyn Clark's popular lace shawl, Flower Basket. She also loves cables.

Through her workshops, Sandi enjoys helping knitters solve problems, especially customizing patterns for a better fit. She worries that knitters "too often have a 'ready-to-wear' mentality" and points out that if someone else drafted a pattern, you can't expect that it will fit your own body perfectly. She advises that we learn to make appropriate changes in patterns so that all our efforts result in "things we can be proud of." Sandi's trusty right-hand girl

Bertha has for many years assisted her in ensuring a good fit for everything she designs and knits. In the photo at the left, Bertha stands next to Sandi, modeling her popular lace Summer Shawlette, knit in cashmere. "What's not to love?" Sandi says with a grin.

One of her many current projects is knitting with handspun collected from spinners all over the world who read her blog. It's hard to underestimate the thrill and sense of a loving community that one would get from whatever comes off her needles some day! In her words,

What we make is who we are, our own stories spun into every yarn, our own hearts in every stitch. As knitters, crocheters, spinners, and weavers, we create community the same way we create a blanket: one very human yarn at a time. What knitter can show off a newly completed sweater without telling her audience where the yarn came from or who the sweater is for? What spinner can resist sharing the name of the sheep whose wool she is spinning or the dreams she has for what the yarn might become? And in the handweaving community, people laugh about 'the weaver's handshake': When two weavers meet, their hands reach out to gently finger the handwoven cloth the other is wearing, even before a verbal introduction is made. The cloth one weaves and wears instantly tells another weaver so much more than a first and last name ever could. The yarns that make up the work of our hands tell our stories — and we hunger not only to hear these stories, but to weave them together in a fabric made of human hearts.

LEARN NO-FEAR STEEKING

Steeking crops up in a number of different knitting traditions. If you hear it casually described as cutting up the center of a just-knit pullover to create a cardigan, for instance, you'll probably cringe. But knitters have perfected techniques for executing this action that are perfectly safe, and the benefits for the approach are many.

For example, if you're following a stranded-knitting chart (or making up your own design as you knit, for that matter), it's far easier to work the entire piece with the right side facing you, both so you can observe the pattern as it develops, and also so you don't have to switch your thinking from working right to left on one chart row to working from left to right on the next. In addition to steeking the center front of a sweater, you can also steek the armholes and the neckline. Kristin Nicholas is so in favor of steeks that she sometimes uses them to knit afghans and scarves in the round. In fact, trying out the technique for the first time on a scarf width is a relatively safe place to practice.

If your project pattern is set up for steeking, it will include a section of stockinette steek stitches (usually five to nine), in the center of which you will later cut the steek. The steek section is often worked in one-stitch stripes or in a checkerboard, which makes it easy to identify the columns of stitches when you are stabilizing and then cutting the steek. You might want to mark the beginning and the end of the steek stitches with stitch markers.

When your knitting is complete, first block the piece (see page 83), and allow it to dry. There are a number of methods for securing your stitches before cutting your steek. Here are instructions for a machine-stitched method as well as a crochet technique.

Machine-Stitched Steek

Identify the two columns of stitches in the center of the steek. To stabilize these stitches, which become the edge stitches after cutting, machine stitch (zigzag) along each of these the two columns of stitches. Next, straight stitch in the "ditch" between the pattern and steek stitches on both sides of the steek. Once all the stitches are secured, use sharp scissors to carefully cut up the middle between the two columns of zigzag stitches. You now have a seam allowance from the edge to the line of straight stitches.

FOR A ZIPPER. If your sweater has a zipper, turn back the seam allowances along the straight stitching, pin, then stitch the zipper in place.

Machine-stitched steek. Use your sewing machine to run lines of zigzag stitching along the two center columns of stitches in the steek. Next, run a line of straight stitches along the "ditch" between the steek stitches and the pattern stitches. Finally, use sharp scissors to cut the strands of yarn between the columns of zigzag stitches.

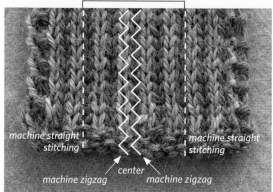

area of steek

machine straight stitching

machine straight stitching

center

machine zigzag

machine zigzag

FOR RIBBING OR BUTTON BAND. If you are adding ribbing or other finish for a button band at the center front or to finish off the armholes, turn back the seam allowances and pick up and knit the stitches along the straight stitching. (Be sure to pick up both strands of each stitch.)

To finish, overcast the raw edges of the steek. For extra security add a second line of overcast in the opposite direction from the first to ensure that no strands of yarn come loose. As wool garments are worn and laundered, this edge will felt slightly, further securing it.

Crochet-Style Steek

For this method you need a length of all-wool scrap yarn and a crochet hook one or two sizes smaller than the size knitting needles you used for the item. Hold the knitted piece so the columns are oriented horizontally (rows are vertical). Identify the column at the center of the steek.

Beginning at the far right edge, insert the crochet hook through one leg of a stitch in the center column and one leg of the stitch in the adjacent column. Pull through a loop of the scrap yarn; yarn over and pull through a loop. *Insert the hook through one leg of the next stitch to the left in the center column and through one leg of the stitch in the adjacent column. Yarn over and draw the yarn through both loops on the hook. Repeat from * to other end of steek. This completes a row of single crochet.

Turn the item 180 degrees. Again beginning at the far right edge, repeat the row of single crochet using the second half of the stitches in the center column just crocheted along with the other half of the adjacent stitches. Work the entire length of the steek.

With a pair of sharp scissors, cut the strands of knitting between the rows of single crochet, taking care not to cut any of the yarn used for the crochet.

Install the zipper or pick up for a button band or other finish as described for machine-stitched steeks, then overcast the crocheted edges to secure them to the inside of the fabric.

Crocheted steek. Using scrap yarn, single crochet along the center of the steek, picking up one leg of the center stitches along with one leg of the adjacent stitches (note the different-colored yarns on the hook) to make each crochet stitch. Turn your fabric and single crochet along the same center stitches, this time taking the other half of the center stitches along with the adjacent stitches (A). When the entire steek is secured, use sharp scissors to cut the strands of yarn between the two columns of crochet stitches (B).

Designing Legends

Today's knitters are blessed with a broad and inspiring selection of patterns from a long (and ever growing!) list of talented designers. When we polled a large group of knitters, designers, and yarn-store owners for the names of designers who have made a special impact not only on style but also on knitters' attitudes to their craft, however, three names were mentioned repeatedly: Elizabeth Zimmermann (sometimes affectionately referred to as EZ), Kaffe Fassett, and Barbara Walker. In different ways the work of each of these three has had an enormous impact on the way we approach knitting.

Knitting Without Tears: EZ's Legacy

Even if today's knitters recognize Elizabeth Zimmermann's name, many may be unaware of the really enormous legacy her attitudes and ideas have had on our favorite pastime. One knitter may know about EZ's famous Baby Surprise Jacket (see page 229); another can tell you where the term (and technique) "I-cord" came from (see page 187). Probably most important, however, was the encouragement Elizabeth gave all knitters to break out, knit because it's fun, and be creative in your own way.

Her books continue to be a reading joy, not only because of the many valuable tips and techniques they offer, but also simply because of her delightfully encouraging voice and quirky sense of humor. She's said to be to knitting what Julia Child was to cooking. Being successful and at the same time enjoying yourself as a knitter is often as simple as recognizing what can be fudged as opposed to when some detail is critically important and, yes, you'd better rip out and fix that mistake. Elizabeth Zimmermann's advice often helps us distinguish between these two options.

One of the most valuable of her legacies is her "percentages" system (EPS), a mathematical formula that helps you determine the number of stitches to cast on for a sweater. The formula is based on the idea that the sleeves and body are usually proportionate no matter what yarn or gauge is used.

"Knit one, purl two,
This sweater, my darling's, for you."

GLENN MILLER
(SHEET MUSIC, C. 1942)

A Kaleidoscope of Color: Kaffe Fassett

Kaffe Fassett is sometimes introduced as a "rock star" of knitting, and indeed his richly colored designs took the knitting world by storm in the 1980s. In 1988 the Victoria and Albert Museum in London mounted a show of his work, the first time a living textile artist received such an honor. He explains that his interest in knitting was sparked when he visited a textile mill in Scotland; on that trip he delighted in the colors of the Scottish landscape and in the discovery that he could find yarns to match those colors. He bought 20 different-colored yarns and some needles and persuaded a fellow traveler to teach him to knit on the way back to London.

Kaffe doesn't just stick to his knitting: he also works in needlepoint, quilting, rag rugs, theater-set design, and painting. Permeating everything he does is a love of, and an immense talent for, expressing color. As the bio on his website says, he's led a "colourful life"! His knitted intarsia designs feature many small areas of color, some of which are reminiscent of the late-nineteenth-century painting technique known as pointillism. Because no one area of color is extremely large, Kaffe recommends using only an arm's length or so of yarn and letting it hang behind the knitted fabric rather than winding it on a bobbin. For those with a fear of tangles, this method is surprisingly unstressful. (For more about Kaffe, see Meet Kaffe Fassett, page 57, Kaffe Fassett on Button Bands, below, and Kaffe Fassett's Tips for on Intarsia, page 255.)

Barbara Walker's Stitch Collections

Truly a woman of many interests and talents, Barbara Walker has written not only a dozen knitting encyclopedias and pattern books, but also another dozen books on topics dealing with religion, cultural anthropology, spirituality, and mythology. Professional designers and amateurs alike find her stitch dictionaries and other references immensely useful in developing their own patterns. Don't worry if you're not lucky enough to have original copies of her knitting books, which began to appear in the late 1960s. Schoolhouse Press has reprinted new editions of most of them, and they are widely available (see appendix for a list). To learn more about Barbara, see Meet Barbara Walker, page 253.

LEARN KAFFE FASSETT ON BUTTON BANDS

Kaffe Fassett insists that any average knitter can tackle his patterns with stunning results, and he encourages knitters to substitute freely and experiment. In spite of this seeming casual approach, however, Kaffe is a stickler about certain things. Button bands should be just as vibrantly patterned as the rest of a sweater, he believes, or they will detract from the end result. And edges can make or break a garment, he warns: "If they are too loose or tight, rip them out and try again."

Not-So-Old Classic Books

In addition to the books of Elizabeth Zimmermann, Kaffe Fassett, and Barbara Walker, several other books from a few decades back are prized possessions of many knitters.

Mary Thomas's Knitting Book was first published in 1938, then reprinted by Dover in 1972; it is still readily available. The little black-and-white cartoons scattered throughout are charmingly retro (see Winding Wools below), but the drawings of techniques are timeless, and the book covers the knitting ground thoroughly. One knitter describes her other book, *Mary Thomas's Book of Knitting Patterns*, as the "Swiss Army knife of knitting."

June Hiatt's *Principles of Knitting* contains detailed descriptions and variations on every technique imaginable, along with copious and clear illustrations. If you stumble on a copy of this mega reference, you might want to grab it. Although it has not been reprinted until recently (Fall 2011), it remains a favorite of many knitters, especially knitwear designers who are lucky enough to have a copy.

James Norbury, a British designer, knitting historian, and author, was another influential knitter of the 1970s. Norbury had his own BBC television show. His *Traditional Knitting Patterns from Scandinavia, the British Isles, France, Italy and Other European Countries* is still available from Dover. He favored long straight needles, so he could hold one needle steady, tucked under his right arm, while the left needle did all the action (sometimes referred to as the "pit method").

If you enjoy collecting stitch dictionaries, look for these two European favorites. *Mon*

Tricot Knitting Dictionaries (several editions) include not only pattern stitches, but also some basic illustrations of knitting and crochet techniques. These books were first published in France in the early 1970s but were then translated into English; it's usually not difficult to find used copies. From Germany, Lisl Fanderl's *Bäuerliches Stricken*, a three-book set, has not been translated into English, but its charts and photographs make it possible to follow the instructions even if you don't read German.

More recently, Japanese knitting (as well as crochet and sewing) books are increasingly popular with American stitchers. Although some have been translated, the distinctive charts, schematics, and drawings make it possible to follow even the Japanese-language versions. This is particularly true of the stitch dictionaries, and Japanese designers' fresh takes on classic designs make these books well worth searching out.

One other lace knitter of the early twentieth century should be mentioned: Herbert Niebling's lace designs are legendary and complex. An English-language collection of his patterns, *Knitted Lace Designs of Herbert Niebling*, has been translated by Eva Maria Leszner from the original German and includes corrections to many of the patterns.

WINDING WOOL

TRAVEL **RESTORE YOURSELF AT A RETREAT**

WHATEVER YOU'RE LOOKING FOR — relaxation, time with fiber friends, inspiration and new techniques — there's a knitting-related retreat or travel experience just waiting to entice you. For most first-timers at such events, the revelation is the warmth and generosity of the community, and the luxury of being able to knit (and spin) and speak in any esoteric knitting vocabulary you wish and find that completely acceptable and, what's more, comprehended. There's often a small marketplace opportunity, as well. It's hard to resist the truly wonderful yarns and fleeces you'll find there — especially with your knitting friends egging you on and any of your usual yarn-acquiring resistance almost completely broken down. (For craft schools, see page 88; for travel-related knitting events, see page 221; for websites, see the appendix. For more ideas, check the classified sections of your favorite fiber magazines.)

COLORADO

KnitAway in the Rockies

Estes Park // coincides with the Estes Park Wool Market in June
Led by Cheryl Oberle

MAINE

Knitting and Yoga Adventures

Monhegan Island // early fall
Weeklong knitting and yoga retreat, led by Lisa Evans

MASSACHUSETTS

Knitter's Review Fall Retreat

Williamstown // November
Organized by Clara Parkes

Moontide Lace Knitting Retreat

Wellfleet, Cape Cod // June

NEW HAMPSHIRE

Squam Art Workshops

Rockywold and Deephaven; also Nags Head, NC // a series of workshops in June, September, and October
A variety of opportunities, including knitting, sewing, printing, and yoga

NEW MEXICO

KnitAway in Taos

Taos // coincides with the Taos Festival in September
Led by Cheryl Oberle

OHIO

Knitters Connection

Columbus
Sponsored by Knitter's Mercantile, a full-service local yarn shop in Columbus, Ohio, this event brings the best of knitting (teachers, products, and students) together for a fun time

VERMONT

Mindful Knitting Retreat

Greensboro // March
Knitting and yoga

WASHINGTON

Madrona Fiber Arts Winter Retreat

Tacoma // February
Classes and vendors

Acorn Street Retreat

Sleeping Lady Conference Center, Leavenworth // June

WISCONSIN

Meg Swansen's Knitting Camps

Marshfield // July
A series of camps and retreats based on EPS (Elizabeth [Zimmermann]'s Percentage System)

Sheep in the City Get-Away

Oak Creek // February
Fashion shows, classes, and guild competitions

THE SWEATER LIFE LIST **123**

Chapter 4

THE Socks LIFE LIST

Never mind that you have to knit two of them, or that a bunch of pointy needles or sometimes intransigent cable loops can at times be annoying, socks remain the feet-down favorite project for many knitters. True, sock yarns are irresistible and plentiful, socks are the perfect small carry-along project, and there seems to be a pattern for every taste and every need. All are reasons enough to tuck a sock project into your knitting bag, but the real hook is the sense of accomplishment that comes from successfully finishing — and wearing — that first pair. You just haven't experienced socks until you've worn well-knit handmade socks, and once you have, there's no turning back. There's always another yarn or another pattern or another person who needs more socks, and after all, socks often take no more than one skein of yarn.

MEET

- Judy Becker
- Sarah Hauschka
- Betsy McCarthy
- Melissa Morgan-Oakes
- Stephanie Pearl-McPhee
- Charlene Schurch
- Sandi Wiseheart

DISCOVER

- Swatch self-striping sock yarns to discover different pattern effects.
- Swatch self-patterning sock yarns to discover their pattern effects.
- Swatch variegated sock yarns with different lengths between color changes.
- Swatch marled sock yarns.
- Swatch tweed sock yarns.
- Swatch wool/silk sock yarn blends.
- Swatch cotton sock yarn.
- Swatch bamboo sock yarn.
- Swatch (and wash) washable wool sock yarns.
- Swatch possum sock yarn.
- Read a history of knitting.
- Find and knit a vintage pattern.
- Visit and explore Ravelry online.

DO/TRY

- Knit one of Cat Bordhi's sock designs.
- Work one of Melissa Morgan-Oakes's sock designs — toe up or top down.
- Knit one of Ann Budd's sock designs.
- Work a Charlene Schurch sock pattern.
- Hand wash hand-knit socks and do not put them in the dryer.
- If necessary, use smaller needles than the pattern calls for, to ensure densely knit fabric.
- Knit and donate a historic Red Cross pattern.
- Choose and join a cause that resonates for you, and contribute your handknits under group guidelines.
- Set up your own group to knit for a cause.
- Knit a pair of argyle socks.
- Knit socks with a cable motif.
- Knit lace socks.
- Knit an ethnic sock pattern.
- Keep a list of all the projects you hope to knit.
- Make Evelyn Clark's Flower Basket lace shawl.
- Start a handspun-sharing project with a group of friends or your guild and knit or weave a blanket.

LEARN

- Memorize (and master) Kitchener stitch.
- Work on ways to avoid "laddering."
- Begin toe-up socks using Judy (Becker)'s Magic Cast On.
- Use the Magic Loop to make socks.
- Learn a variety of cast ons for your toe-up socks.
- Knit the upper half of the leg on a needle that's a size bigger than the one used for the lower part of the sock.
- Learn Elizabeth Zimmermann's sewn bind off for toe-up socks.
- Use a frilled cast on for top-down socks.
- Use a picot bind off for toe-up socks.
- Count rows in legs and in feet so both socks are exactly the same.
- Explore different techniques for turning a heel.
- Expand your knitting techniques by taking classes at a weekend conference.
- Learn how to alter your patterns for a custom fit.

GO

- Sign up for Sock Summit or other sock-knitting retreat/conference.
- Carry in-progress socks wherever you go.

EXPERIENCE

- Knit a sock from the top-down.
- Knit a toe-up sock.
- Work a sock on straight needles ("flat").

- Knit a sock using double-point needles.
- Knit a sock using two circular needles: one sock at a time.
- Make a sock using one circular needle.
- Make two socks at once on one circular needle.
- Choose yarn and stitch patterns with elasticity.
- Use reinforcing threads if you're concerned about wear at heel and toe.
- Choose practical yarns for every-day use; save luxury fibers for "best."

EXTRA CREDIT

- When was the first sock-knitting machine invented?
- Which *did* come first: the sock or the shoe?
- What did Tolstoy have to say about sock knitting?

MORE FOR MY SOCKS LIFE LIST

-
-
-
-

DID YOU KNOW **WOMAN VS. MACHINE**

Machine knitting started in the late eighteenth or nineteenth century with the Industrial Revolution, right? Well, not exactly. The very first stocking-frame knitting machine was invented by William Lee, a British curate, way back in 1589 during the reign of Elizabeth I. There are at least three stories about what drove him to create his invention: Story #1 goes that the young woman he was courting was too busy with her knitting to pay proper attention to his advances. Story #2 has it that his wife was an awfully slow knitter. And Story #3 relates that he was thrown out of Cambridge University for getting married, which wasn't allowed at the time; forced to rely on his wife's knitting skills for income, he came up with the machine that allowed her to knit a whole lot of socks more quickly. Whatever his motivation, it took some time to get his patent approved, because Queen Elizabeth was concerned that machine knitting would threaten the livelihoods of an important cottage industry for hand knitters. The principle behind his machine is still basic to today's versions of sock-knitting machines.

-
-
-
-
-
-
-
-
-
-

Sock Technique Talk

Sock knitting is right up there with sweater knitting as the ideal place to hone your knitterly skills. And since socks often require techniques that are on some knitters' lists headed, "I could never do that," this is a good time to focus on some specific how-tos. Each of these techniques has its use beyond socks, but knitting socks is a great way to discover and practice them.

As with sweaters, you have a number of choices for how to go about your sock projects, and it can be great fun to try as many different approaches as possible before settling on a favorite. For example, you can cast on at the top of the sock and work down, or you can begin at the toe and work up; some patterns even call for knitting socks back and forth on straight needles (called "knitting flat") from side to side, then weaving the edges together when you're done. Most socks are knit in the round, however, using either four or five double-point needles or one or two circulars. You can knit each sock of the pair separately or knit both of them at once. Sock patterns can often be adapted for the approach you prefer, even if they are presented using another technique.

"Sideways Socks." Most socks are knit in the round, but Judith Durant designed these to be knit on straight needles, then joined with Kitchener Stitch down the back. "Turning" the pattern means that the self-patterning sock yarn runs vertically rather than horizontally on the foot.

LEARN FIVE WAYS WITH NEEDLES

The photos here show a variety of needle configurations for working on socks. Each knitter is very likely to develop a favorite. When using four double points, the heel (later, sole) stitches are usually divided evenly between two needles and all the instep stitches are on a single needle; with five double points, the instep stitches are also divided. When using two circulars, the heel stitches are on one needle and the instep on the other, whether you're knitting one or two socks at a time. With one circular, the "Magic Loop" divides the heel stitches and the instep stitches. Study the examples here; for a photo of one sock being knit on one circular needle, see page 141.

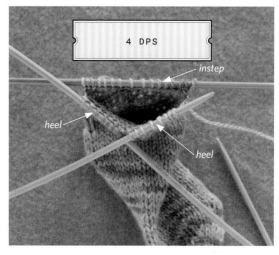

Knitting in Circles

Each approach to circular knitting has its pros and cons, along with its advocates. In my mind, the only bad reason for choosing a method is that that's the way you've always done it. Choosing a different technique may be more appropriate for a special yarn or a specific pattern, or a novel approach may simply capture your imagination and energize your knitting. You may still return to the "old way," but when you do you'll be taking along some new ideas and new tricks that make the tried-and-true work better.

Until fairly recently double-point needles were usually packaged in sets of four, so many of us did our circular knitting with the stitches on three needles, using the fourth as the working needle. But being able to divide your stitches among four needles and work with a fifth means that the piece is closer to "round," so you're less likely to get those annoying "ladders" (loose stitches) at the point where you switch to the next needle. In addition, you can arrange the stitches evenly between the heel and sole, making it easier to keep track of where you are in the sock, as well as involving less need to transfer stitches from needle to needle, which is often the case when you're working the heel and gussets with only four available needles.

LEARN **JIL EATON ON "LADDERING"**

Designer Jil Eaton has this advice for preventing "laddering," that unwanted line of loose stitches that can appear along the length of the sock at the point where you moved from needle to needle when you're knitting in the round on double-points. Jil's trick for avoiding this problem is to pull the first and second stitch on each needle tighter than usual.

The Circular Needle Approach

Designer Cat Bordhi's *Socks Soar on Circular Needles* introduced many knitters to the technique of using two circulars to knit a sock. By dividing the total number of stitches evenly between the needles, it's easy to see at a glance

DID YOU KNOW **WHICH CAME FIRST: THE SHOE OR THE SOCK?**

If you define "socks" as what you wear between your shoe and your foot, then shoes must have come first. This is what Elizabeth Semmelhack believes. Curator of the 2010 exhibit "Socks: Between You and Your Shoes" at the Bata Shoe Museum in Toronto, Ontario, Elizabeth reports that anthropologists have evidence that more than 5,000 years ago Neolithic humans stuffed grass inside their shoes, apparently for greater comfort. According to the exhibit's catalog, "When the 5,300-year-old Ötzi man's body was found in the Alps in 1991, not only had his body been preserved but so had his clothing, including his shoes and 'socks.' The socks were really bunches of grass that Ötzi had stuffed into his shoes."

whether you're knitting the front or back (top or sole) of the sock, as you work. Another advantage of this approach is that you have only two places where you move from one needle to the other (instead of three or four when you use double points), thus limiting the areas where "laddering" can be a problem. Some knitters find that the cable makes it easier to maintain the proper tension across the "jump," as well. Cat followed her first book with two more (*New Pathways for Sock Knitters* and *Personal Footprints for Insouciant Sock Knitters*), offering a further exploration of sock-knitting techniques, including unique ways to "build" your socks.

No More Second-Sock Syndrome

If you're someone who absolutely dreads the idea of starting up a second sock once you've completed the first one, you'll want to try knitting two at once on one circular needle. It's truly not just a parlor trick! Not only do you no longer face "second-sock syndrome," but it's much easier to ensure that each sock is exactly the same size. Melissa Morgan-Oakes has specialized in how to knit two socks at once on one circular needle, working from the top down as well as from the bottom up. Her first book, *2-at-a-Time Socks*, features patterns knit from the top down, and it was followed by *Toe-Up 2-at-a-Time Socks*. (Melissa reminds us that "two-at-a-time is definitely not just for socks. If there are two [or more] of something, rest assured I will be knitting two or more at a time! I use it not only for socks, but also mittens, fingerless gloves, sleeves, baby bootees, glove fingers — anything that comes in pairs, or litters.")

The Story behind Judy's Magic

Judy Becker's "Magic Cast On" has fascinated, and rescued, many knitters who like to work their socks from the toe up. Her description of how she got interested in knitting at all and finally devised her popular technique is full of surprises. For many years Judy explored crafts other than knitting, but she came back to it, she says, "when my son was learning to drive. I needed something to keep my hands busy so that I didn't compulsively clutch at the steering wheel or tear the car door handle off." That's when, out of the blue, she decided to knit a pair of socks. Although she had never knit socks before and didn't know what made her think of it, she guesses that "perhaps it was fate, or serendipity, but thus began my obsession with sock knitting, and my search for the perfect toe-up cast on."

Although she tried many different toe-up techniques, all of which worked perfectly well, for one reason or another she felt each left something to be desired. Then, she relates, "One day while I was recovering from the flu, and sick enough not to be expected to do much, I sat in my rocking chair with a cup of tea at my elbow, all of my knitting books spread around me, and yarn and needles in hand. I tried all the cast-on techniques in the books, whether they were meant to be used provisionally or not, and none was really what I was looking for. Out of frustration, I simply began winding the yarn around my needles in different ways until, suddenly, something worked! At first I couldn't remember what I'd done, but I kept at it until I could recreate the cast on nine times out of ten."

Urged by her knitting friends to share her discovery, she sent an article to Knitty.com. (You can find complete directions for this smooth, invisible cast on in the Knitty archives for spring 2006.) She says that she likes "to think of it as my gift to the knitting community, which has given so much to me." Since being published on Knitty.com, the method has spread far and wide through translation and its appearance in several books (including those of Cat Bordhi and Melissa Morgan-Oakes). Judy says, "I've recently learned that I may have 'unvented' a technique known to some knitters in Estonia, and also perhaps Bulgaria. As far as I know, however, it has never been published in English from those sources."

Judy says that she uses a variety of cast-on and bind-off techniques, depending on the needs of her project. Her final suggestion to knitters is to "learn a variety of techniques, including other toe-up cast ons, so you have a wide arsenal in your knitting tool belt."

LEARN JUDY'S TIPS FOR THE MAGIC CAST ON

* Make sure the same side of the needles is always facing you, and do not turn the needles over.
* Do not get too hung up on which direction the yarn goes around the needles. It really doesn't matter; the "magic" happens in the middle, between the needles. The only thing that will change is the stitch mount. If you find that your stitches are mounted with their leading legs in back of the needle, simply knit those stitches through the back loop on the first round so they are not twisted.
* Move either your right hand or your left hand, but not both.
* When you start to knit the first row, if your needles are parallel to the floor with the tips pointing to the right, the purl bump side should be facing up and the smooth side, down. The photos show a completed cast on on both the right (A) and wrong (B) sides before turning to begin the first row.
* For complete instructions for Judy's Magic Cast On, see the appendix for Judy Becker's blog address. Cat Bordhi has demonstrated this technique in a YouTube video.

Secrets to Sock Success

In spite of these different ways to knit your socks, feet are feet, after all, and their basic "architecture" is the same, no matter the size. Whether you decide to cover them by knitting your socks upside down, right side up, or sideways, first take a thoughtful look at how legs, ankles, feet, and toes are shaped and constructed. This will help you understand what's needed to knit the comfortable, long-wearing socks you aim for. Have you ever heard complaints that hand-knit socks (1) always fall down? (2) are impossible to pull over my instep? (3) bunch up at my toes? Strategic knitting know-how will help you avoid each of these flaws.

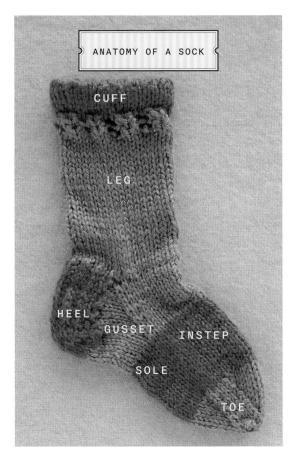

ANATOMY OF A SOCK

CUFF

LEG

HEEL

GUSSET

INSTEP

SOLE

TOE

Off to a Good Start — and All's Well That Ends Well

Choosing the proper cast on (or bind off, if you're knitting from the toe up) is key to a good fit in the leg. It must be elastic enough to slip over the foot and, at the same time, hug the leg comfortably so it doesn't fall down. Here's advice from some sock-knitting experts on how to get a comfortable, practical fit at the top of your socks, whether you start at the top or at the toe.

FROM ANN BUDD. Along with using an elastic cast on for top-down socks, which ensures that the top is nice and stretchy, Ann likes to follow a suggestion she learned from Priscilla Gibson-Roberts: knit the upper half of the leg on a needle that's a size bigger than the one used for the lower part of the sock. You can hardly see it in the sock, but it makes it conform to the shape of your calf better, and it's more comfortable.

FROM MELISSA MORGAN-OAKES. A long tail is Melissa's default cast on for top-down socks. She finds it flexible and attractive, and although she's tried others, she always come back to long tail. For toe-up socks her favorite bind off is Elizabeth Zimmermann's sewn bind off (see Sewn Bind Off, at right). If she's in a hurry, she skips this, however, and opts for doubling the number of stitches on the last round, then binding off normally. She explains her bind off can be tight, and adding the extra stitches just before binding off means she can still get the sock on when it's done.

FROM CHARLENE SCHURCH. Charlene's favorite cast on for top-down socks is a "frilled" cast on. She casts on twice as many stitches as she needs for the sock, then in the first round she works two stitches together around in pattern. (For instance, for a K2, P2 ribbed sock she works K2tog, K2tog, P2tog, P2tog.) The result is that the sock has a decorative bead along the top edge, and this cast on is *never* too tight. For toe-up socks she likes to use a picot bind off. It is decorative and also never too tight, as a standard cable bind off can be. (For one picot bind off, see page 209.)

"The moral of my ode is this:
beauty is twice beauty,
and what is good is doubly good
when it is a matter of two socks
made of wool in winter."

PABLO NERUDA, *"Ode to My Socks,"* TRANSLATED BY ROBERT BLY

LEARN SEWN BIND OFF

Cut your working yarn, leaving a tail two to three times as long as the sock's circumference. Thread the yarn through a blunt-tip needle. *Insert the needle from right to left (as if to purl) through the first two stitches on the needle (A), and draw the yarn through. Next, insert the needle through the first stitch from left to right (as if to knit, B), and drop that stitch off the needle. Repeat from * until one stitch remains. Draw the yarn through that stitch, fasten off, and weave in the tail.

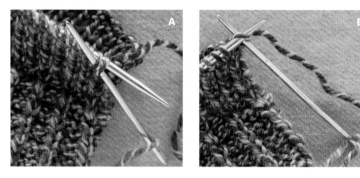

LEARN STEPHANIE PEARL-MCPHEE ON SOCKS

We all love to laugh at ourselves through Stephanie's on-the-mark wit about knitters. But Stephanie is truly a hard-core and extremely knowledgable knitter as well as a humorist. In her book, *Knitting Rules,* among her 10 top reasons to knit socks are frugality, portability, sustainability, versatility, and comfort. Knitting *both* socks of a pair is also character building! But, according to Stephanie, one of the joys of sock knitting is that once you understand the rules and the basic structure of socks, you may no longer need patterns, and she goes on to provide extremely useful advice on the basics that will get you there. The first *Sock Summit,* co-organized by Stephanie and held in Portland, Oregon, in 2009, was a huge success, and at repeat upcoming events, the organizers plan to break all kinds of knitting records.

Doing a Good Turn

Satisfying sock patterns are engineered so that the heel is long-lasting and smoothly forms a perfectly fitted cup for the foot. The measurement from the back of the heel to the top of the instep is quite a bit larger than it is around either the leg or the foot itself. To get from the leg to the wider heel-to-instep area and then once again back down to the narrower diameter for the foot, you "turn the heel." Once you understand the principle (and trust the pattern directions), this can be the most fun part of knitting a sock, because it's very gratifying to watch the three-dimensionality emerge. Although there are many types of heels and ways of forming them, today's Western sock knitters usually turn a heel in three steps. First, if you're knitting from the top down, you work a rectangular flap for the back of the heel, then you shape the cup where the heel rests by working short rows, and finally you pick up along both sides of the heel flap to create the gussets (triangular sections) along the sides. The gussets create the extra fabric needed to accommodate this wider area. You then gradually decrease the gusset stitches until you're back at the same circumference as you had for the leg. You create the heel cup in a different order when you knit toe-up socks, of course, but the final result is similar.

Toe Tips: Make Them to Last and to Fit

The obvious way to ensure comfortably fitting socks is to measure carefully so the heel and toe match your foot perfectly. Too long is just as uncomfortable as too short. It's equally important to avoid a lumpy join at the very end. Many sock patterns worked from the top down weave the opening at the toe of the sock together with the technique known as "Kitchener stitch." With practice this join can be made nearly invisible. Socks are undeniably satisfying to knit, but what's the point of knitting them if they don't fit or they don't last? Here's some advice from the designers.

FROM ANN BUDD. The most dependable way of ensuring that both socks will come out to be the same size is to count your rows, both for the feet and for the legs.

FROM MELISSA MORGAN-OAKES. *For a good fit,* Melissa suggests the following:

* Make certain your gauge is correct, and measure carefully. Keep in mind the idea of "negative ease." Most of Melissa's socks are at least 1 inch less in circumference than the actual circumference of her foot.

* Avoid loose stitch patterns and yarns that don't have good elasticity. Socks take a lot of abuse. You need yarns and designs that stand up to such treatment. Twisted stitches, cables, ribs — anything that draws in is a good choice. Because these designs also make longer-lasting socks, they're good options for daily-wear socks that are also fun and challenging to knit.

For long-lasting socks, Melissa recommends:

* Fiber choice is important. Most of the socks she knits for everyday wear are made from yarns that contain about 15 percent nylon or silk combined with superwash wool. These combinations help make socks wear a little longer.

* Reinforcing threads can be used in heels and toes for added support.

* If durability is important to a specific pair, avoid soft and luxurious fibers. Melissa is careful to save her more sensual yarns for socks that won't be worn daily.

* Hand washing extends the life of any hand-knit item, and socks are no exception. Machine washing of superwash yarns followed by line drying (as opposed to machine drying) helps if you're not a fan of hand washing (and few of us are).

* Designs that focus on stitches that are close to one another or cross over one another generally last longer than those knit in airy, lacy designs.

FROM CHARLENE SCHURCH. Charlene advises that you pay attention to the shape of your foot. Do you have high arches, wide heels, long toes? Most of us don't have "average" feet, so our socks shouldn't be average either. The reason there are so many ways to knit heels is that people's heels come in so many different shapes. Explore what is available, and you may find a different-style heel that makes your socks fit you better.

The best and easiest way to ensure long-lasting socks is to knit the fabric densely enough. Most of the suggested needle sizes and gauges on sock yarns are too loose. Take some time to knit a little swatch to see what happens as you decrease your needle size, and that time will reward you with many more wearings of your favorite socks.

EXPLORE GETTING THE RIGHT YARN MATCHUP

When you're making socks, it pays to consider your choice of yarn, advises Deborah Robson. Many knitters use Merino yarns for socks, which are nice and soft; the fibers are often blended with nylon to increase durability. But some fibers are both soft and durable enough without adding nylon. An example is wool from Bluefaced Leicester sheep, a breed that originated in Northumberland, England, in the early 1900s, or from the Down breeds, like Suffolk or Dorset, which make a nice, cushy sock yarn that has good durability, especially if the fabric is worked at a tighter-than-average gauge. Interestingly, she observes, New Zealand possum can be used for a very soft sock yarn because it's exceptionally fine but doesn't felt.

MORE FOR MY SOCKS LIFE LIST

○ _____

_____

○ _____

_____

○ _____

_____

○ _____

_____

○ _____

_____

LEARN KITCHENER WITH CONFIDENCE

Also known as grafting, this extremely useful technique intimidates many knitters, but if you just take it one step at a time, concentrate, and have a little patience, you can do it without fear. Use it not only for sock toes, but also sweater shoulders or two-piece scarves, or anywhere you need to join an equal number of "live" stitches.

Begin by placing the two sets of live stitches to be joined on separate needles. Hold the needles parallel in your left hand with both tips facing toward the right and with the wrong sides of the knitted fabric facing each other. Thread a blunt-tip tapestry needle with the working yarn. (Cut a long tail at the end of the last row of one set of the stitches, and use that for the graft.)

To set up the sequence, insert the tapestry needle into the first stitch on the back needle as if to knit, and draw the yarn through, leaving the stitch on the needle. Insert the needle into the first stitch on the front needle as if to purl, and draw the yarn through, leaving the stitch on the needle. You're now ready to proceed across the seam.

STEP 1. Insert the tapestry needle into the first stitch on the back needle as if to purl, draw the yarn through, and let the stitch slip off the knitting needle.

STEP 2. Insert the tapestry needle into the next stitch on the back needle as if to knit, and draw the yarn through. Leave the stitch on the knitting needle.

STEP 3. Insert the tapestry needle into the first stitch on the front needle as if to knit, draw the yarn through, and let the stitch slip off the knitting needle.

STEP 4. Insert the tapestry needle into the next stitch on the front needle as if to purl, and draw the yarn through. Leave the stitch on the knitting needle.

Repeat steps 1 through 4 until all stitches have been joined, fastening off the last stitch by drawing the tail of the working yarn through it.

STEP 1

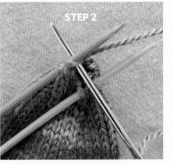
STEP 2

STEP 3

STEP 4

A Good Yarn

Several years ago I was given a large, old-fashioned suit box filled with yarn and needles that had been hidden away in a friend's attic since the 1940s. The majority of the stash inside was fine, khaki-colored 100 percent wool, along with some Boye steel nickel-plated knitting "pins," size 12 (approximately equivalent to a US 1). Here was evidence that whoever had used this material was part of the huge effort, headed by the American Red Cross, to provide not only wool socks, sweaters, and scarves but also cotton bandages for soldiers and sailors during the two World Wars.

Often seen (and photographed) with her knitting (see page 193), First Lady Eleanor Roosevelt launched a campaign to Knit for Defense at a tea at the Waldorf-Astoria in New York in September 1941. Two months after the Waldorf tea party, the cover of *Life* magazine featured a photo of a young girl knitting, and the lead story, "Learn to Knit," advocated knitting as the best way to support the war effort. Because of a wool shortage due to the war, the Red Cross in Seattle even sponsored an effort to teach people to card and spin wool for the cause. I treasure my box of yarn as a connection to a piece of this long-ago history, and I wonder about that knitter and how many socks she (or he) managed to complete. (For historic Red Cross patterns for sweaters, socks, hats, and more, see the appendix.)

The sock yarns you'll find in your LYS today are a far cry from the khaki and navy wools of those war years. Although the fiber quality in the 1940s yarn was actually quite good, the colors weren't anything to write home about. Today's choices — easily as many as three hundred different lines of yarn and continuing to grow — are sometimes awesome, but they go a long way toward explaining what makes sock knitting so addictive, a bit like eating peanuts. You can't knit a pair of socks in every one of the available yarns (probably), but you can dip your toe in!

A painter's point of view. George Luks's *Knitting for the Soldiers: High Bridge Park, c. 1918* is in the collection of the Terra Foundation for American Art, Chicago.

Knitting for the troops. These British women drivers for the Waterloo and Crosby Ambulance Service knit socks and possibly a sweater for soldiers in late 1939.

A blast from the past. Ayrspun Scottish yarn and steel knitting pins may have been used to knit a pattern like "Man's Sock," from a World War II pamphlet reproduced by the American Red Cross.

EXPLORE KNITTING FOR A CAUSE

Even before the World Wars, knitters offered the products of their needles for the good of others, and this has never been more true than it is today.

Individuals and groups provide blankets for homeless shelters, caps for premature babies, and cozy shawls for cancer patients, to mention only a few of dozens of local as well as international efforts.

Local yarn stores and nonprofits in your community may be able to point you to a cause that captures your imagination and your heart. An online search for "knitting for charity" will provide a wealth of possibilities, as well as ideas for how to organize a charity knitting project. Ravelry is another source of information, with a number of groups active in knitting for charity and providing links to specific projects. Here are a few of the most established, representing a variety of needs. The descriptions that follow are adapted from the groups' websites. (For website addresses, see the appendix.)

AFGHANS FOR AFGHANS. A humanitarian and educational people-to-people project that sends hand-knit and hand-crocheted blankets, sweaters, vests, hats, mittens, and socks to Afghanistan. This grassroots effort is part of a tradition inspired by Red Cross volunteers who made afghans, socks, slippers, and other items for soldiers and refugees during World Wars I and II and other times of crisis and need.

CHEMO CAPS. Knitters make hand-knit caps for cancer patients in hospital oncology units and hospice. The caps are made so that cancer patients who lose their hair can have a very soft hand-knit cap to call their own, not only to comfort their heads but also to warm their souls.

HATS FOR THE HOMELESS was created in memory of John Carroll, who died suddenly in 1998, after devoting himself to people less fortunate than he. The project continues a tradition he started.

PROJECT LINUS comprises hundreds of local chapters and thousands of volunteers. Its purpose is first to provide love, a sense of security, and warmth and comfort to children who are seriously ill, traumatized, or otherwise in need through the gifts of new, handmade blankets and afghans, lovingly created by volunteer "blanketeers." Its second goal is to provide a rewarding and fun service opportunity for interested individuals and groups in local communities, for the benefit of children. Contributors to the project have knit (or crocheted) more than three million blankets for children in need since the inception of Project Linus in 1995.

SHAWL MINISTRY. Begun in 1998 by Janet Bristow and Victoria Galo, graduates of the 1997 Women's Leadership Institute at the Hartford Seminary in Hartford, Connecticut, Shawl Ministry was inspired by a love of knitting and crocheting, combined with a spiritual practice that reaches out to those in need of comfort, as well as of celebration. These shawls may be called Prayer Shawls, Comfort Shawls, Peace Shawls, or Mantles, but whatever the name, the shawl maker offers prayers and blessings for the recipient as he or she works, and then sends the shawl off with a final blessing. Sometimes recipients make a shawl for someone else in need, and so the blessings ripple from person to person.

OPERATION TOASTY TOES distributes home-crafted slippers to U.S. troops stationed abroad.

WARM UP AMERICA started in 1991 in a small Wisconsin town with neighbors knitting and crocheting afghans for neighbors in need. Volunteers knit or crochet small sections and then others join them together. Today Warm Up America distributes warm afghans, caps, and other items to tens of thousands of people, thanks to the generosity of knitters and crocheters around the country.

LEARN THE MAGIC LOOP

In 2002 Fiber Trends published a book that featured a technique for working smallish tubes on just one circular needle, instead of using four or five double-points. The book was *The Magic Loop: Working Around On One Needle — Sarah Hauschka's Magical Unvention,* written by Bev Galeskas. The technique may not in fact have been invented by Sarah, but it was the first time it was published, and it was a boon to many sock and hat knitters. You can use the method any time you knit a tube, if your circular needle is too long for the stitches to stretch around it.

THE METHOD. It's important that you use a long cable for this technique (from 30 to 40 inches, depending on the project: shorter for small items, like socks, and longer for sleeves and hats). Cast on the number of stitches you need onto one circular needle and push all the stitches onto the cable. Next, count to the halfway point and pull a loop of cable through between the two stitches at the center of the cast on. With the needle tips facing to the right, push the first half of the stitches onto the front needle. Leave the other stitches on

the cable, with the loop dividing the two groups. Next, join the first stitch to the last stitch (on the cable) so you're ready to work in a round. Keeping the last half of the stitches on the cable and bringing the empty (back) needle into play, knit across the first half of the stitches. Turn. Push the just-knit stitches onto the cable and push the unknit stitches (currently on the cable) onto the needle. As you rearrange the stitches, maintain the loop between the two halves. (If you lose the loop, don't panic: simply find the middle and pull it back out again.) Continue knitting around in this way as directed by the pattern.

Lend me your ears. The key to successful Magic Loop knitting is to maintain a generous loop of cable between the "front" and "back" stitches. The needle configuration looks a bit like droopy hound-dog ears.

Color My Socks

The shelves and bins of sock yarns in every yarn store overflow with color and pattern. Before you make your yarn selection, it's helpful to consider what the options are and how they affect the way the socks will knit up.

VARIEGATED YARNS. These yarns have been dyed in a number of colors that change frequently along the length of the strand, resulting in a gaily patterned, confetti-like effect in your knitting. Until you have some experience with a particular yarn, you may not be able to predict what the fabric will look like when knit up. Depending on how long the color repeat in the yarn is in relation to the circumference of your work, effects can vary a great deal. Usually, each color appears to spiral up a sock, but sometimes short lengths of the same color may appear on top of one another for a number of rows, creating what is called "pooling." You may or may not like this

effect. If you don't like it, there are ways to get around it (see pages 182 and 250).

SELF-PATTERNING OR SELF-STRIPING YARNS are a subset of variegated yarns. Yarn manufacturers dye yarns in multiple colors so that, as the item is being knit, stripes and even small patterns automatically appear in the fabric. In some

LEARN EXACT LOOK-ALIKES

Some knitters enjoy the fun of nonmatching socks and so don't even try for color symmetry. With some planning, however, you can make your socks knit with self-patterning or self-striping yarn match exactly: cast on at the beginning of a color change and then be sure to start your second sock at exactly the same place in the sequence. This works with yarns that dependably repeat the color sequences in the same order and the same length for each color shift, but not all yarns are designed that way. Pull out several yards of your yarn to see if you can detect the pattern and whether it's regular.

All about color and pattern. The length of each color is quite long and the transition between colors gradual in the Noro yarn for these socks; care was taken to identify the color changes so that the socks pretty nearly match exactly.

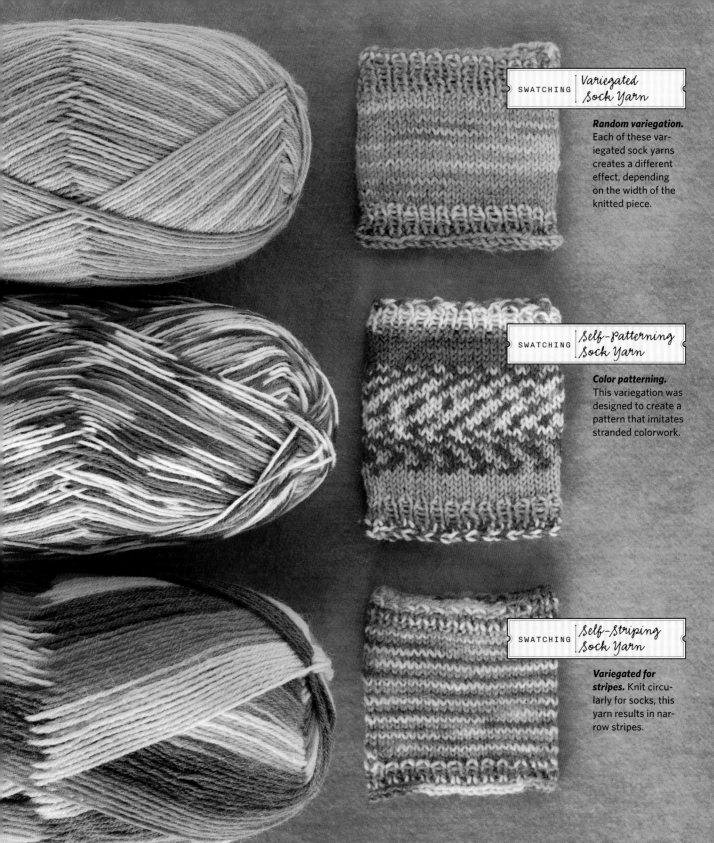

Random variegation. Each of these variegated sock yarns creates a different effect, depending on the width of the knitted piece.

Color patterning. This variegation was designed to create a pattern that imitates stranded colorwork.

Variegated for stripes. Knit circularly for socks, this yarn results in narrow stripes.

yarns the shifts are very gradual, resulting in a watercolor-like blend from one shade to the next over a fairly wide area. Some are almost unnoticeable in the skein, but these subtle shifts can be quite beautiful in the completed item. Other yarns feature more abrupt changes from one color to the next, resulting in stripes that are quite distinct. If the lengths of each color vary, the stripes vary in width. Before you begin knitting, it's worth drawing out lengths of yarn to analyze the progressions so you can take advantage of that yarn's characteristics. If you want your socks to match, you'll need to analyze the yarn and try to start the second sock at the same color shift as the first (see Exact Look-Alikes, page 142).

SOLIDS, HEATHERS, AND MARLED YARNS. When you go sock-yarn shopping, don't overlook what may at first seem a bit staid compared to the multicolor floozies described above. As much fun as it can be to watch the color shifts of self-striping and variegated yarns, socks knit with a solid or heathery yarn may sometimes be a better wardrobe choice. They may also show off lacy, cabled, and other patterns to better effect. Look for solids with different-colored flecks that produce a tweedy fabric. Marled yarns are created by plying two different-colored yarns together. These can be strongly contrasting or just subtly different; the plies themselves may even be variegated. The classic ragg wool sock is a marled yarn, often in beige or gray plied with white but also now often available in other color combinations. (For a photo of marled yarn, see page 12.)

> SWATCHING | *Tweed*

Classic tweed.
For the more conservative among us, tweed is a perfect wardrobe choice.

DID YOU KNOW FOR HISTORY BUFFS AND OTHER CURIOUS FOLK

It's fun to try out the latest intriguing stitch technique or a very stylish design, but there's also something about knitting, as with most handcrafts, that offers a real sense of connection with people who were knitting centuries ago. How were those simple knit and purl stitches first discovered, and how is it that knitters were using them in very different parts of the world? Even if far-flung knitters didn't form the stitches in the same way, they came up with the same result. Can we follow a trail from the first knitter as those ideas spread over the world, and was there really ever a "first knitter"? As Cat Bordhi's book describes it, "Socks Soar" nowadays, but they may also have been the first knitted items, and some of the earliest examples have been traced to Egypt and Spain, from more than a thousand years ago.

There's still a lot to be learned about when and where knitting began, and if you're interested in picking up that trail, you'll want to check out several excellent books on the history of knitting, including Anne Macdonald's *No Idle Hands: The Social History of American Knitting,* Richard Rutt's *A History of Hand Knitting,* and Susan Strawn's *Knitting America;* or explore the website http://knittinghistory.typepad.com/ historic_knitting_pattern.

Vintage patterns hold their own fascination. The Antique Pattern Project (www.antiquepattern library.org) has the following mission: to scan "needlework pattern books that are in the public domain, to preserve them, so we can keep our needlework heritage in our hands. These scans have been photoedited to make them more useful for needle workers, and to reduce file sizes. They are available, for free, to anyone who wants them,

for educational, personal, artistic and other creative uses." You can access copies of their extensive catalog of books and pamphlets, not only for knitting patterns, but also for needlework patterns of all sorts, including crochet, cross-stitch, embroidery, tapestry, and many others. The site also provides reference to other sources of historic patterns and information.

Ingenuity and industry epitomized. This 1855 print shows a shepherd tending his flock while he knits perched on three "stilts" — two for his legs and one to sit upon — to get a better view.

Fibers and Weights

Yarn companies indulge us with the variety of fibers and fiber blends they offer as well as with color patterning. Many sock patterns are written for the equivalent of a fingering-weight yarn, classified by the Craft Yarn Council as "superfine," with a gauge of 27 to 32 inches over 4 inches on US size 1 to 3 needles. You'll find that many yarns classified as sock yarns indeed fit that description. But you'll find wonderful sock yarns and sock patterns in sport and DK weights as well, and you may even move up to a worsted weight for a speedier, easier project, especially if you're looking for socks to wear around the house like comfy slippers or to wear inside your boots.

Many sock yarns are blends of wool and nylon or other synthetics, and knitters are often relieved to discover that many are also machine washable, since socks need more frequent washing than most sweaters and other garments. Check your yarn band carefully for specifications and advice, because even if the yarn is machine washable, it may not be machine dryable.

If you're looking for warm-weather socks, or you just don't care for wool, you'll find plenty of choices in synthetics, cotton, bamboo, and even luxury blends, such as silk or cashmere. Some sock yarns contain some elastic, which helps the socks keep their shape and nicely hug your foot. Sock yarns also often have a percentage of nylon, which makes them more long lasting. (For more about durability, see Toe Tips: Make Them to Last and to Fit, page 135.)

Sock Fabric Design

Almost anything goes when it comes to patterning socks, as is immediately obvious when you see how many wonderful sock-knitting books are available. And because sock knitting is so addictive, it's easy to see that sock knitters are always ready for new challenges. Stranding, cables, and lace are particularly popular, as well as a whole battery of stitch combinations that don't readily fit into those categories. A traditional favorite that periodically makes a comeback is argyle, a style of intarsia that features not only diagonal shapes, but also a line of single stitches that bisect the diagonals to create a plaid effect. Argyles have a very long history, first showing up in Argyll, Scotland, in the sixteenth century. Sir Walter Scott wrote about them in the nineteenth century; golfers favored them in the 1920s; jazz trumpeter Louis Armstrong apparently dug them in the 1930s (photo below); preppies loved them in the '80s, when the argyle style expanded into sweaters and other garments as well; and they're back again in the twenty-first century.

Jazzy socks! American jazz singer and trumpeter Louis Armstrong ("Satchmo") shows off his argyle socks in London during his first tour of Europe in 1933.

MEET MEG SWANSEN

Online knitters can learn Kitchener stitch on YouTube.com. They can stitch-and-bitch the night away with friends, and find a fix for any sort of sweater disaster. Still, every summer more than two hundred knitters, including many older traditionalists but also some twenty-somethings toting extravagant, glittery yarn, take that coveted journey to an out-of-the-way motel in Wisconsin to spend four days in the same room with legendary knitting guru Meg Swansen. These sold-out knitting feasts, an institution since the mid-1970s, are chock-full of knitting technique and her mother's trademark methods for seamless garment construction. They also deliver Meg's favorite gift to knitters: empowerment.

Along with sharing her many favorite tricks — purl-when-you-can, jogless stripes, and "blipless" entrelac are just a few — Meg, the daughter of famed knitter Elizabeth Zimmermann, teaches knitting campers to read their own knitting and rely on that more than on printed instructions.

"I want them to understand stitch movement, to understand what a double decrease looks like," says Meg, "and to accumulate technique, because the more tools you have to work with, the more you can do." Not every knitter wants this kind of education, Meg admits. "If you are perfectly happy to be a blind follower all your life, bless your heart." But like her mother, known to knit while riding on her husband's motorcycle, Meg has never been one for following other people's rules.

A prolific designer and author in her own right, Meg also runs Schoolhouse Press, the mail-order wool- and pattern-supply business Zimmermann began in the 1950s, bucking knitting conventions by offering hard-to-find circular needles and pure wool. Speaking of her mother, Meg reflects, "She brought us up to question everything. It was very lawyerly, in a way. The second we came home from school with something — philosophical ideas, didactic proclamations — she would offer a contrary point of view. She taught us never to take anything at face value."

At camp, as with the retreats Meg holds for knitters who have been attending for many decades, some things have changed since Zimmermann started them in the 1970s. "It's staggering to think that back in 1974 women didn't leave home to do something on their own and leave their children and husbands behind," she says. "The women who did were very bold." Today's campers tend to arrive with more technique, and a strong desire for advanced skills, she notes. But despite the online tutorials and plethora of websites offering knitting advice, many students arrive wanting Meg to demonstrate the Kitchener stitch in person. "It's like the singer who has to sing his most well-known song," Meg says, laughing. And she's happy to do it.

Chapter 5

THE Scarves & Shawls

LIFE LIST

Scarves are one of those comfort projects you never want to leave completely behind. After all, who doesn't need another scarf? A simple scarf on your needles is the ideal take-along for meetings or movies or other occasions when you "just have to knit" but may not be able to pay close attention to a stitch pattern or shaping. Although scarves may be many knitters' first project, no one should ever be apologetic about knitting "only" a scarf. Experienced knitters can find scarf knitting the perfect playground for dipping into a new technique, trying out an intriguing stitch pattern, or exploring the characteristics of a new yarn.

MEET

- Cat Bordhi
- Nancy Bush
- Donna Druchunas
- Melanie Falick
- Kate Gilbert
- Vickie Howell
- Lucy Neatby
- Amy Singer
- Debbie Stoller

DISCOVER

- Search your garden for flower and leaf patterns to incorporate into your knitting.
- Create color palettes inspired by each of the seasons in your garden.
- Check out Knitty.com.
- Seek out all kinds of color and use surprising combinations to spark your projects.
- Choose 10 books from Lost in a Good Book (page 164), and put them on your reading/listening list.
- Read one (or more!) of Debbie Stoller's Stitch 'n' Bitch books

DO/TRY

- Choose a reversible stitch pattern and knit a scarf.
- Make a scarf that will keep someone warm.
- Knit a scarf for glamorous special occasions.
- Work a scarf from the center back down.
- Design and knit a "varsity" scarf using the colors of your home team.
- Knit a striped scarf in which the stripes are different stitch patterns, rather than different colors.
- Work a scarf with a reversible cable pattern.
- Work a bias-knit scarf.
- Make a "shorty" scarf: neck warmer, rufflet, dickey, snood, or cowl, for instance.
- Follow Cat Bordhi's directions for knitting a Möbius scarf.
- Knit one of Cat's Möbius baskets.
- Knit Clapotis or another of Kate Gilbert's designs.
- Knit one of Lucy Neatby's designs.
- Knit a silky scarf — from silk, bamboo, Tencel, or other silky fiber.
- Find a pattern for a Shetland lace shawl and make it for yourself or for a best friend or favorite relative.
- Make one of Donna Druchunas's shawl patterns.
- Knit an authentic Orenburg shawl.
- Make a Faroese lace shawl.
- Incorporate a lace panel in an otherwise plain-knit fabric.
- Insert lace motifs in a stockinette-knit sweater.
- Knit a pattern from Jane Sowerby's Victorian Lace Today.
- Choose a shawl from Meg Swansen's Gathering of Lace.
- Make a project from one of Amy Singer and Jillian Moreno's books.

LEARN

- Create your own design for a completely original scarf.
- Experiment with four different ways to tie a scarf.
- Learn to read and knit at the same time.
- Learn about Estonian lace, and knit one of Nancy Bush's Estonian lace shawl patterns.
- Choose a stitch pattern (or patterns) from a stitch dictionary and design your own lace scarf.
- Learn to "read" your knitting.
- Use a "lifeline" when knitting lace.
- Make Amy's Tuscany Shawl in silk yarn.
- Find people who are into other crafts, such as quilting, sewing, or basketry, and learn what excites them about their work.

GO

- Find and join a knitting group in your area. If you can't find one, start one!
- Visit Estonia.
- Find a time and place to relish a simple knitting project, and appreciate the peaceful pace.

EXPERIENCE

◇ Use the long-tail cast on for a scarf.

◇ Use a knitted cast on for a scarf.

◇ Try a loop cast on for a scarf.

◇ Try a provisional cast on for a scarf or shawl.

◇ Use a twisted cast on for a scarf.

◇ Use a braided cast on for a scarf.

◇ Use a picot cast on and/or bind off for a scarf.

◇ Use Judy's Magic Cast On for a scarf or shawl.

◇ Use an I-cord bind off for a scarf.

◇ Use a three-needle bind off to join scarf pieces at the center back.

◇ Explore patterns by designers in the Twist Collective (see appendix for website).

◇ Unravel a sweater or other item (not knit by you) to discover its pattern design.

◇ Listen to an audiobook about knitting (or any other book) while knitting.

◇ Allow yourself time to enjoy beautiful books.

◇ Knit a lace scarf with qiviut.

◇ Find ways to relax, learn, and knit with friends — even if you can't go to a retreat.

◇ Experiment with nonwool fibers, such as hemp, silk, and cotton.

◇ Relax while knitting a garter-stitch scarf.

◇ Challenge yourself with a Fair Isle design.

◇ Get creative and knit some freeform fabric.

EXTRA CREDIT

◇ Who wrote about a Canadian truck driver who knit while he drove?

◇ Who is probably the most famous fictional knitter of all time?

◇ What famous fictional female detective was an obsessive knitter?

MORE FOR MY SCARVES & SHAWLS LIFE LIST

◇ _____

◇ _____

◇ _____

◇ _____

◇ _____

◇ _____

◇ _____

◇ _____

◇ _____

◇ _____

◇ _____

◇ _____

◇ _____

◇ _____

Off to a Good Start

Whether you work the simplest stitch with a humble yarn or design a complex pattern to show off your skills, being aware of a few scarf-knitting principles will ensure success.

* Choose a stitch pattern that looks good on both sides. The back and front don't have to be identical. In fact, knitting a reversible fabric with a very different look on each side is quite eye-catching. It just shouldn't have a noticeably "wrong" side.

* Unless the pattern stitch is a balanced stitch (contains equal numbers of alternating knit and purl stitches), so it doesn't roll under at the edges and ends, plan on maintaining an edge pattern (usually about 1 inch) in a non-rolling stitch pattern, such as garter, seed, or moss stitch, which will give you a nice flat edge.

* Consider why you need this scarf and how it will be used, and choose an appropriate yarn, from warm and cozy to slinky and seductive. Avoid itchy yarns.

* Choose a pattern that allows the fabric to wrap comfortably and drape nicely. Be sure to swatch, and if necessary, use a larger needle size so your fabric isn't too stiff. Scarves are meant to be cozy. You're not making armor or a neck brace.

* If your pattern has a definite top and bottom (many lace and some stranded patterns do, for instance), you may choose to work the scarf either from the center to the end or from the bottom toward the center, and then work the other half in the same way. If you work from the center down, use a provisional cast on so you can easily pick up the stitches when you knit the second side. If you work from the

DID YOU KNOW — WHAT DO KNITTING AND GARDENING HAVE IN COMMON?

Gardening often attracts the same people who also love to knit, and in the growing season, gardening sometimes even wins out. Garden writer Shirley Remes believes that those of us who both garden and knit do so because each offers similar satisfactions: the tactile pleasure of getting our hands into the dirt or plunging them into fiber; the meditative, relaxing effects they have on us; and the opportunity they offer to create something beautiful.

Shirley polled some gardening/knitting friends to discover more about what makes these two activities twin passions. One friend wrote that "my love of all things botanical shines through in my obsession with the glorious leaf patterns in knitting. It's everywhere and I never get tired of it — in shawls, cardigans, hats." She adores botanical patterns, such as vines and berries, and keeps a category for "leaf" in her Ravelry favorites.

Colors and textures are everywhere in both arts. One knitter compares the layers she loves to incorporate in her shade garden to cables in a knitting project. Both gardening and knitting give immediate gratification as well as teach patience: we get instant pleasure out of turning a cable or planting some annuals in a container, but ultimate satisfaction out of completing an entire garment or a burst of spring color from fall-planted bulbs. As Shirley exclaims, "What great hobbies — so many rewards!"

bottom up, leave the stitches of the first half on a spare needle or stitch holder while you knit the second half, then use Three-Needle Bind Off, page 105, or Kitchener stitch, page 137, to join the center seam.

* Stitch pattern collections are great resources for striking out and creating your own scarf design. Consider using a different pattern for ends and edges (see appendix for suggestions).

Cast On/Bind Off Savvy

Many of us stick to the tried-and-true cast on that we learned when we first began to knit. Among the most likely are the knitted, loop, and long-tail cast ons. But there's a whole other world of possibilities out there, and how you begin can have a very big effect on the appearance of your finished knitting. No one cast on is truly appropriate for every kind of project. For instance, shawls that begin at the center often begin with a provisional cast on that will be invisible as the knitting develops around it. There are even decorative cast ons, such as twisted, braided, and picot (page 209). (See also Judy's Tips for the Magic Cast On, page 132.)

It's just as important to become familiar with the wide variety of bind-off possibilities, too, including applied I-cord and picot (page 209). Some cast ons and bind offs make perfect partners because their structures make them appear almost identical. Check out a good knitting reference for more advice, so you don't find yourself stuck in a cast-on — or a bind-off — rut!

Being two-faced is okay. A simple linen stitch, here worked in a hand-dyed, handspun yarn, is different on each side, but neither side appears to be the "wrong" side.

EXPLORE LINKIN' UP: STITCHIN', BITCHIN', AND OTHER GROUP KNIT-INS

We knitters are social animals, and whether the get-togethers are online or in person, advice is freely given, friendships are formed, and triumphs and tears are shared with a feeling of connection that clearly stretches over time and space. A lot more than just stitches are knitted up!

Simple projects, like socks or scarves, are perfect take-alongs to any gathering of knitters. Or take your knitting problems, and you're sure to get lots of advice. Whether the group calls itself Stitch 'n Bitch or Knit 'n Nosh or Sit 'n' Knit, local yarn shops, community centers, libraries, and churches and synagogues often host regular knitting groups, or you might want to start one yourself. Meetup.com lists existing knitting groups in many areas, as well as suggestions for how to start your own. (For a partial list of Internet resources for finding one near you, see the appendix.)

STITCH 'N BITCH. Thanks to the popularity of Debbie Stoller's books, new Stitch 'n Bitch groups are forming all the time, with more than 400 in the United States and nearly 150 worldwide. The Stitch 'n Bitch website offers suggestions on how to find a group nearby or begin one yourself.

STITCH N' PITCH. Stitch n' Pitch was born when a single knitting-at-the-game event in Seattle, Washington, drew over 1,000 needle artists. Now organized by The National NeedleArts Association, Stitch n' Pitch events are enjoyed at minor and major league games worldwide.

STICKS N' STITCHES. Hockey fans aren't to be outdone: the Columbus Blue Jackets reached out to the knitting world by offering reserved seating at "Sticks n' Stitches" events. Check to see whether your area hockey team is sponsoring such an event. If not, maybe you could convince them to try it.

GUILDS AND OTHER GROUPS. There are other ways to link up regularly with fellow knitters. Consider joining the Knitting Guild Association, which offers a formal Master Knitters program, as well as classes and conferences; membership includes a subscription to *Cast On* magazine. Your local yarn shop may sponsor, or know about, knitting groups in your area. In Canada the Canadian Knitwear Designers & Artisans (CKDA) organization publishes a list of Canadian guilds, including complete contact information.

MEET DEBBIE STOLLER

THERE WAS A TIME when Debbie Stoller hated knitting. "The needles and yarn didn't feel right, the rhythm didn't come, and it hurt my hands," she remembers. This was in spite of the fact that Debbie was enthusiastic about every other kind of needlework from a very early age. When other kids were playing soccer, she happily worked at cross-stitch, embroidery, sewing, and other related crafts — everything but knitting. This isn't to say she didn't keep *trying* to like it, but for many years, the giant sweater she had on her needles grew only about one inch every two years.

Then, in 1993, Debbie cofounded *BUST* magazine (she is now co-owner and editor in chief). Convinced that too much of what used to be considered "just" women's work was looked down on and undervalued, Debbie found great logic in taking up a feminist cause, sometimes referred to as "girlie feminism," that encouraged women to reclaim and embrace domestic crafts. In 1999, she coedited *The BUST Guide to the New Girl Order*, a collection of writings from *BUST* magazine. Setting off on a cross-country tour to promote the book, she decided to go by train because she hated flying. Faced with hours and days just sitting on a train, she threw that big old sweater and a children's how-to-knit book in her bag, deciding to try once more to pick up knitting. "I instinctively tucked one of the needles under my armpit," she recalls, "and all of the sudden, it clicked." The rhythm of the train and the rhythm of the knitting did their magic, and by the time she hit the West Coast, she was hooked.

At the time (1999), yarn stores were few and far between in New York City, but Debbie decided that she wanted to share her new-found obsession, and so she set a time and place and invited a few friends, as well as *BUST* readers, to join her with needles and yarn. The New York Stitch 'n Bitch group was born. Soon after, she wrote a book, which became the best-selling *Stitch 'n Bitch Nation: The Knitter's Handbook*. And other books followed!

Debbie feels that knitting's ascendancy is the result of several cultural trends colliding: many women rejected a global corporate culture seen as unethical and unecological, and turned to making connections with basic tactile pursuits like cooking, sewing, and, of course, knitting. She sees today's beginning knitters taking their knitting to new levels with lace, colorwork, and other more advanced techniques. Debbie is particularly drawn to the social qualities of knitting, and she sees real, in-person interactions as being even more valuable than the online community. When you're in the same room, there's an "exchange of ideas" that women have valued for decades, and Debbie clearly treasures being part of that long heritage.

Knitting the Classics...
and Beyond

Your scarf wish list is likely to be pretty long, considering all the classic and contemporary patterns you have to choose from. Refer to the appendix for a list of recent scarf and shawl pattern books. Ravelry has dozens of scarf groups, including groups that knit for charity; scarf swaps; techniques; KALs; and even Harry Potter scarves. Cracking open the scarf door is like opening an overstuffed closet — dozens of possibilities are likely to come tumbling out.

Knit for the Home Team

The varsity scarf, with lengthwise stripes, is usually quite long and knit by casting on enough stitches to give you the length you want. You then knit across the width of the scarf. The "varsity" part comes from the tradition of working the stripes in your favorite school's colors. You don't have to be outfitting yourself for the Big Game, however: it's fun to create this striped scarf in whatever colors you wish. Make the stripes whatever width you choose, all the same or of varying widths.

EXPLORE JUST FOR FUN

Knitting can be more than just practical, and there are times when you'd rather wrap a dainty necklace around your neck instead of a warm, cozy scarf. For a change in texture, abandon your big needles and fat wools, and choose instead fine needles and yarn and go for pure ornament. This necklace, knit on US 0 needles in shiny 5/2 pearl cotton (available in a wonderfully wide range of colors), is quick and easy to knit. The seed beads at the tip of each "triangle" add a touch of panache to the design. Research edging patterns for ideas on how to design your own jewelry. Even if the pattern is written to be used with, say, worsted-weight yarn, you can often follow it using much lighter weights and smaller needles to get the delicate effect you're looking for.

* When you change colors, leave longish tails (at least 8 inches) that can be used as fringe when the scarf is complete. You'll probably want to augment these with additional lengths of yarn, depending on how narrow you make your stripes.

* Instead of color changes, let texture make your stripes by working a different stitch pattern for whatever width you want for the stripe.

* Alternate both stitch patterns and colors: for instance, one color stripe in garter stitch, another color in stockinette, the next in seed stitch, and so on.

A scarf of a different stripe. Casting on for a scarf knit lengthwise does require a lot of stitches, but it's relaxing to knit the long rows without interruption, and the "length" (which is the scarf width) is only as wide as you want it — or until you run out of yarn.

Cables in Reverse

When knitting a cabled scarf, it's best to choose a pattern that's reversible so your scarf shows no wrong side when the wind whips it around. Reversible cables are comprised of a purl 1, knit 1 rib: the purl stitches contract and "disappear" on both sides of the fabric, leaving the knit stitches dominating, for a stockinette effect. Several contemporary designers, including Veronik Avery, Lynn Barr, Lily Chin, Teva Durham, Norah Gaughan, and Iris Schreier, have explored reversible stitch patterns. (See appendix for specific titles. For a description of basic cabling, see Capable with Cables, page 113.)

Some knitting trickery. Cables would seem to be the perfect design element for a scarf, but they are undeniably unattractive on the wrong side — unless you know how to make reversible cables. The "trick" is to work the cable in K1, P1 ribbing, so that the purl stitches recede and disappear on both the right and wrong sides, leaving the knit stitches to fill out the surface of the cable on both sides. To maintain the no-wrong-side feature of this scarf swatch, the cable sits on a field of seed stitch.

SWATCHING | *Reversible Cable*

Mysterious Möbius

Named for the nineteenth-century German mathematician who first described it, a Möbius strip has only one surface. To explore the concept, take a strip of paper a couple of inches wide and six or seven times as long, give it a half twist, and tape the ends together. You'll discover that you can run your finger along the paper, traveling along the entire surface and arriving back where you started without crossing the edge. If you use knitted fabric, rather than paper, you can take advantage of the properties of a Möbius to make a scarf with a nice drape. This approach is only a simulation, however, and not what Cat Bordhi calls a "native-born" Möbius. Cat has developed a cast-on method that makes it possible to create a Möbius loop from the moment you cast on. The result is, as Cat describes it, "graced with the miracle of mirror symmetry and an infinite round that continues until you decide to bind off." (See Cat Bordhi's Möbius Magic, at the right.)

LEARN CAT BORDHI'S MÖBIUS MAGIC

Inventive designer, author, and teacher Cat Bordhi has taken hold of the possibilities inherent in the Möbius to create designs that are as much fun to knit as they are to wear — or play with. In her two books on Möbius knitting, *A Treasury of Magical Knitting* and *A Second Treasury of Magical Knitting,* she presents a total of 74 projects, from scarves to bags and baskets, all based on the concept of Möbius design.

Her favorite gift for nearly all occasions is one of her felted Möbius baskets, for, she says, "They mesmerize everyone from young children to the most jaded adult. This mysterious, beautiful, and practical container has one continuous surface and one continuous edge. If one follows the outside surface up the handle, it becomes the inside surface, which becomes the outside surface, on and on. I've made ivory-colored Möbius baskets for wedding gifts, orange versions with ribs and tendrils for Halloween, and terra cotta ones for housewarming presents. These baskets are imbued with a sense of the sacred, for they represent the confluence, harmony, and unity of all life."

One of Cat Bordhi's Möbius baskets.

MEET KATE GILBERT

"Hideous" is the way Kate Gilbert describes her first sweater. But there's much more to it than that. Kate was 16 and, having been curious about knitting for years, happened upon the Cary Grant film *Mr. Lucky*, in which the movie star learns to knit. "I want to do that," she thought, so she headed to a craft store for yarn and needles and taught herself.

But it was with her subsequent trip to the library, where she found a book of patterns for sweaters knitted in one piece, that things really began to happen. Kate, with years of handmade papermaking and Ukrainian Easter eggs under her belt and no one around to discourage her, decided to draft her own design. The result was enormous, ill-fitting — and inspiring. Next came an intarsia project, then a sampler afghan.

"I learned a ton," she says. "I had no one telling me, 'That's hard.' I had no idea."

Kate, now a Montreal-based designer, grew up in Rochester, New York, attended the State University of New York at Buffalo, and later worked in New York City for graphic designer Milton Glaser and for *BUST* magazine, founded by knitting expert Debbie Stoller. In 2001 she moved to Paris to be with her boyfriend (now her husband). It was there, teaching English and knitting in her spare time, that she made and sold her first pattern, Anouk, an intarsia flower pinafore designed and named for a friend's baby. Since then, many of Kate's designs have become hot knits: the Sunrise Circle Jacket, Wisteria Sweater, Bird-in-Hand Mittens, and the Clapotis, a bias-knit scarf.

What do her widely varied designs have in common? They often have "somewhat unorthodox construction," like the Sunrise Circle Jacket's overlapping half circles in the front. And she strives to make each one fun to knit. "I try not to knock off other people's clothing designs," says Kate. "Sometimes I see a silhouette I like, or something sewn, and I think, how would that look knit?" But she generally doesn't go to fashion as her first source for ideas. Rather, ideas come from plants, motifs, ironwork patterns.

These days, finding time for knitting and designing is a challenge; she has a young daughter to care for and a quarterly online magazine, *Twist Collective*, to produce. Still, designing is integral to Kate's life, whatever the pace. "I can't *not* design things," says Kate. "It's kind of the perfect job for me."

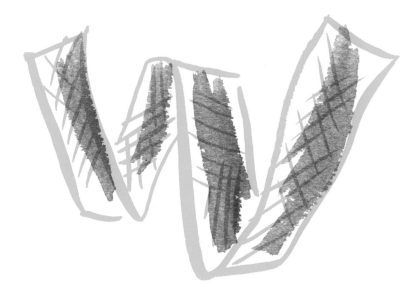

Sometimes It's Okay to Be Biased

If the direction of your rows of knitting runs diagonally across a square or rectangle, your scarf or shawl will be stretchy. We like stretchiness in our scarves, shawls, and blankets, because even when we wrap them snugly, they have elasticity, allowing us to move. One popular example of this style is Kate Gilbert's Clapotis scarf, which is not only worked corner to corner but also features dropped stitches to create an open pattern perpendicular to the rows. (See the appendix for Internet addresses for Kate Gilbert's Clapotis and Cheryl Marling's Tudora.)

Small, but Indispensable

Neck warmers, scarflets, ruffs, dickeys, snoods, cowls, and the like represent a family of scarf relatives that are the shorties, and all make very useful wardrobe accessories. A simple neck warmer is a tube that's elastic enough and large enough to slip over your head. Some button, others are designed with an eyelet to draw the end through. Cheryl Marling's Tudora, for instance, is an example of a buttoned version.

Lucy Neatby's Double Knits

Lucy Neatby calls herself a "mechanic" of knitting. As long as she can remember, she has had an insatiable curiosity about how stitches are constructed and how they work together. At one point she even unraveled a purchased gansey sweater to analyze its construction. As she says, this addiction is "a safer sport than hang gliding."

For years she has been fascinated by holes, and several of her scarf designs feature an unusual technique for "incorporating fresh air in your knitting." Knit lengthwise, the oblong holes in these designs are parallel to the rows, creating an open fabric with nice drape.

She finds double knitting another technique well suited to scarves, because it creates a reversible fabric. She likes to lightly stuff some of the shapes that form her design, in order to accent the whimsical "bubbles" or hearts scattered over the length of the scarves.

Lucy feels that fear of failure often holds knitters back, but exploring the inventive ways she puts stitches together in her designs can make knitting a truly joyful experience. She likes to demonstrate that a single knit stitch looks happy and in harmony with its neighbors. Forcing or twisting a stitch into an unnatural position may mean that you're practicing "stitch abuse" instead of keeping your stitches properly aligned in the fabric.

Happy stitch. Lucy Neatby and the Dolly Mamas created this Lucy doll, complete with Lucy's "happy stitch" tattoo. (See appendix for the Dolly Mamas.)

Lucy's Bubbles. This cleverly designed scarf is not only worked in double knit, but the bubbles are lightly stuffed, giving them a bit of dimension — and whimsy. The multicolor yarns, especially the more brightly colored one, make a very gradual change from one color to the next, creating a lovely watercolorlike wash effect.

LEARN NEXT TO NOTHING: DECADENT SILKINESS

IF THE SCARF YOU WANT TO MAKE *really* won't touch your skin and you mostly care about its being warm, a little bit of scratchiness may not matter. But in fact, it's likely that you'll want to pull that scarf up around your chin once in a while, so fiber content is ultra important. Some knitters admit that silkiness is up at the top of their fave-fiber lists. One of these knitters is Jenny Bakriges (for more about Jenny, see pages 269 and 281). In Jenny's view "silken" can refer to moth-made silk, but it can also include Tencel, bamboo, and any of the fibers than shine and feel like real silk. "They slither and tease and make one feel rich, just by virtue of experiencing them. Plus, color and silk make beautiful music together: rich and complex, almost naughty. Silk can sing in the simplest of patterns and it can reign supreme in the fanciest situation you can think of to put it in."

"I love to use silk in anything next to the skin," Jenny says, "where there's nothing to get in the way of me and pure bliss."

All tied up. Fashion often dictates the way we fasten our scarves. A popular and efficient method is simply to fold the scarf in half, drape the folded scarf around your neck and draw the ends through the loop created by the fold, as shown in the drawing at the bottom right. For a change, if your scarf is long and supple enough, you might want to experiment with more twists and turns shown here, or simply drape it, shawl-like over your shoulders with a single tie.

EXPLORE LOST IN A GOOD BOOK

Some knitting demands every bit of your attention, but there are those mesmerizing, repetitive projects that seem almost to knit themselves once you learn the pattern, and that's when a good book can make life just about perfect.

You may discover that you're one of those knitters who can in fact read and knit at the same time. (If you've never tried it, maybe you could add this skill to your Life List.) But even if you're not there yet, audio books are widely available, so with your mind on the book and your hands occupied with your knitting, you'll stay blissfully out of trouble.

In the following books knitting may be integral to the theme or simply a delightful surprise that brings a character to life. This is a very short list of the many possibilities; add your discoveries to it as you encounter knitters and knitting in whatever you're reading.

Knitting-Themed Series

* Kate Jacobs's Friday Night Knitting Club series
* Elizabeth Lenhard's Chicks with Sticks series, a trilogy for young adults
* Debbie Macomber's Blossom Street series

Not Really Just-about-Knitting Novels

BALZAC AND THE LITTLE CHINESE SEAMSTRESS, *by Dai Sijie; translated from the French by Ina Rilke.* Set in China during the days of the Cultural Revolution, this novel tells the story of two teenage boys who have been sent to a mountain village to be "re-educated." The book is filled with wonderful characters, including the mother of the boys, who confesses, "As for me, although I seem to be busy knitting this blue sweater, what I'm really doing is composing poems in my head, while my hands are occupied."

KNITTING, *by Anne Bartlett.* Grief, the healing power of friendship, and knitting as the bond combine in this short novel set in Australia.

THE KNITTING CIRCLE, *by Ann Hood.* A semiautobiographical story of a group of knitters who share their stories of tragedy and the accompanying stages of grief and, in the process, experience friendship and healing.

THE LACUNA, *by Barbara Kingsolver.* Harrison Shepherd's formative and tumultuous early life is spent in Mexico with the Diego Rivera family, where he served as a cook and also got to know Leon Trotsky. When he later settles in Asheville, North Carolina, he becomes a popular writer. His assistant and devoted admirer, Violet Brown, is a knitter and, in one of the touching moments in the novel, gives Shepherd a pair of "soft gray wool gloves" that she hand-knit for him, the first birthday gift he has ever received.

THE SHIPPING NEWS, *by Annie Proulx.* Knitting figures often in this novel set in Newfoundland, Canada. Proulx includes the rather horrifying description of the "don't-do-this-at-home" activity of a truck driver who "had his arms sticking through the steering wheel, knitting away like a machine" as he "barreled" across Nova Scotia.

SMALL CEREMONIES, *by Carol Shields.* Yarn found in a nonknitting household becomes a source of mystery in Pulitzer Prize–winning author Carol Shields's novel.

A TALE OF TWO CITIES, *by Charles Dickens.* Madame Defarge is probably the most notorious knitter in literature. As the French Revolution was brewing, all the women in her Paris neighborhood spent the day knitting (as Dickens relates, "the fingers of the knitting women were vicious"), but Madame Defarge's knitting had a menacing and, we finally learn, vengeful character: she stitched a code in which she recorded the names of individuals she believed deserved death because of their arrogant mistreatment of the lower classes. Dickens chillingly described her constant knitting as she alertly took in all that was going on around her, always knitting on "with the steadfastness of Fate."

THE VOYAGE OUT, *by Virginia Woolf.* In Woolf's first novel Mrs. Elliot proclaims, "I'm proud of my knitting. I think things like that run in families. We all knit well. I had an uncle who knitted his own socks to the day of his death — and he did it better than any of his daughters, dear old gentleman."

Books about Mill Girls

Playing with yarn and making fabric was obviously not always about fun. As the textile industry developed in the United States during the nineteenth century, it provided advantages and new opportunities for many, but those opportunities also had their downside. For a good read about this era, here are some novels that provide interesting insights on life in the mills. If your curiosity about this era is aroused, you might look for an out-of-print collection of journals, diaries, newspaper accounts, and interviews of girls who worked in the mills: *The Lowell Mill Girls: Life in the Factory,* edited by Joanne Weisman Deitch.

AN AMERICAN TRAGEDY, *by Theodore Dreiser.* Recently included in *Time* magazine's list of the one hundred best English-language novels written between 1923 and 2005, Dreiser's story is set in upstate New York in a collar-making factory. Based on an actual event, it centers around a loss of innocence and ultimate tragedy for both main characters. Tobias Picker adapted the novel into an opera, which premiered at the Metropolitan Opera in New York in 2005.

FORTUNE'S ROCKS, *by Anita Shreve.* This time the young girl's downfall comes *before* running off to the textile mills.

LYDDIE, *by Katherine Paterson.* Although this book is categorized for children ages nine to twelve, it's a classic story of the trials and tribulations of a Lowell mill girl that many adult fiber lovers will enjoy. And of course, you can share it with a young friend as well and together admire the determination that carries this young girl through.

UNRAVELLING, *by Elizabeth Graver. Unravelling* tells the story of a young teenager who leaves her family farm in New Hampshire to make a life for herself in the "City of Spindles" — Lowell, Massachusetts. This is a beautifully written novel, not only about the New England textile industry of the nineteenth century, but also of a mother-daughter relationship.

Novellas and Short Stories

HEART OF DARKNESS, *by Joseph Conrad.* Conrad writes about two "uncanny and fateful" women whom he describes as "dark-clothed knitters of destiny" as they sat "guarding the door of Darkness" and knitting black wool.

◗ **"ROMAN FEVER,"** *by Edith Wharton.* Two middle-aged American women with their daughters are tourists in Rome. Knitting is an important theme in the story, and although some readers have seen the knitting as implying that that's *all* women can do, others find much different symbolism in the way Wharton describes her characters and their work.

Mysteries

And for mystery lovers, here are some books that untangle more than just yarn (this is only a partial listing of each author's books):

◗ **AGATHA CHRISTIE'S MISS MARPLE MYSTERIES:** Any and all! To the uninformed eye, Jane Marple seems like a sweet, harmless grandmotherly type, completely absorbed in her knitting, an attitude that hides the fact that her steel-trap analytical mind is busily gleaning important details from the conversations and events taking place around her. Her ability to put all this together unfailingly leads to solving the crime.

◗ **MONICA FERRIS.**
Blackwork; Thai Die; Unraveled Sleeve

◗ **SALLY GOLDENBAUM.**
Death by Cashmere

◗ **MARY KRUEGER.**
Died in the Wool; Knit Fast, Die Young

◗ **MAGGIE SEFTON.** *Dyer Consequences; Fleece Navidad; Dropped Dead Stitch; Skein of the Crime; Double Knit Murders: Knit One, Kill Two* and *Needled to Death*

Books about Knitting

◗ **A HISTORY OF HAND KNITTING: THE COMPELLING HISTORY OF THIS ANCIENT CRAFT,** *by Richard Rutt.* The book traces the history of this craft from ancient times to the present, examining museum collections, literary evidence, and popular legends.

◗ **KNITLIT,** *collected by Linda Roghaar and Molly Wolf.* A series of three books — *Knit Lit: Sweaters and Their Stories . . . and Other Writing about Knitting; KnitLit (Too): Stories from Sheep to Shawl . . . and More Writing about Knitting;* and *KnitLit the Third: We Spin More Yarns* — including stories, essays, anecdotes, and recollections by all kinds of knitters who are passionate about their craft.

◗ **KNITTING AMERICA: A GLORIOUS HERITAGE FROM WARM SOCKS TO HIGH ART,** *by Susan Strawn.* A comprehensive history of knitting in America from Colonial times to the present, with color photos of vintage pattern booklets, posters, and postcards.

◗ **KNITTING HEAVEN AND EARTH: HEALING THE HEART WITH CRAFT,** *by Susan Gordon Lydon.* Written when the author knew she was dying, this profound book describes how the sensual pleasures of yarn, color, and knitting gave Lydon strength and perspective in the face of family tragedy, as well as her own diagnosis with breast cancer. Her first book was *The Knitting Sutra: Craft as a Spiritual Practice.*

◗ **NO IDLE HANDS: THE SOCIAL HISTORY OF AMERICAN KNITTING,** *by Anne Macdonald.* Excerpts from diaries, letters, and personal remembrances present the picture of the importance of knitting in America, from colonial until present times.

MEET ANN BUDD

SOME KNITTERS ARE ARTISTS WHO USE YARN as their medium. Ann Budd, however, considers herself more an engineer who knits.

A native of Boulder, Colorado, where she still lives, Ann learned to knit as a child when her father brought the family to Switzerland for a sabbatical in the late 1960s. Attending a village elementary school, she was soon knitting bootees and more. She took to the craft, but when she returned to Colorado, she kept it a secret, because traditional women's crafts were "uncool."

In college Ann studied science, earning a master's in geology and planning for a career in the oil industry. While she waited for her dream job to come along, she kept busy working in a local yarn store, where she learned to weave, as well as to alter and create patterns for customers. That in-between job changed her life. Even after she landed her dream job, she kept knitting and weaving in her spare time. And then, in the late 1980s, she married and began to rethink her career. She took a job at *Handwoven* magazine, and later, after her three sons were born, she worked as a managing editor, then senior editor of *Interweave Knits*, eventually moving into designing knitwear.

With *The Knitter's Handy Book of Patterns* and several other titles to her credit, Ann, someone who always likes to know how things work and why, has become an authority on creating and tailoring patterns. "I feel like I'm where I ought to be. I don't think of myself as a designer, I think of myself as an engineer," says Ann.

An avid sock knitter who has around 30 hand-knit pairs in her drawer, Ann recently devoted herself to experiments with the heels of socks, trying to find the best round-heel look with a toe-up design. "I try to figure out patterns that require the least amount of fuss, and I like to have some clever aspect to it. With socks, it's often a cast on, a way to integrate the top edge into the patterning on the leg," she says.

In her book Knitting Green, *Ann turned her inquisitive eye to the questions surrounding planet-friendly knitting: what makes a yarn sustainable, for instance, and which dyes have the least environmental impact?*

The project was illuminating, she says, because it showed that the issues are complex. "There are no black-and-white answers," she reflects. For instance, bamboo grows so fast that it is easy to harvest and replace, yet it requires a lot of chemicals to transform it to a usable fiber.

Having watched the growth of the knitting industry over the past 25 years, she finds environmental awareness just one of the interesting developments. Ann enjoys the explosion of yarn choices; she also applauds the innovative construction of garments. "It's very exciting. You look in the very old pattern books, and things were just . . . normal. Now, anything goes!"

Classic Shawls

I like to think of shawls as scarves' grown-up sisters, especially if the shawl is lace knit. For centuries, in many different cultures, the place to showcase lace-knitting abilities has been by creating a shawl. You might want to make your first lace project something smaller than a full-size shawl, but once you gain confidence and you're hooked by the allure of creating delicate and exquisite patterns, you'll be more than ready to explore further.

Although lace often looks complex and difficult, in reality many lace patterns are rhythmic and relaxing to knit, making lace knitting a very satisfying and endlessly fascinating experience. It can seem almost like steps in a dance, once you learn the rhythmic repeats. In the simplest of terms, lace is created by pairing yarn overs that create holes, with decreases that (eventually) maintain the total stitch count. The lace pattern emerges depending on the way these increases and decreases are arranged and how they shift from row to row or round to round.

Time-Honored Traditions

Many cultures have age-old lace designs that are part of their proud fiber tradition. The finer the yarn and the more intricate the patterning, the greater the knitters' skills could shine. Because the design possibilities are almost endless, lace knitting can be addictive, so beware!

SHETLAND. One of the most famous Shetland shawls is the wedding ring shawl, so called because it is so fine that a 6-foot-square shawl

can be pulled through a wedding ring. Examples of Shetland lace go back to the seventeenth century. Queen Victoria owned several items knit in Shetland lace, thus helping to popularize the style. According to Donna Druchunas, who has written several books on lace knitting, the key to Shetland lace is that although it looks complicated, it has fairly simple repeats and small lace patterns, allowing the knitters to make the shawls more quickly and, ipso facto, make more money.

As with all lace, Donna reminds knitters that when measuring gauge, be sure to wash and block the swatch before measuring, especially if you'll be stretching the lace while blocking to smooth out the texture and open up the holes.

ORENBURG shawls are knit with a yarn spun of the very fine down of the Orenburg goat, which is combed from the animal (rather than

LEARN PUZZLE POWER

For Lori Gayle, a technical knitting editor and lover of lace knitting, "Figuring out lace patterns provides the same satisfaction as completing a crossword puzzle."

sheared) and then often plied with a fine silk thread for strength. Known to have been knitted about 250 years ago, these shawls share their cobweb-like quality with that of Shetland shawls, and like the Shetlands, the finest ones can be drawn through a wedding ring. Orenburg is a city on the Ural River southeast of Moscow, near the Russian border with Kazakhstan.

ESTONIAN. Estonian lace shawls are the product of a cottage industry nurtured for nearly two centuries by the talented women of Haapsalu, whose story has been vividly told by Nancy Bush in *Knitted Lace of Estonia*. The typical shawls were 40-inch (or larger) squares that featured a center pattern as well as border and edging patterns. According to Nancy, in addition to traditional nature motifs, Estonian knitters created designs named for well-known people, from Greta Garbo to Swedish royalty.

FAROESE. You can identify the lace shawls of Denmark's Faroe Islands by their butterfly-wing shaping, created by knitting from the bottom up and decreasing along the center back; they are usually knit in garter stitch so that they are reversible. Traditionally worked in natural-colored wools, their shaping gives them a lovely drape and makes it easy to keep them in place on your shoulders; some are made with long ends that may be tied around the waist, as well. Sheep are so ubiquitous to the islands, that it's thought that the name "Faroe" can be traced back to the ancient word for sheep.

Getting the gold ring. Orenburg shawls, like many Shetland shawls, are knit with such fine down yarn that they can be pulled through a wedding ring.

A Shetland lace shawl. Edged with the tree and crown pattern and knitted in the early 1930s, the shawl center features an unusal join between the patterns that results in flowerlike motifs.

MEET NANCY BUSH

For Nancy Bush, one of life's magical moments occurred just as they do in a storybook, the heroine happening upon an obscure, antique volume that changes her life forever. Nancy was standing in a Utah library at this pivotal moment, opening a book about Estonian traditional clothing from the nineteenth century for her research on knitted socks. In studying the photographs of Estonian people and their patterned hand-knits, something clicked for her.

"I knew, standing there that day, that I had found my life," she says. The patterns spoke to her, she recalls, and while she knew little about Estonia, it looked familiar, as if she'd been there before. Since that day in the early 1990s, Estonian knitting has become Nancy's passion. The author of several books, among them *Folk Knitting in Estonia* and *Knitted Lace of Estonia,* she teaches at conferences throughout the year, offering workshops on knitting Estonian lace and other Estonian knitting traditions, knitting socks with traditional "top-down" construction, and more. She also runs an online mail-order yarn and supply business, The Wooly West.

Nancy loves the aesthetic aspects of Estonian knitting — the complex use of pattern, the designs that vary from one island to the next, the knitting techniques and embellishments. But she also loves the way knitting is part of the country's ethic of self-sufficiency. "If they needed something," she says, "they made it themselves."

Nancy, who grew up in Salt Lake City, Utah, graduated from the University of Utah in the mid-1970s with a degree in art history, focusing on Japanese folk art. After college, she decided to learn a craft and was drawn to textiles. So she began studying weaving, first in San Francisco, then in Sweden, where she also took up knitting. Back home in Utah, she worked in a bookstore before opening up her own yarn shop and then moved into teaching and writing books.

She was researching her first book, *Folk Socks,* when she stumbled upon the book about Estonia. Three years later, in 1995, she was on a boat in the Baltic Sea, approaching Tallinn, the Estonian capital. She's visited more than a dozen times since then, witnessing growth that's included new hotels and more tourism. But that first visit, just a few years after Estonia regained its independence in 1991, following decades of Soviet occupation, stays with her. On the train in Tallinn, riding alongside older women, she delighted in seeing their traditional knitted berets and mittens; she also loved watching the local knitters at work.

"It was still so rural," she marvels. "We traveled to a couple of the islands, and it was like going back in time."

Success with Lace

While it's true that some awesome lace *is* truly challenging, often what looks difficult is not as impossible as it might seem if you take your time and follow some simple habits of knitting. Here are some basics that may help.

❊ **YARN AND NEEDLE SIZE.** To show your lace off to best effect, choose a smooth, fine yarn with two or more plies. (Some traditional lace knitting is done with singles, but these are exceptions to the usual.) Be sure to use large enough needles that the holes and the rest of the pattern are clearly defined. (The needles are likely to be a larger size than is recommended on the yarn band, unless it specifies "for lace.")

❊ **GAUGE.** Lace tends to stretch, so keep in mind that you may need fewer stitches per inch than you would need using the same yarn and needles for a denser-knit fabric. For instance, if you'd like to insert a 2-inch lace panel along the front of a sweater knit in stockinette, and your gauge for the stockinette is eight stitches per inch, you may need only six stitches in the lace pattern to maintain the correct circumference for the sweater. Another reminder to make swatches and measure your gauge!

❊ **NEEDLE MATERIAL.** Experiment with needles. If your yarn is slippery, it's all too easy to drop stitches, and you may therefore appreciate the mild toothiness of wood or bamboo needles.

❊ **CAST ON AND BIND OFFS.** Be sure to cast on and bind off loosely. Again, because the lace area will be stretchy, you don't want the edges to be tight. Some cast ons and bind offs are especially suitable for lace: check a knitting reference book for suggestions.

❊ **KEEPING TRACK.** In her book *A Gathering of Lace*, Meg Swansen offers several excellent tips for lace knitting. Although she doesn't usually use markers as she knits, she makes an exception for lace. "Because of all the yarn overs, it's more difficult to read where you are," she says. She suggests tying pieces of wool in a contrasting color around the needle as markers and making use of the "lifeline" (see The Security of Lifelines, below). In addition, she advises, "You have to monitor it, you have to keep paying attention" to make sure the pattern is vertically aligned. As always, she urges knitters to learn to "read" their own knitting, because it's easy to misread charts.

LEARN THE SECURITY OF LIFELINES

Especially helpful to new lace knitters, the lifeline is a temporary thread inserted through a row of stitches in an unpatterned row at the beginning or end of a pattern repeat. If you discover you've made a mistake but can't figure out how to fix it without ripping out, you have that safety net of held stitches that you can confidently pick up. If you run a lifeline on the first (or last) row of a pattern repeat, you'll always know exactly where to begin the pattern after you've ripped out.

Deb Robson describes this easy way to run a lifeline: while the unpatterned row is on the needle, thread a lightweight, slick strand of yarn into an eyed needle and run that needle through the stitches, right along the knitting needle that's holding them. You'll find it's easier to run the eyed needle along the bottom side of the knitting needle (that is, where the stitches' "feet" are), rather than along its upper loop). Nylon fishing line and dental floss both make good lifelines. If you have problems above your lifeline, you can pull the knitting off the needles, and rip back to the lifeline, which keeps the work from raveling further. Slide the knitting needle along the path defined by the lifeline and begin knitting again. Leave the lifeline in place, but be sure not to pick it up and knit it as you work the next row.

Design Your Own

Stitch collections, such as Barbara Walker's 1971 *The Craft of Lace Knitting,* hold the tools you can use to design a simple scarf or shawl in a lace pattern.

If you decide to design your own, note the pattern multiple and cast on the appropriate number of stitches for the width you want. For a 20-inch-wide shawl, for example, if your stitch gauge is 6 stitches to an inch, you need about 120 stitches. But if the pattern multiple is 18,

"Frost Flowers." Many traditional stitch patterns, such as this one, taken from Barbara Walker's *A Treasury of Knitting Patterns,* represent themes from nature, including snowflakes, feathers, birds, and flowers.

you need to cast on either 108 stitches (for an 18-inch-wide shawl with 6 pattern repeats) or 126 stitches (for a 21-inch-wide shawl with 7 pattern repeats). If you plan for a knitted border, be sure to include the border stitches in your cast-on stitch count. In the example above, you might knit the lace pattern centered on 108 stitches with a 6-stitch border on each edge to achieve the 20-inch width you're aiming for. Don't forget that lace is often very stretchy, so you'll usually gain quite a bit of length and width when you block the finished piece.

Exploring Traditions

If you're more comfortable beginning with a published pattern or you're interested in learning firsthand about different ethnic knitting traditions, you'll find a number of excellent books to guide your exploration.

Nancy Bush's books on Estonian lace (see page 169) present a full, inspiring picture of Estonian lace, complete with tips and techniques, as well as its fascinating history. Donna Druchunas's *Arctic Lace: Knitting Projects and Stories Inspired by Alaska's Native Knitters* contains the cultural background along with the patterns of the people who specialize in knitting lace with that very special fiber: qiviut.

Jane Sowerby's *Victorian Lace Today* gives us the tools, techniques, and patterns to re-create nineteenth-century lace in twenty-first-century forms, all tantalizingly shown in beautiful photographs. Meg Swansen's *A Gathering of Lace* includes elegant lace patterns from all over the world for not only scarves and shawls, but also sweaters, vests, socks, and gloves. (See the appendix for complete information on these and more lace pattern books.)

LEARN MIXING AND MATCHING

In her classic book *The Craft of Lace Knitting,* Barbara Walker suggests how to incorporate lace into an existing pattern by inserting it either along the length of the item or placing single elements as desired over the face of the fabric. When several lace patterns are used next to one another, they are referred to as panels; when a lace pattern is set against a background pattern it is known as an insertion. This mix-and-match technique offers a multitude of opportunities to enhance all kinds of knitted projects.

MEET LINDA LIGON

It's amazing what can happen when someone simply follows her interests — especially when that someone is Linda Ligon.

In the late 1980s, Linda had already founded Interweave Press, which specialized in publishing books and magazines about arts and crafts, when she got interested in herbs. She was so interested that she launched *The Herb Companion*, a magazine that was among the first to identify and pursue the nation's growing interest in the culinary and medicinal properties of plants. That led to a sister publication, *Herbs for Health*, which, in turn, led to Linda's trip to the Amazon to visit with a shaman. There she fell in love with the jungle, the highlands, and, as an avid weaver, the traditional textiles of Peru. That eventually led to the 2010 Tinkuy de Tejedores, a first-of-its-kind gathering of native weavers from Peru, Bolivia, Guatemala, and other Latin American countries.

Linda's contribution to the world of fiber, however, really began with an earlier, one-thing-leads-to-another tale. It was 1975, and she was living in Loveland, Colorado. A schoolteacher with two young children and another one on the way, Linda had decided to stay home to care for her newborn. But it wasn't long before an idea was taking shape in her mind. Weaving had become very popular, and yet there was little literature available to weavers.

"There was so much interesting stuff related to weaving going on in the western states. I decided to start a nice little magazine for people in the region," recalls Linda. She had worked on her own high school and college yearbooks, and later, as a teacher, she had mentored students working on a high school newspaper, so she had picked up typesetting, page design, and other skills. Linda set out on a trip to Santa Fe, interviewing and photographing weavers. Back at home, she sat at her dining table and put together the first, 24-page issue of *Interweave*. She took it to a printer, and then gave the copies away.

Next, a local weaving store gave her a grocery bag full of sales receipts to sift through, and she put together a mailing list. Only a few years later, the magazine was self-supporting; she started another magazine, *Handwoven*, filled with patterns and projects. "It took off," she remembers, but its success didn't come without controversy: some weavers felt that other weavers shouldn't need "recipes" for their projects, but should rely on their own imagination and ideas instead.

Demand for patterns eclipsed the negative voices, however, and by the time Linda sold Interweave to Aspire Media in 2005, it had grown into a media company that included *Interweave Knits, Piecework, Fiberarts*, and more. Interweave has now published nearly 300 books, runs 30 websites, and sponsors several craft programs on public television.

Linda remains deeply involved: she's the creative director, a member of the board of directors, and works at Interweave 40 hours a week on new media projects such as videos and electronic magazines with animated graphics. In her free time, she plays cello and weaves. She's pleased to see the resurgence of interest in handcrafts, and the way new technology contributes to it. "There's a lot today that feels like the '60s and '70s," she said. But now, there's apt to be a laptop on that dining table where the very first issue of *Interweave* came to life.

EXPLORE THE JOY OF THE FIBER COMMUNITY

Many fiber lovers have discovered the special joy of breaking away from regular schedules and chores to spend a few days or a week doing nothing but knitting, spinning, or weaving with friends who share their love of creating beautiful fibery objects to see, touch, and cherish.

You'll find a wide variety of opportunities not only coast to coast in North America, but worldwide as well. For instance, three annual events that have become special favorites for many over the years are Meg Swansen's Knitting Camps in Wisconsin, Clara Parkes's Knitter's Review Fall Retreat in Massachusetts, and the Madrona Fiber Arts Winter Retreat in Washington. (For more information about these and other retreats, see Restore Yourself at a Retreat, page 123.)

KNITTING CAMP. Rosi Ziegler, recently a first-time "camper," described her Wisconsin retreat experience as not only helpful for improving her knitting skills, but also inspiring as she explored tables stacked with sweaters, hats, and scarves that both Meg Swansen and her mother, Elizabeth Zimmermann, had knit. "It was like stepping into a museum and being told it's okay to touch anything you want — even to wear anything you would like," she explains, "and it was so rich to have so many examples of various techniques to touch, examine, and go back to over the course of the week." Seeing items that she remembered from watching EZ on her PBS television series more than 25 years ago, she mused, "What an endorsement for good wool and good care!"

KNITTER'S REVIEW FALL RETREAT. Clara Parkes keeps her retreat small and, with the return of many participants who have come each year, promotes a special kind of encouragement for each knitter's and spinner's development as a fiber artist. Inspiring classes are designed to challenge even experienced knitters, and a special guest and the sharing of goals and accomplishments are features of this supportive retreat.

MADRONA FIBER ARTS WINTER RETREAT. Like Clara Parkes, Suzanne Pederson, who codirects the Madrona retreat, sees the Washington event as a way of generating a sense of community for those who come. The organizers provide the classes and the place, but the participants themselves create what the retreat offers them. Mother-daughter pairs, college roommates, and others have attended for many years.

For listings of these and other festivals, workshops, and retreats, see Fiber Festivals, page 42; Back to School, page 88; Knitting Trip Adventures, page 221)

MEET VICKIE HOWELL

WHEN VICKIE HOWELL WAS SEVEN OR EIGHT, her mom gave her a crochet hook, knitting needles, and sewing supplies. The first thing she remembers finishing was a seersucker dress for one of her dolls. "I was pretty darn proud of the fact that I thought to use one of her existing dresses to trace around onto two pieces of fabric. Then I hand-sewed them together," she says. "Of course, it didn't fit, but I didn't care because I made it myself!" "Do-it-yourself" has been Vickie's mantra ever since.

A mother of three, she started a small Web business right after her first child was born, selling handmade things for moms and babies. "It was really more of a hobby than anything else, though — something to feed me creatively while I got used to my new role as a mother."

It wasn't until she got the job as the host of the television show Knitty Gritty that she turned her DIY passion into a career. "I felt that getting that job was a huge gift from the universe, and so I had a responsibility to make the most out of it," says Vickie. "Before the first episode even aired, I'd pursued my first book deal. Since then, I've continued to hustle one opportunity into another so that, hopefully, I'll be able to do the work I love for many years to come."

Among her many books is *Craft Corps*, a compilation of profiles of both professional and amateur crafters; it is rooted in Vickie's strong belief in crafts as a path to self-sufficiency and community. When she isn't working, Vickie gravitates toward small projects she can expect to finish — accessories, home decor items, baby clothes, and cardigans with simple lines but a funky edge.

One of the lessons she's learned from knitting is that "life is better in color." Says Vickie, "Before I started knitting, my favorite color was black. Knitting in black, though, can get pretty boring after a while, so I branched out into colors. Now, I love teal, gray, turquoise, orange, chartreuse, olive, and yellow. I still love black. But knitting taught me that infusing a little color into my life makes the overall picture a much richer experience."

Vickie loves knitting for its versatility. "If you need to relax, you can zone out knitting a garter stitch scarf. If you need a challenge, you can work on an intricate Fair Isle sweater. If you need to express your creativity, you can freeform knit a mystery piece. (For information about freeform knitting, see Freeing Up Your Inner Knitter, page 248.) If you need something portable to fill your subway commute time, you can knit socks. Knitting gives you what you need from it."

Chapter 6

THE

LIFE LIST

Our hats can be the ultimate expressions of our individuality, like a cherry on top of a sundae or a cedar waxwing's flirty crown. Even the most conservative of us is sometimes daring enough to at least flaunt a pom-pom, and just think of some of the fairly outrageous hats, from jesters to monkeys to pumpkins, we're willing to put on the heads of our babies!

Handspun hats. This Moroccan craftsman displays his colorful hats as he knits yet another creation.

Like other smallish projects, knitting a hat is a great way to explore a technique that's new to you, whether it's lace, stranded knitting, or knitting in the round. And hats are even quicker to knit and handier to take along than socks. A key ingredient to the success with any hat project is the yarn you knit with. For perhaps no other garment is yarn choice more important: even someone who tolerates wool sweaters may mind too-itchy wool over his forehead.

LIFE
THE
KNITTER'S
LIST

Learn it · Explore it · Do it · Check it off!

HATS

MEET
- Linda Ligon
- Jillian Moreno

DISCOVER
- Make a hat using only yarn(s) from your stash.
- Knit a traditional Andean ch'ullu.
- Experiment to see if "trading places" works for you.
- See if Elizabeth Zimmermann's method for joining in the round works for you.

DO/TRY
- Line a hat with a nonitchy fabric.
- Use cashmere yarn for a hat.
- Start a hat at the crown with a jaunty I-cord.
- Use pom-poms to top off your hand-knitted hats.
- Attach a tassel to the crown of a hat.
- Knit I-cords for ties on kids' hats.
- Use I-cords to extend earflaps on Peruvian- or ski-style hats.
- Work an I-cord as a button at the center of a hat's crown.
- Attach three or more I-cords at the center of the crown for a tassel effect.
- "Curl" an I-cord at the crown by threading the bind-off tail back through the cord.

- Knit a hat in your favorite sports team's colors.
- Knit a watch cap.
- Knit a ski hat with earflaps.
- Knit a ski hat with a folded top.
- Make a double-knit ski band.
- Knit a stocking cap.
- Knit a "ponytail" hat.
- Knit a turban.
- Knit a beret.
- Knit a Scandinavian hat.
- Knit a felted hat with a brim.
- Knit a cloche.
- Knit a snood.
- Knit a balaclava.
- Make a hat as gift for someone you love.
- Knit a pattern from one of Jillian Moreno and Amy Singer's books.

LEARN
- Experiment with different ways of marking the beginning of rounds.
- Experiment with different ways of disguising the jog in stripes when knitting circularly.
- Make a cozy headband or hat using a double-knit stitch pattern.
- Be inspired by Jillian Moreno and learn to spin.

GO
- Travel to Peru.

EXPERIENCE
- Play with texture and scale by combining thick and thin or smooth and fuzzy yarns in one hat.
- Use a loop cast on to begin a hat from the top down.
- Try Margaret Radcliffe's techniques for avoiding "pooling."
- Give your interests room to take you in new creative directions.

EXTRA CREDIT
- What trade-protectionist law was enacted in fifteenth-century England?
- What are the colorful hand-knit Peruvian hats called?
- Name five historically influential women who were avid knitters (don't peek).

MORE FOR MY HATS LIFE LIST
- _____
- _____
- _____
- _____

A Word about Yarns

The Yarn Harlot Stephanie Pearl-McPhee's self-deprecating descriptions of her stash resonate with thousands of us knitters because we all suffer from the I-need-that-yarn syndrome at one time or to one extent or another, and it's a relief to share and confess — and laugh at ourselves! Knitting a hat is an excellent way to make dents in your stash and use up odds and ends from other projects, as long as you keep several things in mind.

COLOR. For best results have enough of one basic yarn that it can become the anchor and theme around whatever other colors you add.

WEIGHT. If you use more than one color, whether stripes or stranded knitting, the yarns usually need to be close to the same weight. Sometimes it's fun to break this rule in order to get an interesting texture, for instance, by alternating thick and thin or smooth and fuzzy yarns.

COMFORT. Most important for hats: Avoid itchy yarns at all costs. Cashmere almost always satisfies, but many smooth Merinos or Merino blends are just fine, and plant fibers (cotton and bamboo, for example) are also successful, though not as warm or as elastic. Scan the descriptions of yarn on pages 17–38, however, because you may discover some surprises that will be perfect for your next hat. And because many hat patterns require only about a skein of yarn, this is a good project for experimenting with unfamiliar (or expensive) yarns.

GAUGE. If warmth is what you have in mind, be sure you knit at a gauge that creates the fabric density required to keep the wind at bay. On the other hand, hats that are too hot are annoying, and they need a bit of stretch as well in order to be comfortable. Stitches that are too tightly packed may result in a hat that's both too hot and too stiff. Too much stretch, however, and you'll find the hat down over your eyes, especially if it gets wet and stretches even more. (Each of these concerns is yet another gentle reminder of the importance of swatching!)

LEARN   LOOK FOR THE SILVER LINING

If you really want to knit a hat with wool that might be a bit on the scratchy side (or the wearer is particularly sensitive), consider lining the hat with silk fabric or synthetic fleece fabric or a knitted fabric of a less-scratchy fiber. It's usually effective to line only the part of the hat that sits on the forehead (about 3 inches). If you use woven fabric, remember that it won't stretch, so you'll have to take care to get the fit just right.

Top Hat Techniques

Hats are great projects for technique building, particularly of your circular knitting, since many, if not most, hat patterns are knit in the round. You may want to use double-point needles for the entire project, if all the stitches will fit on three or four needles. For hats you should probably choose double-point needles that are at least 7 or 8 inches long, so the stitches don't fall off the ends as you work. Or you may prefer to use a circular needle for the wider part of the hat and move to double points when there are too few stitches to fit around the circular. (Or, use the Magic Loop technique, page 141, for the crown.) Here are some tips for success from the experts.

AVOIDING THE TWIST. Once you've cast on the required number of stitches, you need to join the first and last ones to make your continuous circle. Almost every set of pattern directions you'll encounter reminds you not to twist your stitches around the needle when you make that join. To get a clear look at your work, lay down your needles (whether double-points or a circular) on a flat surface big enough that you can arrange the entire piece in a circle, and untwist the cast on so the bottom of every cast-on stitch faces into the middle of the circle. Now you're ready to make your join.

ELIZABETH ZIMMERMANN ON AVOIDING THE "BUMP." Elizabeth Zimmermann suggested a join that is almost invisible: cast on one more stitch than your pattern calls for. When you've ensured that your stitches are all aligned properly and not twisted, slip the last cast-on stitch to your left needle and knit it together with the first cast-on stitch, using the tail from the cast on held together with the working yarn. You're now at the correct stitch count and your circle is joined. When you come back to this stitch on the next round, be sure to knit the double strand as a single stitch.

An invisible beginning. Here, the extra last cast-on stitch has been slipped to the left-hand needle to be knit together with the first stitch, using both the working yarn and the tail, for just this first stitch.

BETSY MCCARTHY ON AVOIDING THE "BUMP."
Another way to avoid the little bump on the bottom edge of the hat between the first and last stitches is to have them "trade places." Here's how Betsy does it: Pick up your work, holding your needles so the first cast-on stitches are on the needle in your left hand and the last ones are on the right. Use the tip of your right-hand needle to move the first cast-on stitch (now on the left-hand needle) to the right-hand needle.

Keeping your working yarn behind the needles, use the left-hand needle to tease the last cast-on stitch (now sitting second to the stitch you just moved to the right-hand needle) up and over the transferred stitch, and move it to the left-hand needle. Gently snug up the yarn and you're ready to begin knitting the stitch you just transferred to the left-hand needle.

MARKING THE BEGINNING OF ROUNDS. Once you've made your join so perfectly invisible, it may become difficult to spot the beginning of each round. One of the simplest ways to keep track is to look for where your cast-on tail is attached. As the fabric lengthens, however, it becomes difficult to spot the exact stitch that begins the next round. If you leave a quite long tail, you can weave it to the front and then to the back on subsequent rounds as you progress. Or you can just place a stitch marker to identify the spot. If you're using double points rather than circulars, however, place your marker after the first stitch, so it won't fall off the needle.

TOP-DOWN CAST ONS. Use a loop cast on that can be tightened to hide the hole once the hat is complete. Or for a jaunty accent, begin with a short I-cord, and increase to the necessary number of stitches for the crown once the I-cord is the desired length. (See Top It Off!, page 186.)

DID YOU KNOW **COVERED BY LAW**

Remember when your mom insisted that you wear your hat, even when none of the other kids were wearing theirs? That was bad enough, but what if the law of the land required you to wear your hat, and not only that, what if it stipulated what that hat should look like? In fifteenth-century England, this was pretty much the case because of a trade-protectionist law that prohibited wearing any imported hats. A century later a new cap law required that all males of a certain class over the age of six "shall wear upon the Sabbath and Holydays, one cap of wool knit, thicked and dressed in England" or they would be fined.

One of the most popular of these knitted hats was known as the Monmouth cap, named for the Welsh town of Monmouth on the Wye River. Knit in stockinette stitch in a heavy yarn from a breed of sheep whose fleece felted easily, it featured a wide hem that was turned to the inside, a knitted loop on the back edge, and a knitted "button" on top.

The medieval knitters (always men) were called "cappers." By the 1600s these caps were standard gear for both soldiers and sailors. They were even listed as "practical clothing" for both the Massachusetts and Jamestown settlers, and word has it that Captain John Smith offered a Monmouth cap to Powhatan, Pocahontas's father.

MORE FOR MY HATS LIFE LIST

◇ _____

_____

◇ _____

_____

◇ _____

_____

◇ _____

_____

Color in the Round

Margaret Radcliffe specializes in explaining the sometimes small but very important details that make knitting more fun and your projects more successful. Here are her thoughts on multicolor circular knitting.

AVOIDING THE JOG IN STRIPED HATS. Because circular knitting creates a continuous spiral, the beginning of each round steps up on the first stitch of the preceding round, which creates a telltale "jog" in stripes. To disguise the step-up jog, when you come to the first stitch on the second round of a new color, slip it purlwise, with yarn in back, then complete the round. When you're weaving in tails, weave each tail into the stripe that matches it in color, bringing the stripes into alignment as you do so. Alternatively, knit into the stitch below the first stitch,

Ready for the downhill. Not only the hat, but the sweater as well, shows off this Swedish stranded knitting design.

and complete the round, then weave tails into the matching stripes as just described.

AVOIDING TOO-TIGHT STRANDED-KNIT HATS. Knitting too tightly is a common pitfall of stranded knitting (carrying two or more colors all the way around). This is disastrous for hats: you may have gotten the gauge that gives you exactly the right circumference for your hat, but even a slightly too-tight carry of the nonworking yarn can turn a comfortable hat into a vise if you carry the nonworking yarn too tightly. These strands don't stretch, as the knitted stitches do. Check frequently to ensure that you're leaving the correct amount of slack in your carried yarns.

Margaret warns, however, that you don't want too much slack or your fabric will be flimsy, and holes may even appear at the color changes, instead of being sharply defined. Spread out the stitches on the right-hand needle so the fabric is flat, then knit the first stitch in the new color, taking care not to tighten it. An even better way, she says, is to turn the hat inside out, and (for stockinette) purl around, instead of knitting. With the stranding on the outside, you're much less likely to make the mistake of pulling it too tight. Peruvian knitters often use this technique for their *ch'ullus* (see page 184).

AVOIDING UNWANTED POOLING. When the same color appears on two or more adjacent rows, creating a little irregularly-shaped puddle of color, it's known as pooling. Both the length of each segment of color in the yarn as well as the width of your knitted piece affect the tendency of color to pool — or not. Swatching is the only way to determine the outcome, and because the results are very different depending on the width of your hat, as well as on whether you're knitting flat or in the round, your swatching must test actual size and method of knitting. Achieve the effect you like by using various textured stitches, working a pattern with slipped stitches, or alternating a solid-color yarn with each row (or round) of the multicolor yarn.

Double Your Pleasure

Although many hats are knit in just one layer, nothing beats a double-thick knitted fabric for keeping ears warm when the winds howl. This is a particularly popular knitting technique to use for ski bands, but it's also useful anywhere you want reversible or extra-cozy fabric.

The following describes just one of several ways to double knit, and it results in stockinette on both sides of the fabric. All of your stitches are on one needle (in other words, both layers of knitted fabric), with twice as many as you need to get your gauge. (If you want 20 stitches per 4 inches, you'll need to cast on 40 stitches.) As you work, you alternate knit and purl stitches across each row (or round), so that as you look at your needle, you see the wrong side of the back layer and the right side of the knit layer. In other words, as the fabric develops, the wrong sides of each layer are facing, and you are always creating two layers as you knit. In order to achieve color patterns, such as stripes, checks, lettering, or other graphic elements, you use a different color for each layer. The shapes are formed by "exchanging" the layers, usually by following a color chart. For example, to change colors from back to front, you use light yarn for knit stitches that you've been working with dark yarn, and dark yarn for those you've been working with light. The knit and purl sequence remains the same, however. It is essential that you bring both yarns to the front when purling and both yarns back when you're knitting, so that no stray yarn carries over top of the fabric on either side. The resulting fabric is completely reversible, with the elements on one side of the fabric being negative images of those on the other. (For books on double knitting, see the appendix.)

Looking down into double knit. If you look carefully at the stitches removed from the needle tips, you can see that the purl stitches have popped to the back and the knit stitches to the front, revealing the space between them. Once replaced on the needles (alternating colors like the adjacent stitches), they will be knit and purled alternately, creating the back and front of the fabric in the same round.

DID YOU KNOW ANDEAN HATS

Put together alpacas, a wide variety of native dye plants, and cold weather, and you have the materials and inspiration behind the multicolored and imaginative Andean hats, or *ch'ullus*. The knitters are often men, who from a young age take pride in knitting their *ch'ullus* on small-gauge needles with tightly spun alpaca yarn (or sometimes sheep wool) that is brightly colored with natural dyes. The first *ch'ullu* that a child receives is traditionally knitted by his father. The hats are knit in the round on four or five needles using a style of knitting similar to that of the Portuguese, in which the yarn is tensioned by bringing it from around the back of the neck. (For more about Portuguese knitting, see page 68.) Children learn to spin as early as two or three years of age, and become skilled at knitting (or weaving) by the time they are about seven. The designs include not only animals, birds, human figures, and geometrical patterns, but also messages spelled out in lettering. Earflaps embellished with tassels (called *t'ikas*) and sometimes white beads are a characteristic feature of these distinctive Andean hats.

Before and after. A Peruvian boy holds a black lamb, with a llama right by his shoulder, wearing his brightly colored *ch'ullu* (left). *Ch'ullus* and other Peruvian knits and handwovens are on display (right).

MEET AMY SINGER

"Dream job" is the way Amy Singer talks about her work. Amy is founder and editor of Knitty, which she describes as a Web magazine with "a sense of humor and absolutely no doily patterns." In each quarterly edition Knitty lets her put her own special mark on the knitting world, making sure the site offers lots of modern lace patterns, for instance, plus cardigans and socks (which are among her favorite projects). Amy, who coauthored *Big Girl Knits* and *More Big Girl Knits* with Jillian Moreno, makes sure the patterns offer a wide range of sizing. And she loves to feature fun, whimsical pieces.

Amy, who lives in Toronto, Ontario, spent 20 years working as a proofreader in the advertising industry, picking up graphic and website design skills as she went. In 2002, hoping to add another skill to her résumé and eventually free herself from the drudgery of proofreading, she decided to create an online knitting magazine and found herself in her favorite work situation so far, working for herself while immersed in a favorite pastime. In 2006, she was able to quit her day job to work on Knitty full time.

"I love that we are able to publish designers of all ages and experience levels," Amy comments. "There's no barrier to entry here; if you can provide a good submission from the pattern to the photos, you're equal to every other designer we've ever published."

Amy got her start in knitting at age six, with help from her grandmother. In the late 1990s she was passionate about quilting but took a break when repetitive strain injuries in her hands made the hobby too difficult. One year,

at the holidays, she decided to knit hats for her quilting friends. "That's when I realized where my heart really was," says Amy.

Because she is highly allergic to wool, Amy's own designs feature fibers such as silk, cotton, and hemp. "Most of the fibers in the nonwool world have very little (if any) stretch," she notes. "They're more about drape than structure. Sometimes you can use tricks to make them hold their shape, but mostly, you just have to pick different projects. I'm thankful for nonwools with Lycra or elastic, because those allow me to knit socks and other things that have to hold their shape."

Among her favorite handknits are a silk shawl from a pattern from Scottish designer Ysolda Teague, and her own Tuscany shawl, in two Handmaiden yarns, Silken and Sea Silk (the photo below is of Amy knitting Tuscany in Tuscany). "My favorite discovery is that silk makes beautiful lace and blocks like a dream," says Amy. "I love how silk feels against the skin, and the warmth it gives. A simple shirt always looks better with a lace shawl around my neck."

LEARN TOP IT OFF!

Plain hats may be spiced up with embellishments that include pom-poms, tassels, or I-cord. You might even want to consider adding pom-poms to the ends of your I-cord.

MAKING POM-POMS

MAKING TASSELS

Pom-poms

These fuzzy balls can be as large or as small as you like.

STEP 1. Cut a piece of stiff cardboard that is as wide as you want your pom-pom to be, and cut a slit halfway across one side. Wrap yarn around the cardboard 50 to 125 times, perpendicular to the slit, depending on the pom-pom's diameter and the yarn's weight. Keep the strands evenly spaced and don't overlap them too much in the center. Insert an 8-inch length of yarn under the wrapped yarn, using the slit to access the wrapped yarn on both sides of the cardboard. Tie it tightly around the whole bundle of yarn (for extra strength you may want to double the tie).

STEP 2. Slide the tip of your scissors under the wrapped yarn at both edges, and cut through the yarn. Remove the cardboard. Fluff out the yarn to form the pom-pom, and trim ends to form a neat, even ball. Use the tail ends of the tie to attach the pom-pom.

Tassels

Like pom-poms, these can be modest or daring. You can even attach more than one, if desired. The method for creating them is similar to that for pom-poms.

STEP 1. Cut a piece of stiff cardboard that is the length you want your tassel to be. Wrap yarn around the cardboard as many times as desired, depending on the yarn weight (for instance, about 25 times for worsted weight and about 15 times for bulky weight). Insert an 8-inch length of yarn under the wrapped yarn at one edge of the cardboard, and tie it tightly around the whole bundle of yarn (for extra strength you may want to double the tie).

STEP 2. Slide the tip of your scissors under the wrapped yarn on the edge opposite the tie, and cut through all layers. Wrap another 8-inch length of yarn around the tassel about ¾ inch below the top knot, tie tightly, and allow the tail ends to blend into the rest of the tassel. Trim the bottom of the tassel to even the ends. Use the tail ends from the first tie to attach the tassel.

I-Cord

An I-cord is a narrow cylinder knitted on two double-point needles. This extremely useful knitted embellishment is credited to Elizabeth Zimmermann, who named it "I-cord," short for "Idiot Cord," because it's so simple to make. You can make it different diameters by changing the number of stitches you use, but three or four stitches is most common.

1. Using double-point needles, cast on the number of stitches desired (if you're using a pattern, it will specify how many are needed).

2. Do not turn your needle. Instead, shift the needle to your left hand, and slide the stitches back to the other end of the needle so the first cast-on stitch is the first stitch at the tip of the left needle. Knit the first stitch as usual, bringing the yarn from the last cast-on stitch behind the work (knit this first stitch fairly tightly).

3. Knit the remaining stitches.

4. Repeat steps 2 and 3 until the cord is the desired length.

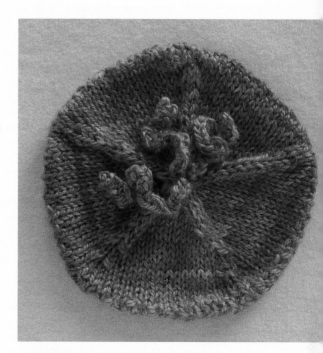

Twirly top. The tails of each of the three I-cords at the top of this beret were drawn through the lengths of the cords and pulled to tighten slightly until they formed squiggles.

The possibilities for I-cords on hats range from practical to fanciful:

- Use them as ties on kids' hats.
- Create the classic decoration at the tip of earflaps on Peruvian- or ski-style hats.
- Make a buttonlike accent by placing a short I-cord at the center of the crown.
- Attach three or more I-cords at the center of the crown for a tassel effect.
- At the crown make an I-cord, then thread the bind-off tail back through the length of the I-cord, and pull gently to create a squiggly cord. Make several for a whole bunch of springy cords. (See photo above.)

EXPLORE CLASSIC HAT DESIGNS

Styles come and go, of course, but some classic hats never seem out of style and are always popular. Many designs reflect the ethnic origins of the styles.

"PONYTAIL" HAT

FELTED HAT WITH BRIM

STOCKING CAP

JULIET CAP

BALACLAVA

CLOCHE

BERET

NEWSBOY CAP

KLEIN BOTTLE
CAP

WATCH CAP
WITH POM-POM

WATCH CAP

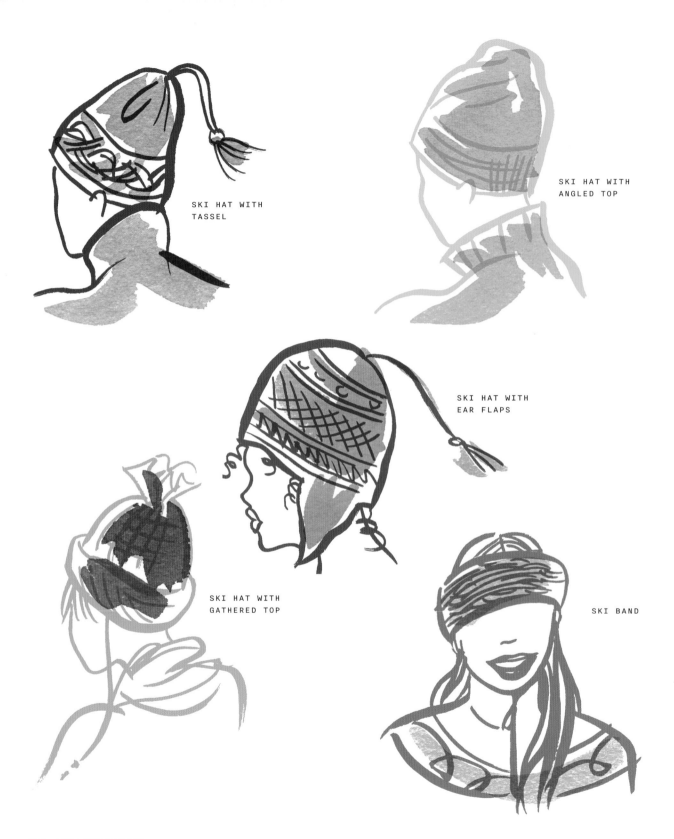

SKI HAT WITH
TASSEL

SKI HAT WITH
ANGLED TOP

SKI HAT WITH
EAR FLAPS

SKI HAT WITH
GATHERED TOP

SKI BAND

MEET JILLIAN MORENO

FOR DESIGNER JILLIAN MORENO, love is the feeling she gets when she gives the gift of a handknit — the hat, for instance, she knit for her husband of her own handspun yarn, with a reverse-stitch heart hidden in the rolled brim.

"It's such a tangible way to show you love someone or respect them," says Jillian. "When my kids or husband go out in the world with my handknits on, I feel like I'm sending them out in a little bubble of protective love."

The author of *Big Girl Knits*, an avid spinner, and ad manager of Knitty.com as well as editor of *Knitty's* "little sister" section on spinning, dubbed Knittyspin, Jillian entered the world of knitting in her mid-twenties, when she signed up for a class. But she was already a fiber person. "Even as a kid, I had little stashes of fabric and yarn. I didn't do anything with them but keep them, rearranging them, draping and tying them around my stuffed animals.

"My mother, who grew up in Germany during World War II, had to make things when she was growing up. She later hated anything homemade or crafty. It reminded her of the struggles of the war," says Jillian. "Consequently, I didn't grow up with crafts and came to the land of crafting late."

Jillian was working at Hill County Weavers in Austin, Texas, when she designed her first pieces, the Rockstar and Latifa scarves that are available on Knitty.com. (The Rockstar pattern, which uses a faux-fur accent yarn, comes with a warning: "Strangers will pet you when you wear this scarf.")

In 2006 she published *Big Girl Knits*, marking what she and coauthor Amy Singer call an "up-sizing revolution" and helped bring larger sizes into the mainstream. The book, driven by her own frustration at the lack of "plus-sized" designs, is filled with original patterns from leading designers and lots of tips for choosing flattering sweater shapes and customizing designs for various body types. *More Big Girl Knits* followed two years later.

"At the time of *Big Girl Knits*, two-hundred-plus knitting books were being published each year and nothing, nothing on plus-sized knitting or how to shape knitting for your body," notes Jillian. "Now I'm so happy to see magazines and books regularly go up to 2X, and there are all kinds of books, magazine articles, and blog entries about fitting your body — from how to choose a pattern to making adjustments in commercial patterns to designing your own patterns."

These days, from her home in Ann Arbor, Michigan, Jillian spends her time designing, teaching classes to adults and children, working on *Knitty* and Knittyspin, and — whenever she finds the time — spinning on one of her three wheels.

"I love the magic of fluff to yarn, running my hands over every inch of the yarn," says Jillian. "Both knitting and spinning are creative expressions for me. I use them to inspire myself for the other parts of my life and express the inspiration the rest of my life brings. It's a satisfying circle."

Several years ago there was a lot made of various film stars and other public figures who were caught knitting. But some celebrities, especially in the world of politics (and especially, it seems, U.S. presidents' wives), were avid knitters much further back in history, and some of them were quite influential in popularizing the craft.

MARTHA WASHINGTON. The first First Lady was reported never to lay down her knitting, constantly clicking her needles, even as she ran a large household and received her guests.

QUEEN VICTORIA. After Prince Albert died, Queen Victoria took up spinning to occupy herself. She let her fondness for Shetland knits be known and so gave a boost to that important cottage industry. She herself knit and crocheted scarves for soldiers.

SOJOURNER TRUTH. Born into slavery in the late eighteenth century, but later freed, Sojourner Truth was quite a woman, fighting injustice as both an abolitionist and a women's rights activist. She is said to have at one time spun 100 pounds of wool to fulfill her sense of obligation to one of her several owners.

GRACE COOLIDGE. Known as an especially skillful knitter, Mrs. Coolidge often donated her knitted items as fund-raisers at bazaars and raffles.

LOU HOOVER. Mrs. Hoover had a delightfully creative and more casual approach to her knitting: rather than rip out mistakes, she advised repeating them to create new patterns — a version of one of my own favorite sayings, "It's not a mistake, it's a design element."

I Sell the Shadow to Support the Substance.
SOJOURNER TRUTH.

A woman of principle. African-American abolitionist and women's rights advocate Sojourner Truth sits for her photo with her knitting in her lap (about 1870).

KIRSTEN FLAGSTAD. This twentieth-century Norwegian soprano was said to spend backstage intervals at the opera house playing cards, drinking cognac or stout, and knitting sweaters and scarves for her family. Known for her great Wagnerian roles, she would casually lay her knitting aside minutes before going onstage to stun opera audiences with her gorgeous voice. For a BBC radio poll, she claimed that the one luxury she would want if she were stranded on a desert island was "knitting needles and wool."

ELEANOR ROOSEVELT. Showing up at important meetings with her famously voluminous knitting bag, Mrs. Roosevelt was once referred to as "First Knitter of the Land." She vigorously promoted the idea of knitting for the troops during World War II, and a photo on a White House Christmas card from the war years shows her holding her knitting. She especially enjoyed socializing and knitting with friends. (I'll bet she'd have loved a Stitch 'n Bitch group.)

MADELEINE ALBRIGHT. A Wellesley alum who remembers the clicking sound in classrooms coming from knitting needles rather than laptop keyboards, Albright is said to have enjoyed the relaxation that knitting brought throughout her career.

More women to admire! At the top is soprano Kirsten Flagstad, knitting as she waits for her next entrance in an opera at Covent Garden, London. Below, this photograph taken of his mother by Eleanor Roosevelt's son in the 1930s was used to promote the safe, time-saving features of air travel for women. The quote below the photo read, "I never cease to marvel at the airplane."

Chapter 7

THE

Gloves & Mittens

LIFE LIST

If scarf knitting is comfort knitting, then mittens and gloves are like soul food for the knitter. There's something down-home and old-fashioned about mittens. Perhaps a bit underappreciated by our southern neighbors, who don't need them as much, we northerners can't do without them for at least half the year. Consequently, some of the handsomest and most classic mitten designs and techniques come from Scandinavia, Scotland, Russia, and Latvia, as well as New England and the Maritimes in North America.

GLOVES & MITTENS

Learn it · Explore it · Do it · Check it off!

MEET
- Robin Hansen

DISCOVER
- Join a special interest group on Ravelry.
- Check Ravelry and publishers' websites for pattern errors before beginning to knit.
- Follow bloggers that you particularly like — check out whom they're following, too.
- Subscribe to online magazines, newsletters, and sites that feature patterns.
- Find apps that support and enhance your knitting life.

DO/TRY
- Knit a classic Norwegian mitten in red and white with a salt-and-pepper palm.
- Knit a pair of traditional Swedish or Norwegian mittens following the twined-knitting method.
- Work Lovikka mittens.
- Make Latvian mittens using traditional designs.
- Knit a mitten pattern from one of Robin Hansen's books.
- Make a pair of "wet" mittens and full them for a custom fit.
- Knit a pair of thrummed mittens using bits of fleece or short pieces of colored yarns.
- Work a pair of double-rolled mittens.
- Knit fingerless gloves for outdoor work and sports.
- Knit fingerless gloves in cashmere, trimmed with beads, for something extra fancy.
- Make a pair of fingerless gloves with a flap.
- Work a pair of "shooter's gloves," with thumb and "trigger finger" separate.
- Create some lovers' mittens for your favorite lovers.
- Make a pair of mittens with a self lining.
- Embellish your mittens or gloves with lace, beads, or embroidery.
- Make a pair of traditional Sanquhar gloves.
- Knit a pair of matching mittens using self-patterning sock yarn.
- Jot down your hand measurements and use them to get perfectly fitted mittens.
- Keep a notebook with the hand measurements of everyone you knit mittens for. (Measure them for socks, sweaters, and hats while you're at it!)

LEARN
- Practice stranded knitting in the round.
- Follow the waste-yarn method to save stitches for a thumb opening.
- Work in double-knit for glove fingers.
- Add embroidery to a pair of hand-knit mittens or gloves.
- Weave contrasting-color yarns along rows or lengthwise down columns of knit stitches.
- Add classic Scandinavian braided ties and tassels at the mittens' wrist.
- Work a folded picot edge at the cast on of gloves or mittens.
- Work a picot bind off on mittens or gloves.
- Make a rolled (or double-rolled) edge on your mittens or gloves.
- Use the I-cord bind off for mittens knit tip down.

GO
- Visit Latvia.
- Visit Nova Scotia.

EXTRA CREDIT
- What links NATO, Latvia, and mittens?
- Why has Scandinavian twined knitting become something of a lost art?
- What suggestion about mitten patterns did a doctor make during the Civil War?

MORE FOR MY GLOVES & MITTENS LIFE LIST
- _____
- _____

Classic Mittens and Gloves: Styles and Patterns

Mitts, mittens, gloves — we cover our hands for warmth and protection or simply for fashion, and when we accomplish both at the same time, so much the better. This chapter contains some suggestions for mitten and glove styles you might like to sample. Note that many of the patterns that have become traditional for mittens and gloves include a feature that also makes them extra warm: stranding, felting, or thrums, for instance. (For a sampling of books featuring patterns in all these styles, see the appendix.)

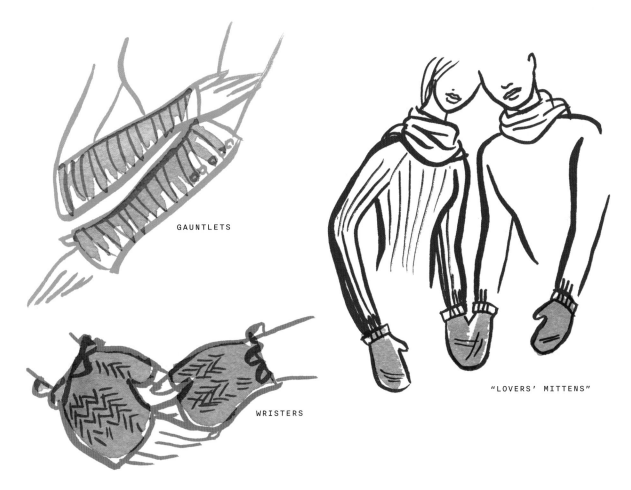

GAUNTLETS

WRISTERS

"LOVERS' MITTENS"

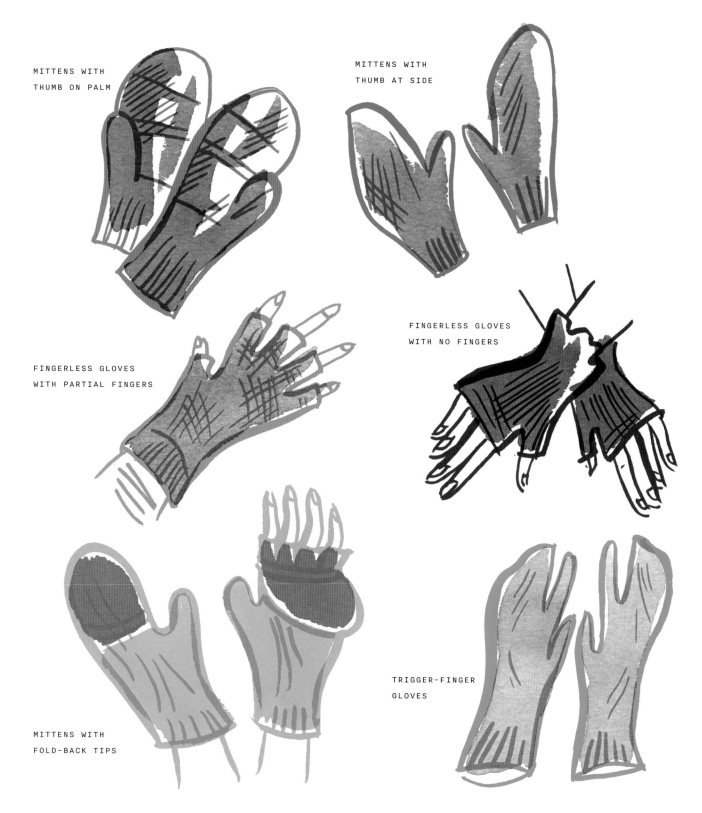

MITTENS WITH
THUMB ON PALM

MITTENS WITH
THUMB AT SIDE

FINGERLESS GLOVES
WITH PARTIAL FINGERS

FINGERLESS GLOVES
WITH NO FINGERS

MITTENS WITH
FOLD-BACK TIPS

TRIGGER-FINGER
GLOVES

Going International

NORWAY. The traditional star motif often seen on these cheerful classics originated in nineteenth-century Selbu, Norway. Worked in stranded patterning in two or more colors (often red and white or black and white), the mittens from Selbu also feature alternating colors in the ribbing, small motifs on the palm in contrast to the large star on the back of the hand, and pointed mitten tips. The small motif often used on the palm is called "salt-and-pepper" and is created by a simple alternation of two colors across a row, then staggered from row to row. Generally, these mittens have no gusset. Instead, "waste yarn" holds the place for the thumb until the rest of the mitten is finished. Your first encounter with this technique may throw you off, not only because you wonder why on earth you have to knit this little scrap of yarn into the palm of your mitten, but also your very understandable trepidation about creating a hole in the middle of your work when it's later time to pull out the waste yarn. It's not quite as daunting as cutting your first steek, but it may be a close second. To see how it works, see Waste . . . and Want Not, page 200. (For twined mittens, another Scandinavian style, see Robin Hansen on Twined Knitting, page 202.)

A Norwegian classic. The large star design, striped cuffs, and pointed tips are typical of mittens from Selbu, Norway.

LEARN WASTE . . . AND WANT NOT

You may come across a pattern that calls for what is sometimes known as an "afterthought" thumb. Rather than protruding from the side of the hand (which, when you think of it, is how our hands are naturally shaped), this thumb may rest completely on the palm, creating a sort of flap. The advantage of this location is that it doesn't interfere with whatever complex pattern you are working on the back of the hand. You prepare for this by "saving" thumb stitches that you can go back to after you've completed the rest of the mitten.

The maneuver works like this: At the place where you'll later work the thumb, drop the working yarn and knit a specified number of stitches using a short length of scrap (waste) yarn. Next, slip these waste-yarn stitches back onto the left-hand needle, pick up your working yarn once again, and knit across in your pattern and then on around the mitten.

When you complete the mitten tip, you go back to the waste yarn stitches and carefully remove the waste yarn. Then, pick up the newly "live" stitches that appear at the top and bottom of the opening (the stitches that up until then were held by the waste yarn). Pick up a stitch or two at each side of the opening to avoid any gaps that may appear, then knit your thumb using those stitches.

You may find this waste-yarn technique useful for other purposes, such as slits for pockets in a sweater.

"Saving" thumb stitches. The red waste yarn has been knit in, then slipped back to the left-hand needle to be knit across with the working yarn (A). As you remove the waste yarn stitch by stitch, pick up the newly "live" stitches above and below the opening to create the thumb stitches (B).

SWEDEN. *Lovikka* mittens are the ultimate when you're looking for cozy warmth. A popular style coming out of northern Sweden in the early twentieth century, these mittens are worked in a heavy yarn, which is fulled (felted) to thicken them further by agitation and hot water (see page 285). The mittens are then brushed, inside and out, creating a lovely halo effect. Bright embroidery and a braided tassel embellish the cuffs.

You'll find *twined knitting* in Danish and Norwegian mittens as well as in Sweden, but the method originated in Sweden more than three

Swedish Lovikka mittens. Knit with heavy yarn, these mittens are felted and brushed to create a thick and warm fabric, then embellished with colorful embroidery at the cuff and finished off with tassels.

centuries ago. Although the knitting process is rather slow, the fabric it creates is firm and warm — great when you want long-wearing mittens in chilly weather. The yarn traditionally used for twined knitting has a Z twist as its final (plying) twist (see Why the Ply? on page 48). Unless you spin your own, Z-twist yarn may be difficult to find, so if you have to give up the search, it's possible to successfully work twined knitting using ordinary yarn.

To create the distinctive construction, you alternately knit a stitch with one strand of yarn coming from one end of a ball of yarn (the outside, for instance) and then the next stitch using a strand from the other end (the inside). Always take the yarn for the next stitch *over* the yarn used for the last one. If you use S-twist yarn, you may have to let the twist back into your yarn from time to time by allowing the ball to hang free and naturally rotate to retwist. (This can be pretty challenging if you're using both ends of the same ball, so it might be easier to use two separate balls if you find this is necessary.) Twined knitting creates a fabric that not only is sturdy but also shows off the variety of lovely stitch patterns common to the style. (For more on twined knitting and a photo of a swatch knit in this style, see Robin Hansen on Twined Knitting, page 202.)

LATVIA is the site of discovery of the oldest mitten known to exist, estimated to have been made in the thirteenth or fourteenth century. It's appropriate that this long-lost article was discovered in a region with such a strong tradition of mittens. The elaborate patterning and distinctive colors of Latvian mittens make them an important source of national pride. Even in summer, women used to tuck these stunning knit mittens into their waistbands to show them off. An old Latvian tradition required mittens to be part of a bride's hope chest; some brides knit several hundred pairs, which were given to in-laws and others who helped plan the wedding. Not only was it expected that every young girl knit this mountain of mittens before her wedding, but, unless she didn't care about public opinion, no two pairs of mittens could be worked in the same design. Every symbol used in these intricate designs had a meaning (or in some cases, multiple meanings), usually based on a connection with a specific deity, and each was coupled with a wish.

DID YOU KNOW **A VERY WARM WELCOME** When NATO held a summit in Riga in the fall of 2006, summit guests received mittens hand-knit by Latvian men and women, ages 30 to 86. In all, the knitters made 4,500 pairs! Each pair featured a unique design worked in traditional symbols, patterns, and colors (with men's more reserved and women's brighter). The colors, rather than the designs, are more closely associated with various regions of the country. As its organizers explained, the project was "a special source of national pride, because it combined tradition, culture, and history with something of lasting practical value that could be enjoyed around the world."

EXPLORE ROBIN HANSEN ON TWINED KNITTING

Twined knitted mittens come from the mountains of Sweden and Norway, where the technique was preserved and in hiding for three centuries along with right-hand knitting.

Robin Hansen describes twined knitting in this way: Twined knitting was used throughout northern Europe and the Middle East whenever a firm, flat edging was needed, such as on scooped necklines or stocking tops. Today it turns up in eastern European and Middle Eastern knitting as a decorative edging, often called "braided edging," although the effect of the two-color twined purl is more like a series of sideways chevrons than braid.

Twining samples. Margaret Radcliffe's swatches and gloves illustrate some of the many decorative stitches, as well as cast ons and bind offs, characteristic of twined knitting.

The apparent reason for twined knitting's demise in many regions has to do with the spread of the German or continental method of knitting in much of Europe: holding the working yarn in the left hand makes it difficult to twist the two strands while knitting. At the same time other noncurling edgings (garter stitch and ribbing, for instance) were developed that could be worked with left-hand knitting.

In twined knitting two strands are worked alternately, usually two ends of the same (quite small) ball. The strand for the present stitch is brought consistently either under or over the strand just used, creating a half-twist between stitches. The stitch gets its name because the repeated half twists resemble twine laid along each round on the purl side. The knit side is typically quite flat and firm, and the fabric has only slight elasticity. Twined knitting is almost invariably worked in the round.

Swedish twined knitting is typically ornamented with patterns of raised stitches created by alternating (without twisting) knit and purl stitches with the purl strand held continuously on the front of the work. The elegant, raised patterns made on the right side by these purl floats add punch to the knit stitches. The smooth, firm surface of the knit side is also an excellent ground for embroidery.

Norwegian twined knitted mittens are made with the inside (purl side) on the outside, which shows off the twined effects, including two color and herringbone. The inside is often lined, either with a sewn-in pile or with six rows of sewn-in, duplicate stitches (called *napping*) done with a softer wool yarn.

Although working twined knitting initially seems slow, the resulting fabric is firm, warm, and durable and, depending on the yarn and ornamentation, can also be quite elegant.

North American Favorites

Robin Hansen's work on mittens and mitten-knitting traditions in Maine and the Maritimes is an invaluable source of traditional patterns, interpreted for twenty-first-century knitters. Patterns from her 1983 *Fox and Geese and Fences* are included in a new collection, *Favorite Mittens* (for specifics, see the appendix). Some especially popular patterns include New England "wet" mittens and "stuffed" mittens.

WET MITTENS are the iconic fisherman's mitts. Worked in medium wool yarn with plenty of sheep's lanolin still in it, these sturdy workman's mittens are shrunk "on the job": The fisherman dips the mittens in seawater, then tosses them on the deck and walks on them while hauling traps. Now and then, he dries them on the engine manifold, wets them again, and walks on them some more. By the end of the day, they have shrunk to fit his hands. Each day, before using them, he wets them, wrings them out, and puts them on wet. Maine fishermen swear that wool, the great insulator, keeps you warm when wet, even better than when dry.

When you knit your own version of these, you can replicate the fishermen's routine by vigorously scrubbing the finished mittens on a washboard in your kitchen sink, subjecting them alternately to hot soapy water and ice-cold rinse water until the fabric is fulled and shrunk about 20 percent.

Not for the faint-hearted. This Nova Scotia fisherman wears the iconic fisherman's mitts as he pulls his oars off the Grand Banks.

STUFFED, OR THRUMMED, MITTENS have evolved over time. "Thrums" are the ends of a warp left at the back of the loom when the woven fabric is completed. They are too short to reach through the heddles to be woven. Because yarn was too valuable to just throw away, thrifty weavers who were also knitters cut these pieces into short lengths, which they knitted into mittens and caps for added thickness and warmth.

Today, most knitters no longer use actual thrums for these mittens. Only the name "thrummed mittens" remains, and only in parts of Newfoundland and Labrador. Today's knitters make "stuffed mittens" with short, doubled-over lengths (4 inches) of carded fleece, bunches of pencil roving, or locks of washed but uncarded fleece. The fleece is knitted along with the working yarn at intervals, say every fourth stitch in every third round. The tips of the fleece fluff to the inside, and the spots of color where the fleece has been caught into a stitch gaily dot the outside. When worn, the fleece felts inside, creating an even warmer and more luscious mitten.

You don't need to limit your stuffing to mittens, by the way: it works well for caps and puffy vests as well. Nor do you have to limit yourself to natural sheep colors, or even to fleece. You can revive the thrifty thrum tradition by using little bunches of leftover yarn.

DOUBLE-ROLLED MITTENS. Robin describes double-rolled mittens in this way: They were possibly invented somewhere in eastern Canada and New England and until recently were mainly seen in museums. Edna Mower, a French Canadian knitter late of New Hampshire, brought them back into use and popularity. Knitted with a strand of unspun, carded wool carried behind the work by knitting over and under it, the mittens are thick but flexible and wonderfully warm. Although knitted on fine needles, they are of a common mitten tension of about six stitches per inch, because the carried roving forces the stitches apart, showing through to the knit side with a wonderfully raggy, north-country look. "Double" refers to the double thickness of the mittens; "rolled," to the roll of roving.

From the early 1900s double-rolled mittens were worked holding the yarn in the right hand. Short pieces of fleece or roving were wrapped

Stuffed for warmth.
Thrummed, or stuffed, mittens are created by knitting bits of fleece into the fabric every few stitches, every few rows. The puffiness will settle down as the fleece becomes felted inside with wear.

around the working yarn with each stitch, always wrapping in the same direction. Edna found this tedious, so as a child she invented the over-and-under carrying technique using pre-carded mill rovings. (Find out more about Edna Mower and double-rolled mittens in Robin's *Flying Geese & Partridge Feet*; see appendix for information.)

What's Old Comes 'Round Again

FINGERLESS GLOVES ("wristlets" or "wristers") have taken off in popularity over the past few years. It's not that they're a twenty-first-century discovery (the American Red Cross included wristlets on their list of items to "Knit for Sammie!" during World War I), but the fact is that they really are comfortable, they really do make you warmer (even though your fingers aren't covered), and they can be a satisfyingly quick-to-knit project. Some versions are daintily knit in lace patterns with fine, often luxury yarns, perhaps embellished with beads. At the other end of the spectrum are sturdy mitts suitable for fishing, biking, and other outdoor activities when you need warmth but want your fingers free. Some fingerless gloves have holes for your fingers; some have a partial thumb, which helps keep them in place.

VARIATIONS ON THE THEME. Some fingerless gloves have a flaplike mitten tip attached to the back-of-the-hand side of the glove, which can be pulled off of or over your fingers as needed.

Another cross between a mitten and a glove is the "shooter's mitten," which has a thumb and forefinger, but a single covering for the other three fingers. This form could be useful to anyone who wants the warmth of a mitten, combined with some of the freedom of movement of a glove. Its name obviously comes from the fact that it frees up the trigger finger, but it's just as useful for cross-country skiers who need to adjust their bindings or for urbanites who need to grab their metro cards in a hurry. The concept goes back at least as long ago as the Civil War: you can find a pattern for these gloves, which were intended to be knit for the soldiers, in the *New York Times* archives from December 1861.

A much more romantic mitten variation is the "lovers' mitten," which features a left-hand mitten for one person, a right-hand mitten for his or her partner, and a third double mitten, knit with two cuffs but with one oversized hand roomy enough for two hands to keep each other warm inside.

Another comfortably warm mitten is worked so it has a self-lining. You use a provisional cast on and knit the mitten as usual. You then go back to the cast-on stitches and remove the provisional cast on so you can pick up the stitches and knit another, identical mitten off in the other direction. When completed, tuck the one inside the other for a comfortable, lined, very

DID YOU KNOW? TO THE EDITOR

This letter to the editor appeared in the Thursday, November 6, 1861 edition of the *New York Times*:

"As you recommend the employment of 'nimble patriotic fingers' in making mittens or gloves for the army, I would suggest that the mittens be made with a first finger as well as thumb. It is quite difficult to pull a trigger with a mitten of the usual shape, and the finger could be used or not as required. Mittens are much warmer than gloves, for the same reason that four children would be warmer in one bed than sleeping alone. Very respectfully, A PHYSICIAN."

warm mitten. (Basic knitting techniques books, as well as online videos show several different provisional cast ons.)

Up for a Challenge?

When you're ready to step up from fingerless gloves and mittens, it's time to take on the challenge of knitting "real" gloves. Knitting gloves isn't really that much more difficult than knitting mittens. You just have to enjoy knitting in the round, and you need a little patience. (*Note:* It's also possible to use a double-knit technique to knit the tubes required for glove fingers.) With each finger separate and not cozily exchanging heat with the rest of your hand, many people find that gloves aren't as warm as mittens. Aside from that disadvantage, they do seem dressier than mittens and can even be elegant, and they allow you more control when you need your fingers to work independently.

Among the most impressive traditional gloves are those from Scotland. Although the knitting cottage industry that developed in the small town of Sanquhar in southwestern Scotland by the late-eighteenth century was short-lived, the characteristic two-color geometric design that was worked on both gloves and "stockings" has survived. In the nineteenth century these gloves were worked in a sturdy yarn blend of wool and cotton or flax called *drugget*.

A Scottish specialty. Because they were comfortable and hard wearing, these gloves from Sanquhar, Scotland, became a popular item for riding and driving. About a dozen patterns were developed, often named for visiting dignitaries, such as "Cornet" and "Duke of Wales."

DID YOU KNOW **THROW DOWN THE GAUNTLET** Reflecting their origin as the protective gloves that were part of a medieval knight's suit of armor, gloves with long, sometimes flared cuffs are called gauntlets. Usually, these gloves are complete, fingers and all, although you may also run across a fingerless variety that covers the wrist and then extends to nearly elbow length. Today, you're likely to see this style for such disparate uses as a fashion statement or part of the uniform of a member of a marching band or drum corps.

MORE FOR MY GLOVES & MITTENS LIFE LIST

◇ _____

◇ _____

_____

◇ _____

_____

Mitten- and Glove-Knitting Techniques

Many of the tips and techniques that are useful to know when knitting socks are also helpful when you're working on mittens or gloves. Although you may find some patterns for mittens written to be knit flat (on two straight needles), most are knit in the round so there's no potentially uncomfortable (or weak) seam. Here are a few things to keep in mind:

YARN AND GAUGE. To many minds wool is the most obvious choice for gloves and mittens, because it provides warmth even when wet (check out those New England fisherman's mitts, page 203). And since the most likely reason you want mittens or gloves is to keep your hands warm, it's important to get a gauge that not only meets the pattern requirements but also gives you a fabric that is dense enough to keep out the cold, while at the same time not so stiff that you can't bend your fingers.

If you like multicolored mittens or gloves, but aren't in mood to work a stranded or intarsia pattern, you can turn to the variegated and self-patterning yarns that you love for socks. In fact, many sock yarns work beautifully for mittens and gloves, or look for slightly heavier weights of variegated yarn, still with interesting color effects.

STRANDING. When you knit in the round with more than one color (which you'll be doing if you make the Scandinavian, Latvian, or Scottish

Two ways with multicolor yarn. Rather than make the mittens on the left match, I enjoyed the relaxing flow of the gradual color change and let them both be individuals. The self-patterning sock yarn used for those on the right seemed to ask for a more formal treatment.

LEARN FIT LIKE A GLOVE

Fit is just as important for your mittens as it is for your socks. You want enough room for your fingers to wiggle a bit at the top so they aren't constricted — being able to move them around keeps your fingers warmer. You also want the tip of your thumb to go all the way to the tip of the mitten thumb, with the base of the thumb settling comfortably into the valley between your thumb and index finger. If you're making gloves, not only your thumb, but each of your fingers expects this same kind of perfect fit. "Too long" can be even more awkward in gloves than in mittens.

Robin Hansen gives the following advice for getting your mittens and gloves to fit perfectly. First, keep the following three "rule-of-thumb" proportions in mind:

❈ Your thumb is one-third the length of your hand.

❈ Your thumb "leaves" your hand one-third of the way to your fingertips.

❈ Your thumb's circumference is 40 percent of the distance around your hand.

To put these proportions to work as you knit, Robin Hansen suggests that you measure your hand from the crease at the base of your palm to the tip of your middle finger. Divide that number by three, and you'll have the length of your thumb. Add another thumb length for the cuff. To find a comfortable girth for the mitten or glove, measure around your hand above the first knuckle on your index finger, including the tip of your thumb. A mitten or glove made to these proportions has the thumb exactly in the middle lengthwise. Here's the formula:

Hand length ÷ 3 = thumb length

Hand length + thumb length = a good finished length, including cuff

---

Hand circumference (including thumb tip) ÷ 2 = finished width

---

Hand circumference × 0.40 = thumb circumference

---

styles described here), you need to take particular care not to pull the carried yarn too tightly across the back. This is especially true when you move from one needle to the next if you're using double-point needles. As you complete each needle, take a moment to check and make sure you've got some slack in the carried yarns. When you change needles, if your pattern continues to need the same color for the first few stitches on the next needle that you used for the last stitches, catch up that nonworking yarn in the last stitch on one needle before moving to the next, to help keep the yarn from "taking a short-cut" around the corner.

SIDE THUMBS VERSUS PALM THUMBS. Where to put the thumb is one of those points of controversy among knitters who have definite ideas about which approach is the most comfortable, or the most iconically mittenlike. If you're working on one of the authentic ethnic styles, of course, the decision will have been made for you by the pattern and the tradition.

Mittens (as well as gloves) that are designed with a thumb that tapers out at the side require extra fabric to accommodate the thumb. You create this space by working a gusset, gradually increasing the number of stitches beginning just above the cuff. Once the piece is wide enough to accommodate the widest part of the hand, the thumb stitches are set aside on stitch holders or scrap yarn while you continue to knit to the tip. Some mittens and gloves have no shaping to accommodate this area but are wide enough to be comfortable without it, or the gusset may be placed in a different location, rather than at the base of the thumb.

An alternative to creating a thumb gusset is to place the thumb at the side of the palm of the hand, and use waste yarn to hold a place for it where you can come back to knit in the thumb later. For information about this approach, see Waste . . . and Want Not, page 200.

The Frosting on the Cake

When your mittens or gloves are serving more than just practical purposes, and you want them to make a fashion statement as well, you can have fun embellishing them in any one of a number of ways. Take a page from an ethnic style that you admire, or branch out with something more contemporary and unexpected. The cuffs, in particular, are just waiting for something dramatic and unique:

BEADING Working one of the beaded techniques into your cuffs is fun and handsome. (See page 259 for information about beading.)

BRAIDED TIES. Some Scandinavian mittens feature a colorful braided and tasseled tie woven through the fabric at the wrist. (See photo on page 200.)

PICOT EDGE. A folded picot edge makes a particularly sweet and lacelike trim for gloves and mittens. See Pretty in Picot at right for one pattern for a picot edge. You'll find several other variations in stitch dictionaries.

EMBROIDERY. Kristin Nicholas has made embroidered embellishment a specialty on her knitwear. As you can see in some of her work, such as the photo on page 210, for instance, you don't have to limit your embroidery just to the cuffs: embellish the back of the hands, or for that matter, treat the whole mitten to stitchery.

SWATCHING | picot

Firm and fine. Picot not only makes a delicate trim for mittens, socks, and gloves, but because it is formed by doubling the fabric back in a hem, it also provides stability to the edge.

LEARN PRETTY IN PICOT

You can work picot as part of the cast on or the bind off. The following are basic instructions for both, but you can change the look depending on your whim and your yarn by changing the number of stitches included in each "point."

PICOT CAST ON. Work about 5 rows in stockinette stitch. On the next wrong-side row, knit 1, *yarn over, knit 2 together; repeat from * to end. Purl the next row (including all the yarn overs), and continue with the rest of your pattern. When the item is finished, turn the first 5 rows to the inside to form a hem. The picot row is along the edge, magically forming regularly spaced points all the way across where the yarn overs and stitches knit together are. Whipstitch the hem in place on the inside. This method was used at the bottom of the swatch above.

PICOT BIND OFF. At the beginning of the bind-off row, *cast on 2 stitches, then bind off these 2 stitches and the next 2 stitches in the normal way (4 bind offs in all). When 1 stitch remains on the right-hand needle, slip that stitch back onto the left-hand needle as if to purl; repeat from *. When all but 1 stitch is bound off, cut the yarn and draw the tail through the stitch to fasten off.

Here are some ideas to get you started; refer to an embroidery stitch dictionary as well as ethnic patterns for more ideas and examples (see appendix for resources).

※ Use classic embroidery stitches such as lazy daisies, feather stitch, and satin stitch.

※ Weave contrasting-color yarn along rows or lengthwise down columns of stitches.

※ Use the knit stitches as a "grid" for placing embroidery stitches.

ROLLED OR DOUBLE-ROLLED EDGE. Work reverse stockinette by purling around for about 1 inch, then work stockinette by knitting around. The reverse stockinette section naturally turns under, creating a neat roll on the right side. For a double roll, knit the first inch or so, then purl for about an inch before again knitting around (in other words, stockinette for 1 inch, reverse stockinette for 1 inch, then stockinette). Both pairs of mittens in the photo on page 207 have double-rolled edges.

I-CORD EDGE. If you knit your mittens from the top down, use an I-cord bind off for a firm, nicely finished edge (see I-Cord Bind Off, below).

Knots and flowers. Two simple embroidery stitches, French knots and lazy daisies, punctuate the stripes and lift these mittens out of the ordinary. A Kristin Nicholas design.

LEARN I-CORD BIND OFF

Cast on 3 stitches to the left-hand needle. Knit 2, then knit 2 together (the last cast-on stitch and the first live stitch; the photo at the right shows the "knit 2 together" as the last stitch knit). Do not turn: the first 3 stitches on your right-hand needle are now the I-cord stitches. Slip these stitches back onto your left-hand needle and again knit 2, knit 2 together. Bind off all stitches.

EXPLORE ONLINE
TAPPING INTO KNITTING

The online fiber world couldn't be more energetic. The knitters' version of Facebook is Ravelry, where, once you join, you can keep track of your own knitting projects, your plans for what you want to do next, and your needles and yarn stash.

You can also find photos of projects completed by other Ravelry users (and share your own) and join forums that discuss patterns and techniques, as well as thousands (true!) of groups with special interests, such as lace knitting, hand dyeing, spinning, weaving, knit-alongs, charity efforts, and all kinds of other fiber-related activities.

Knitting magazine and book publishers, knitting designers, yarn stores, and yarn companies often have websites. Other Internet knitting resources include everything from personal blogs, podcasts, online magazines, and newsletters to pattern sources and how-to references. Because knitting websites abound and new ones constantly crop up, it's not practical to offer more than a sampling here. Many have multiple missions, so surfing is the best way to discover what each has to offer and which best meet your needs and taste.

If you haven't explored Web possibilities, here are some suggestions to help you get started. For some specific names and addresses, see the appendix.

BLOGS. When you discover a blogger you especially enjoy, you might want to click through to other bloggers he or she follows.

PODCASTS. As expert knitter and editor Wendy Preston puts it, "Podcasts are NPR for knitters. . . . They are free, cater to a wide variety of interests, and provide hours of knitting entertainment." You can learn what various podcasts are all about by searching Ravelry's Podcast Group. Listening to and participating in these offers a sort of virtual community when you can't get to a festival or retreat. Some have created apps and others have associated blogs.

ERRATA. Before beginning a new pattern, check out the publisher's website or Ravelry for errata and advice. Unfortunately, mistakes can crop up in even the most carefully edited pattern, but online resources often make it possible to head off problems before you begin your project.

RESEARCH. Surf Google, Yahoo!, and other search engines for yarns by specific brand, weight, and fiber; guilds and other organizations to join; fiber farms; specific techniques; yarn stores or fiber festivals in areas where you live or visit; favorite knitting designers; and so on.

VIDEO. Check out YouTube and other video clip websites when you need a refresher for some technique you only half remember, or when you come across a reference to something you've never learned. It's good to look at several examples: knitters often take slightly different approaches to any one procedure, and you can learn something from each one and make it your own.

E-MAGAZINES AND PATTERN COLLECTIONS. Whether you're looking for the perfect pattern, news about the latest yarns, or advice about the best cast off for toe-up socks, do some exploration of the various e-magazines and pattern collections you can find online.

Chapter 8

THE

Bags

LIFE LIST

Is there anyone who can't find a use for yet another bag? Creating a bag gives us knitters plenty of freedom to experiment with techniques. You can leave the need for a perfect fit out of the equation, and if the spirit moves you, give your creative expression free rein and go wild. Bags also give you a chance to try out different kinds of yarns, from sturdy hemp and linen to slender silks and Tencel or the bulkiest of wools, depending on how you plan to use your bag. As with any other project, the key is to choose the yarn that best suits the purpose of your bag. Nowhere is "form follows function" more true.

In addition to what you choose for your yarn, some stitch patterns are more appropriate than others for a bag, again depending on the use you plan for it. Unless you're knitting a net-like fabric for something like a market bag, you should probably choose a stitch pattern, yarn, and yarn gauge that isn't too stretchy. This is particularly true if you're making knitted straps or handles for any bag. Slipstitch patterns are often good choices, because they tend to have limited elasticity and are therefore more stable. One I particularly like for both handles and bags is called "Linen Stitch" (see No Time to Stretch, page 220).

MEET

◇ Judith Durant

DO/TRY

◇ Make a sturdy knit-felt bag for your laptop.

◇ Use hemp or linen to make a stretchy market bag.

◇ Cut plastic strips from used grocery bags and use them to knit a *new* plastic bag.

◇ Knit a silk drawstring pouch for carrying jewelry or other valuables when you travel.

◇ Make a '20s-era beaded bag for dress-up occasions.

◇ Teach someone else to knit when you travel.

LEARN

◇ Use a stranded pattern for a knit-felt bag.

◇ Explore each of the five main types of beaded knitting techniques.

◇ Look for stitch patterns that don't stretch and use them for bags or bag straps.

◇ Explore the ethnic fiber traditions of places you visit.

GO

◇ Go on a treasure hunt in museums to see how many paintings include needlework of some kind.

◇ Collect postcards of paintings that depict knitting, weaving, spinning, or sewing.

◇ Search out fiber-related activities in every city you visit: yarn stores, knitting groups, yarn crawls, and so on.

◇ Put three of the "yarn-friendly" cities on page 218 on your list of places to go — add three more that you discover on your own.

◇ Discover knitting-themed vacation options and book one in the next year.

◇ Visit farms that focus on raising animals for fiber.

◇ Choose a cruise for your knitting travel adventure.

◇ Pick a knitting travel adventure that takes you to a continent or country you've never visited.

◇ Search out fellow knitters wherever you travel and strike up conversations with them.

MORE FOR MY BAGS LIFE LIST

◇ _____

◇ _____

◇ _____

◇ _____

◇ _____

◇ _____

◇ _____

◇ _____

◇ _____

◇ _____

◇ _____

◇ _____

◇ _____

◇ _____

TRAVEL ART SPOTTING: PAINTINGS OF KNITTERS

The next time you visit an art museum, you might like to do some sleuthing to see if you can detect anyone knitting — or, for that matter, weaving, spinning, or sewing — in any of the paintings. You're likely to discover fascinating details about ordinary household life in works painted centuries ago.

It can be unexpectedly touching to recognize the connection you have with these characters, who will very likely come to life for you in a new way through something as simple as fiber. When you locate one of these treasures, be sure to check at the museum bookshop to see if a postcard or poster of that particular painting is available.

In Praise of the Needlewoman: Embroiderers, Knitters, Lacemakers, and Weavers in Art, by Gail Carolyn Sirna is an excellent book containing a collection of examples of artwork spanning several centuries. I'm sure this is only the tip of the iceberg, however. Here are just a few examples, with the museums where you can find them. For an online peek at them, search for these images by artist and title.

CLOTILDE, *by Louis Paul Dessar* (Musée Nationale de la Coopération Franco-Americaine, Bléran-court, France)

COAST SCENE, *by Edith Hume* (Victoria and Albert Museum, London)

KNITTING FOR THE SOLDIERS: HIGH BRIDGE PARK, C. 1918, *by George Luks* (Terra Foundation for American Art, Chicago, Illinois) (see page 138)

THE KNITTING LESSON, *by Jean-François Millet* (Clark Art Institute, Williamstown, Massachusetts) (below)

THE YOUNG BRIDE, *by Mary Cassatt* (Montclair Art Museum, Montclair, New Jersey)

YOUNG KNITTER ASLEEP, *by Jean-Baptiste Greuze* (Huntingdon Library, Art Collections, and Botanical Gardens, San Marino, California)

Never too young to learn. Jean-François Millet's *The Knitting Lesson* is part of the collection of the Clark Art Institute, Williamstown, Massachusetts.

Useful Techniques

Some knitting techniques are more suitable for bags than others, and choosing the most appropriate one is just as important as selecting the right yarn. Here are just two approaches for very different kinds of bags: felted knitting and beaded knitting. Another useful technique for eye-catching bags is intarsia, which is described beginning on page 254.

Fit for Felt

Felt, including both "wet" felt and fulled knitting, is an obvious choice for workhorse bags, such as your knitting bag or a laptop cover (see page 285 for more about the different kinds of felting). Patterns for knitted felt are readily available in books, magazines, and online (for suggestions, see the appendix). For best results keep the following advice in mind:

Soft look, sturdy feel. Felting the knit adds thickness and stability, ideal for bags. Kathleen Taylor's two-color work here is softened by felting and brushing.

SHRINKABILITY. Be sure the fiber you choose will shrink. Many animal fibers are willing to felt, as long as they haven't been treated to be machine washable. Animal fibers blended with non-shrinking fiber (especially synthetics) are usually unacceptable, as well. More loosely spun fibers usually full more readily than tightly spun ones.

STRANDED PATTERNS. Textural stitches are usually not a good choice for knitted felt, simply because the shapes of the stitches tend to disappear in the fulling process, with the result that your efforts are wasted. On the other hand, stranded knitting can be very effective: although the individual stitches may blur and not be apparent, the overall painterly effect is often very pleasing, as you can see in the photo at left.

GAUGE. Check your gauge. Patterns for felted knits usually give you a "preshrunk" gauge measurement, and you'll find that that's considerably looser than what you would normally look for with any yarn. Larger needles and fewer stitches per inch are the rule. This allows the stitches room to move around during the process, and movement is one of the factors that makes felt. When they have plenty of room to move, the fibers blossom and fill the holes as the fabric changes character during the fulling process, becoming thicker and denser.

THOROUGHNESS. Don't be afraid to keep agitating the piece until it's the thickness you're looking for. Because it's true that you can't remove shrinkage, be sure to monitor the felting progress so you don't take it too far. On the other hand, it's also true that you don't want a sleazy fabric, especially for a bag. Look for a firm feel with densely packed stitches: you shouldn't easily see the shapes of the individual stitches.

FINISHING. If you wish, you can brush the fulled fabric with a stiff brush, such as a cat brush. This gives the surface a nice halo that further hides the individual stitches.

> *"It is easy to say how we love new friends, and what we think of them, but words can never trace out all the fibers that knit us to the old."*
>
> GEORGE ELIOT

LEARN BAG STYLES

✻ **FOR A STURDY BAG TO HAUL YOUR STUFF** or protect your laptop: Knit and full a wool bag. You'll get the perfect cushioning, plus pizzazz.

✻ **FOR "GREEN" SHOPPING** that renounces the ubiquitous plastic bag: Knit your own hemp- or linen-mesh market bags. Or take on the plastic bag itself: Cut bags into "endless" 2- to 3-inch-wide strips by starting at the bottom of the bag and spiraling upward; then use this plastic "yarn" to knit a colorful, sturdy bag.

✻ **FOR SHEER LUXURY:** Fashion a dainty silk drawstring pouch to hold your jewelry when you travel.

✻ **FOR ELEGANCE** at a concert or a ball: Create a stylish beaded purse straight out of the Victorian or the '20s eras.

SWATCHING | *Linen Mesh*

Stretchy but strong. Combine a no-stretch yarn like linen with an open pattern, such as faggoting, and some other laces that by their nature stretch, and you have the makings of an excellent market carryall.

TRAVEL YARN-FRIENDLIEST CITIES

Are you shy about knitting on the subway? Discouraged by the dearth of yarn stores in your community? Dying to find some knitting friends to hang out with? Some cities have developed a reputation for being knitter-friendly. If you live near or visit any of these, you might want to take notes on how they've achieved their fiber friendliness and perhaps import some of these ideas to your own community. Perhaps you'll also want to add some of these destinations to your "life list."

Other places to find organizations and activities in your area are such websites as Meetup, Ravelry, and Stitch 'n Bitch. Look, too, for "yarn crawls." Yarn crawls are self-guided tours of participating yarn shops and craft stores in an area — think "open house" tour; they usually include special offers, small gifts, and raffles as part of the day's fun. Knitters in yarn-friendly cities love to invite other knitters to discover their many LYSs by organizing tours of shops. (See appendix for websites.)

BOSTON, MASSACHUSETTS. A Ravelry group organizes several yarn crawls in the city, and there are also quite a few Stitch 'n Bitch groups in Boston. The Greater Boston Knitting Guild hosts monthly meetings, members receive discounts at several local shops, and the group supports Boston-area charities, such as the Dana-Farber Cancer Institute and the Women's Lunch Place.

CHAPEL HILL, NORTH CAROLINA. The Raleigh/Durham/Chapel Hill Triangle supports a healthy knitting community with lots of fiber Meetup groups and lively yarn shops.

CHICAGO, ILLINOIS. Active groups include Stitch 'n Bitch, Chicago Knitters Unite! and the Windy City Knitting Guild. Stitch n' Pitch with the Chicago White Sox and the city's many yarn shops make Chicago a very sympatico destination for knitters.

LOS ANGELES, CALIFORNIA. LA has a number of welcoming yarn stores, as well as several Meetup groups, including Yarn Projects from the Heart, which organizes charity knitting and crocheting.

MINNEAPOLIS, MINNESOTA. The active Minnesota Knitters' Guild sponsors a popular day-long workshop and fiber fair, Yarnover, in April each year; the guild also has a tradition of organizing a variety of public service projects.

NEW YORK, NEW YORK. Opportunities to join several groups, including Meetups and Stitch 'n Bitch, make New York one of the yarn-friendliest cities. The Big Apple Knitters Guild hosts monthly meetings; members receive a bimonthly newletter, discounts to guild workshops and retreats as well as participating yarn shops, and access to a guild library of knitting books and videos. Sit 'n' Knit New York City has well over 1,000 members citywide. New York is also a great place to take part in a Stitch n' Pitch game.

PORTLAND, OREGON. Although a relatively small city, Portland is multiply blessed with yarn stores, and it hosts a yarn crawl in the "dreary" time of year (early March). Groups include a rotating Stitch 'n Bitch group and the Portland Knitting Meetup group.

SAN FRANCISCO, CALIFORNIA. San Francisco hosts a number of groups and guilds, as well as many fiber-friendly museums, including the Museum of Craft and Folk Art and the museum at the California College of Arts and Crafts.

SEATTLE, WASHINGTON. Groups include the Seattle Knitters Guild, which has a lending library and newsletter; the Knitting School, which offers weekend workshops and year-long classes for machine knitters; Seattle Purly Girls; North-End Knitters; and several Stitch 'n Bitch groups. The Seattle Mariners was the first team to host a Stitch n' Pitch Night.

VICTORIA, BRITISH COLUMBIA. Home to many fiber artists (including the Bitchy Bees and the Victoria Knitters Guild), Victoria holds a week-long FibreFest/Knit Out each June.

WASHINGTON, D.C. The Yahoo group Knitting-N-The-City organizes monthly knit and crochet gatherings, and the DC Knitters' website lists many area groups, yarn stores, and other resources, including links to Stitch & Bitch DC. The Stitch DC yarn store's blog also helps coordinate knitting activities.

Beaded Bags

Explore the possibilities of beaded knitting on a bag: beads can provide elegance and glitz, as well as welcome weight, to hand-knit purses. Bead-embellished knitting is an excellent technique for "dress-up" bags, in particular, and a small bag is an ideal project for learning how to knit with beads. As knitting designer and editor Judith Durant explains in her book *Knit One, Bead Too*, there are several techniques for incorporating beads into your knitting as you go:

* *Bead knitting,* which the Victorians loved, pretty much covers the surface of the fabric with beads. It also offers you the opportunity to make pictures or other graphic multicolor designs.
* *Beaded knitting* is done by allowing a bead or beads to lie between stitches. When you increase the number of beads between stitches from row to row, the fabric flares out: think '20s flapper style!
* *Slipstitch bead knitting* floats the beads on top of slipped stitches.
* *Carry-along bead knitting* has the beads strung on a supplementary piece of yarn that you bring into play as desired.
* *Hook bead knitting* allows you to add beads without prestringing, by sliding them onto individual stitches with a crochet hook. This can save wear and tear on delicate yarn.

Beading on the go. Judith Durant combines beads and cables in a bag that's both dressy and practical. The beads provide welcome weight to the piece.

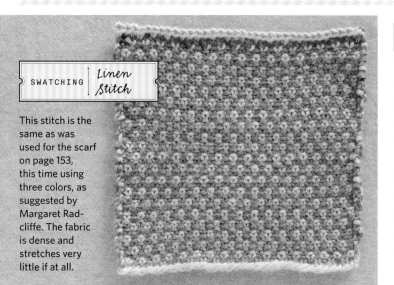

SWATCHING | *Linen Stitch*

This stitch is the same as was used for the scarf on page 153, this time using three colors, as suggested by Margaret Radcliffe. The fabric is dense and stretches very little if at all.

LEARN NO TIME TO STRETCH

This simple Linen Stitch pattern must be worked on an odd number of stitches. It's a great stitch pattern when you need something for bag handles or other items that have little stretch, even when knit in wool.

Row 1: K1, *slip 1 with yarn in front, K1; repeat from *.
Row 2: K1, P1, *slip 1 with yarn in back, P1; repeat from *, ending K1.
Repeat these two rows throughout.

TRAVEL KNITTING TRIP ADVENTURES

Massachusetts knitter Joan Kwith was determined to buy some local yarn while traveling in Patagonia. Unable to speak the language, she went from shop to shop making knitting motions, until a friendly shopkeeper led this "crazy tourist" to just what she was looking for.

Travel is always an exciting adventure, and making connections through fiber, as Joan did, even without language, makes it rewarding in a whole new way. For many of us a dream vacation would make textiles an important part of that trip to an area of the world that's new to us. Here are just a few organizations that offer this kind of themed travel (for website addresses, see the appendix).

◇ **ALASKA FOR FIBER FANATICS.** Dream a Dream Tours offers several knitting and spinning adventures in Alaska for "fiber fanatics," including visits to a musk ox farm, glaciers, and the Alaska State Fair.

◇ **BEHIND THE SCENES ADVENTURES** are specialty trips for small groups with common interests in traditional festivals and celebrations, ethnic textiles and indigenous costume, archaeology, cultural history, art, and architecture. They feature "exotic destinations, savory local cuisine, flamboyant festivals, gorgeous scenery and remote villages where the people still make all their own exquisite textiles." Recent trips included Thailand, Laos, Peru, and India.

◇ **CRAFT CRUISES** offers a tempting menu of craft-theme-based cruises to literally all parts of the world. In addition to knitting, they offer cruises devoted to crocheting, beading, handspinning, needlepoint, and mixed media, as well as Christmas and kids.

◇ **CRAFT WORLD TOURS** offers small-group international travel programs that have been specially designed for people interested in the handcrafts, folk arts, village life and customs, and traditional lifestyles of other cultures. Recent trips included Mexico, Myanmar (Burma), India, Guatemala, Uzbekistan, Ecuador, Morocco, and Romania.

◇ **FIBER SUMMIT SERIES ABROAD (FSSA)** is based in the Italian Tyrolean Alps and Venice and offers programs for knitters, crocheters, hand spinners, weavers, quilters, dyers, students of kumihimo (a Japanese braiding technique), and enthusiasts of temari (Japanese thread-covered balls), embroidery, and other needle arts in various settings around the world.

◇ **JOYCE JAMES TOURS.** Past trips have included Scotland, Wales, Ireland, France, Iceland, Italy, and Turkey.

Chapter 9

THE Kids-Knit LIFE LIST

There's nothing like the news that a baby's on the way to spur mothers-to-be and grandmothers-to-be to dig out some needles and yarn, even if they've never knit before or if their knitting needles have been gathering dust (or rust) for decades. The wonderful surprise to new and former knitters alike is the evolution in the patterns and yarns that make knitting "little" things a whole lot more fun than ever before.

Although it can still be lovely to work up a traditional white, pale yellow, pink-for-girls, or blue-for-boys "layette," it's totally appropriate, and probably more welcome now to most new moms, to go for rich, bright colors. Penny O'Sullivan, a garden designer and writer in New Hampshire, believes that every new baby must have a red blanket, which she's certain stimulates their blossoming brains. In addition to "wow" colors, you can choose from dozens of yarns that are not only cloud soft, but also machine washable.

Yankee Knitter's
Bunny Sweater

LIFE
THE
KNITTER'S
LIST

Lean it · Explore it · Do it · Check it off!

KIDS-KNIT

MEET
- Susan Anderson
- Debbie Bliss
- Jil Eaton

DISCOVER
- Look into "green" fibers for baby items.
- Find stories of children and craftspeople in other countries and discuss them with your children.

DO/TRY
- Knit something in bright red for every new baby on your list.
- Knit a baby blanket, and if you don't know a baby to give it to, find a charity that organizes knitting for a cause.
- Knit for the future: give items that will fit when the season's right for them.
- Create a knitted heirloom for that special baby you know.
- Knit a perennial favorite: Elizabeth Zimmermann's Baby Surprise Jacket.
- Knit a pair of wool soakers.
- For a toy with real personality, knit a doll or stuffed animal with some pizzazz.
- Knit a new wardrobe for a child's favorite doll.
- Knit matching sweaters for your child and his or her doll.
- Ask at your local school if you can offer some classes in knitting or other fiber arts.

- Use pretty colors and quality yarn when teaching a new knitter.
- Choose five books from the list on pages 231–232 and read them to a child.
- Make a replica of an article from a child's favorite book and present it (and the book) as a gift.
- Talk with your kids about where the fibers in the clothes came from; read about the plants or animals that provided them.
- If you're a spinner, teach a child to spin with a stick or with a drop spindle.

LEARN
- Get creative about color choices when knitting for babies and children: choose the unexpected.
- Follow the experts' advice on safety considerations: check for secure attachments and safe stuffings and closures.
- Teach a child to finger knit.
- Learn some rhymes that remind your students the steps in the knitting process.
- Read about sheep, then visit a farm, especially at lambing or shearing times.

GO
- See if your public library has reading circles for kids, and volunteer: choose fiber-related stories.

EXPERIENCE
- Experiment with different very soft yarns when knitting for babies.
- Learn about the qualities of natural wool that make it optimal for baby clothes.
- Try to remember who taught you to knit — and what you made.
- Teach a sister or brother, daughter or son, granddaughter or grandson, niece or nephew how to knit.
- Set aside time to share knitting and knitting books with the people you love.

EXTRA CREDIT
- What's a "wool soaker," and why would anyone ever want to knit one?
- What famous fictional wizard loved knitting patterns?

MORE FOR MY KIDS-KNIT LIFE LIST

- _____
- _____

Designing for the Young

A number of designers have made designing for children their special world (although each of them designs imaginatively for adults as well). Among these designers are Susan B. Anderson, who designs not only garments but enchanting and imaginative toys that are as much fun to knit as they are to play with; Debbie Bliss, who has published more than a dozen books of patterns for babies and kids, as well as created her own lines of yarns, many of which are particularly suited to knitting for babies and toddlers; Jil Eaton, whose Minnowknits patterns show off her colorful line of Merino yarn; and Ann Norling, who is especially known for her fruit and flower caps for kids. They share their advice about what to consider when knitting for babies and young kids.

Susan Anderson's Advice

SOFTNESS FACTOR. Susan says, "Consider the yarn fiber content and how soft the yarn is. Softness is important because babies have sensitive skin. I tend to lean toward cotton and cotton blends for this reason when knitting for babies. When knitting a gift for someone else's baby, cotton is the safest route by far. However, this doesn't by any means rule out wool and wool blends when knitting for babies. There are many types of extremely smooth and soft wool that are suitable for a baby's skin. I often refer to yarn softness as the 'itch factor.' Babies and kids are much more sensitive to the feel of their clothes than adults are, and they will let you know about it. I think my best advice is to be aware that if you knit something itchy or scratchy for a baby or a child, it most likely won't get worn much. Unfortunately, I know this from experience.

WASHABILITY. "Equally important is whether or not you can wash the yarn either by machine or hand without much trouble. All babies are messy little things, so without a doubt their clothing, blankets, and toys will need frequent washing. Most labels give you recommendations on how to wash the yarn. Cottons wash wonderfully in the machine. Mercerized cotton is especially easy, because it can be thrown in the dryer as well, whereas some cottons respond best to air-drying to retain shape. Superwash wools are always great for baby items for the same reason. I have made baby garments in all kinds of wools, some easily washed by machine and others washed gently by hand only. My best recommendation here is to know your recipient.

Some parents don't mind washing baby items by hand and laying them out flat to dry; some parents do mind taking this extra effort. What I don't want to happen is to knit an item, gift it to a new baby, and not have it worn or used due to the yarn I selected. That's no fun at all."

COLOR SELECTION. Susan continues, "Parents want to shout from the rooftops the news about their new baby girl or baby boy. That's part of the fun of having a baby. This is why color selection at this time in life can become sort of a declaration of gender. I think at other phases in life color selection may not be as important. I have never been a huge pastel fan so I try to mix up colors, and I often use lots of colors together

Upsa daisy! Fun to knit, adorable to wear — who could resist Susan Anderson's Upside-Down Daisy hat?

for baby items. Brights and neutrals and rainbow hues are all fun and acceptable for babies of both genders. I have to warn you, though, that as soon as a shade of pink is thrown in a knitted item, it could be considered 'girly' by some. I honestly never worried about this with my own boys and girls. I mixed up the color range pretty well for my kids, and we all loved it. Knowing the family you are knitting for and their general style will be a good clue as to whether they will stick to traditional baby colors or be a bit more adventurous. I say, why not shake it up a little?"

SAFETY ISSUES. When it comes to safety, Susan advises, "The rules for clothing, toys, and bedding for babies are constantly changing. My youngest child is 10 years old, and in this last decade there have been so many safety recommendations added to the list that it is difficult to keep up. Of course, safety for babies is always the important thing to consider. Here are some general things I keep in mind when knitting for babies:

* Don't put ties or long strings on baby garments.
* All stitching of small pieces should be incredibly secure. I use carefully hidden knots to secure ends when color changes occur and when I attach parts on toys. You don't want parts to come off or to become loosened in baby items. Knots are usually a no-no in knitting, but for safety's sake, I break the traditional rules in this instance. I often make a small knot with the ends to secure and then weave the knot in and trim it.
* Stuff knitted toys for little ones only with fiberfill, not poly-pellets. Poly-pellets can sneak through the fabric and become a choking hazard. Poly-pellets are wonderful for older kids and adults because they give a heft and balance to knitted toys.

- If the toy is for slightly older kids, enclose the poly-pellets in a fabric bag before putting them inside a toy. This prevents the pellets from leaking through the fabric.
- I don't use buttons on clothes for infants. Instead, I use zippers or make other sorts of knitted closures when possible.
- Organic and natural dyes are highly appreciated in hand-knit baby items. Gentle is best when it comes to babies."

Debbie Bliss's Advice

- "Choose baby pattern designs that are practical as well as stylish. Babies can't tell you that the yarn is itchy or that those buttons down the back are uncomfortable to lie on!
- Remember the caregivers: Easy-to-wash is an important feature for most busy, young families.
- Take particular care to sew buttons on firmly so they don't come loose and then might easily be swallowed. Equally important, but maybe less obvious: Avoid hairy yarns, such as mohair, which can be ingested.
- Avoid using any kind of tie around the baby's neck."

Jil Eaton's Advice

- "First and foremost, always choose the very best materials you can find when knitting for babies and children. These precious garments often become heirlooms, so you want fine materials to last over time. Never use acrylics, as they leach oils from your hands and often pill when worn.
- Take washability into consideration: You can easily find beautiful superwash wools, as well as wonderful no-rinse wool washes. To use

the no-rinse washes, simply fill your washing machine, use the lowest setting, soak the garments for 20 minutes, then go directly to spin; air day, and you'll have lovely, clean garments."

Knit an heirloom. Special occasions require a special yarn, like Judith Durant's silk-alpaca christening blanket.

Getting Practical

Here are some other considerations, both practical and safety oriented, to keep in mind as you knit for babies.

DRESSING UP. Choose a pattern that's easy to put on and take off the baby: necklines should be generous, for instance. You might consider sweaters and jackets that open down the back.

SAFETY FIRST. Be sure you attach buttons very securely. You might even want to forgo buttons and use Velcro closures instead. Avoid using ribbons or cord any longer than about 6 inches.

GO GREEN. Many young families are concerned about the environment and the kinds of products their children wear, as well as what they eat. Many yarns perfect for babies and kids are organic, which means the yarn, its processing, and its dyes (including the dye processes) are all ecologically responsible (see page 39).

YARN CONTENT. Whether or not you go for machine washability, babies will probably be happiest in soft yarns, such as Merino wool, cashmere, cotton, or bamboo. The finer the yarn and the less textured, the smoother and more comfortable the garment is likely to be.

PLAN AHEAD. As much fun as it is to knit for very little babies, they just don't stay little for very long. In fact, it's amazing how quickly they grow, so you might decide that a gift for a new baby should be size 12 months instead of 3 months, so that there is more time to appreciate it. Also, do some math to calculate what age and likely size the child will be in the season most appropriate for the item you're knitting. You don't want to knit a warm, cozy sweater that might fit in July when it won't be worn but be outgrown by chilly November.

Baby-soft bamboo. Gitta Schrade's design is shown in both 100 percent bamboo (pink) and a bamboo-cotton blend (variegated).

Classic Patterns

When knitting for babies, it's always satisfying to knit traditional designs that may sometime become family heirlooms. One of the most classic of classic baby patterns is Elizabeth Zimmermann's Baby Surprise Jacket.

The story behind the "birth" of this jacket is also classic EZ. She writes of trying to decipher a bonnet pattern written in German, only to give up in despair of its turning into anything. When she threw the strange item down in frustration, she took a second look at it because it occurred to her that it looked something like a jacket. She soldiered on to complete what has become a must-do (and most enjoyable) project for every knitter. The charm of knitting this somewhat-unorthodox pattern for the first time is the inevitable feeling that you're sharing Zimmermann's puzzlement-turned-eureka as you fold the completed garment just so, and find that it really does become a very handsome jacket. The possibilities for working it in a variety of color combinations are pretty much bound to make you want to knit more than one.

"There is no right way to knit; there is no wrong way to knit. So if anybody kindly tells you that what you are doing is 'wrong,' don't take umbrage; they mean well."
ELIZABETH ZIMMERMANN

Recipe for a classic. For decades, the popularity of Elizabeth Zimmermann's Baby Surprise Jacket is due almost as much to the fascination of its unusual construction, with infinite color patterning possibilities, as to how good-looking and practical it is.

DID YOU KNOW — WHAT'S OLD BECOMES NEW AGAIN

Along with environmental consciousness has come interest in some amazing qualities of wool. Wool is one of the best fibers for wicking away moisture that you can use. As wool absorbs moisture, it carries it away from the skin and provides insulation against both cold and heat, which makes it not only comfortable but also less likely to foster conditions for diaper or other rashes. Wool knits are also stretchy and soil resistant; in addition, the lanolin contained in wool can provide some water repellency. All these factors combine to make knitted wool diaper covers (or "soakers") once again popular with many young families. You can find several patterns for soakers online (for website addresses, see the appendix).

Just for the Fun of It

Knitting for babies and children doesn't have to be just garments.
Hand-knit dolls and toys are a delight to make, and a number of designers, including Susan Anderson, have made these a specialty.

Gail Callahan points out that knitting toys is a great way to practice techniques: the projects are relatively small, but they often involve shaping that requires a series of interesting increases, decreases, and short rows. When you assemble the various pieces of an animal or doll, and especially when you create its facial expression, you may be startled as the creature almost seems to come to life. (For safety tips regarding knitting toys, see Designing for the Young, page 225.)

In addition to knitting the toys themselves, many knitters have happy memories of knitting clothes for their dolls as one of their first knitting projects. Barbara Walker designed and knit clothes for more than four hundred 12-inch dolls, including Barbie, Ken, superheroes, and pop-star figures. Melanie Falick's *America Knits* contains a photo of two of these, and *Threads* magazine published an article about the collection in the October/November 1990 issue. Kids, especially, are happy to knit simple tubes to fit their dolls, but if you're looking for something with a bit more style, Nicky Epstein published two books with clothes for Barbie dolls.

Multiplying bunnies. It's hard to knit just one of Susan Anderson's playful bunnies, designed to be knit in soft organic cotton.

EXPLORE READ TO ME! CHILDREN'S FIBER FAVORITES

To anyone who can't imagine being without a project on their knitting needles, it can be astonishing to discover that many kids have no idea what goes into the clothes they wear. Was my sweater knit, crocheted, woven? Is my hat made of wool, cotton, bamboo? Not a clue! Yet many of the best-loved, most long-lasting children's books have knitting or a related fiber craft as their theme.

Here are just some of the top favorites that create ways for kids and young adults to learn about the plants and animals that grow the fibers they wear, as well as the processes involved in making their clothing. (For more suggestions, see the appendix.)

◇ **ANNIE AND THE OLD ONE,** *by Miska Miles.* When Annie's Navajo grandmother says that she won't die until Annie's mother completes the rug she's weaving, Annie secretly unweaves the rug to hold back the time of her grandmother's death.

◇ **CHARLIE NEEDS A CLOAK,** *written and illustrated by Tomi dePaola.* To make the new coat he needs, Charlie gets help shearing, dyeing, weaving, and sewing from a flock of delightful sheep.

◇ **A GIFT FROM THE LONELY DOLL,** *written and illustrated by Dare Wright.* In one of the favorites of the Edith and Little Bear books, Edith is knitting a scarf for Mr. Bear and, typically, is teased by Little Bear that it's going to be much too long.

But Edith solves that problem, and Mr. Bear, of course, loves his scarf.

◇ **THE GOAT IN THE RUG,** *by Charles L. Blood and Martin Link; illustrated by Nancy Winslow Parker.* A young Navajo girl, Geraldine, tells how she wove a traditional rug using the clip from her "friend" Glenmae, a goat.

◇ **GOODNIGHT MOON,** *by Margaret Wise Brown; illustrated by Clement Hurd.* For decades *Goodnight Moon* has been a favorite bedtime book in which the "quiet old lady whispering hush" sits knitting in the moonlit room where a young rabbit resists sleep by wishing goodnight to each object he can see.

◇ **THE HARRY POTTER SERIES,** *by J. K. Rowling.* The Harry Potter series includes many knitters. Mrs. Weasley's hand-knit sweaters (sometimes knit by magical needles without her guidance) are not always welcome gifts; Hermione passionately knits to liberate house elves (and the house elf Dobby himself also knits); even Dumbledore and Hagrid (whose sensitive nature is hidden within his giant frame) knit.

◇ **HOMER PRICE,** *by Robert McCloskey.* "Mystery Yarn," one of the six short stories in this classic collection, relates the tale of Miss Terwilliger and her hand-knit robin's-egg-blue dress and how she outfoxed two men who were competing to be the first to ask her to marry.

◐ **IS YOUR MAMA A LLAMA?** *by Deborah Guarino; illustrated by Steven Kellogg.* Each of baby llama Lloyd's friends describes their mothers in charming rhyme.

◐ **LITTLE WOMEN,** *by Louisa May Alcott.* In this beloved classic, who can ever forget the four March girls, knitters all, especially rebellious Jo, who grumbled, "I can't get over my disappointment in not being a boy . . . I can only stay home and knit, like a poky old woman."

◐ **THE LORAX,** *by Dr. Seuss.* The Lorax, a wise old creature who "speaks for the trees," tries to defend his idyllic environment and its animals from the Once-ler, a conniving businessman who turns native Truffula trees into unnatural all-purpose garments.

◐ **THE MITTEN,** *written and illustrated by Jan Brett.* After begging his grandmother to knit him snow-white mittens, the boy promptly loses them in the snow. But as the story unfolds, the ever-expanding mittens fill with wild animals.

◐ **RUMPELSTILTSKIN,** *adapted from the story by the Brothers Grimm and illustrated by Paul O. Zelinsky.* The unforgettable story of the miller's daughter who got help from Rumpelstiltskin when she was ordered to spin straw into gold. Wonderful illustrations!

◐ **SHALL I KNIT YOU A HAT? A CHRISTMAS YARN,** *by Kate Klise; illustrated by M. Sarah Klise.* The hat that Mother Rabbit knits her son is such a hit that they decide she should knit one for each of his friends as Christmas gifts. The animals are skeptical of their unusual gifts until it begins to snow and the hats become welcome shelter. The author and illustrator are sisters.

◐ **SHEEP IN A JEEP AND SHEEP IN A SHOP,** *by Nancy E. Shaw; illustrated by Margot Apple.* Two rhymed stories full of the funny and silly misadventures of a flock of sheep that young children love.

◐ **SOPHIE'S MASTERPIECE: A SPIDER'S TALE,** *by Eileen Spinelli; illustrated by Jane Dyer.* Sophie the spider's incredibly beautiful and unusual webs are unappreciated until she meets a young pregnant woman and spins an amazing blanket for her baby-to-be.

"I was merely reading the Muggle magazines," said Dumbledore. "I do love knitting patterns."

J.K. ROWLING, *Harry Potter and the Half Blood Prince* (2005)

Passing the Needles Along

With children in the picture, you've got a great opportunity not only to knit *for* them, but also to knit *with* them. Do you remember who first taught you to knit? I do: my father. I never saw him sit around and knit, but he'd learned how, probably from his mom, and I was sick in bed, so he grabbed the chance to entertain me. I still remember the yarn, too: bright red and pretty darn thin! Little could he have known how many years of "entertainment" he was giving me.

When something you do gives you great pleasure, you can't help being enthusiastic about it and wanting to share it. Even if you don't think of yourself as a teacher, if you love to knit or spin or weave, find someone to teach. You'll not only have given someone the gift of a new creative skill, but you'll very likely receive an equally powerful gift when their faces show that they "get it." Over and over, knitters report that their most memorable and satisfying knitting-related memory is the joy of teaching someone else to knit.

Like adults, some kids are product oriented and want to have an idea what they're going to do with their knitting; others just enjoy the process. In either case make sure they have nice yarn in a color or colors they like and needles that are not too long and that they can be comfortable with (see Melanie Falick on Teaching Children to Knit, page 237). For the product-oriented types, simple squares can be turned into beanbags or pouches for storing treasures. For the more ambitious or those with longer attention spans, a scarf is a great first project. Keep the stitch count low: 20 or 25 stitches with a heavy worsted or bulky yarn is enough to get some rhythm going, but not so much that the project grows too slowly.

If you're interested in teaching in a public school setting, Cat Bordhi offers an entire curriculum, along with her inspiring experience teaching knitting in her community of Friday Harbor, Washington. The curriculum also includes a listing of websites and books for teaching kids to knit and a kids' reading list of nonfiction books about knitting, as well as fiction with knitting as a theme (for information see the appendix).

DID YOU KNOW RHYME TIME

When you and your student are ready to move on to needles, here are some old-time rhymes that may help reinforce the steps. (They may help adult learners, too!)

FOR THE KNIT STITCH
In through the front door,
Up over the back,
Peek through the window,
And off jumps Jack.

FOR THE PURL STITCH
Down through the bunny hole,
Around the big tree,
Up pops the bunny,
And off goes she! (or he!)

LEARN FINGER KNITTING

Some kids enjoy learning "needle-less" knitting, a.k.a. finger knitting. It's easiest to learn if you use bulky yarn. Use the finished product as a belt, strap, or even a fun, skinny scarf. Knit with a non-stretchy yarn, such as cotton, it could be used as a pet toy or collar. Here's how to do it.

STEP 1 (CAST ON). Place your left hand so your palm faces you. Lay the yarn tail between your thumb and index finger. Wrap the yarn counterclockwise around your index finger, then behind your middle finger, over your ring finger, and behind your little finger. Continue winding by going back the way you came but now wrapping over your little finger, behind your ring finger, over your middle finger, and under your index finger. Repeat this same pattern out to your little finger and back to your index finger, this time placing the yarn just above the first wrap. Don't wrap too tightly, and don't let the strands of yarn overlap one another.

STEP 2 ("KNITTING"). Beginning at your little finger, lift the bottom strand of yarn up and over the top strand and off the tip of your finger (the top strand stays put). Do the same on each of your other fingers in order (ring, middle, index).

For subsequent rows, beginning at your index finger, wrap each finger one more time (out and back) as you did to cast on. Once again pass the bottom strand up and over the top strand and each of your fingertips in turn.

STEP 3 (BIND OFF). When your knitting is as long as you want it, stop wrapping after you've passed a whole row off your fingers. (The yarn is at the left, next to your index finger, and each finger has only one strand of yarn on it.) Lift the loop off your little finger, and place it on your ring finger. Lift the bottom strand over the top strand and off your finger, then move the loop off your ring finger onto your middle finger. Repeat this sequence with each finger until only the index finger holds a loop. Cut the tail and draw it through that loop, and pull snugly to fasten. Fasten off the beginning tail as well.

Tip: If you have to lay down your knitting before it's complete, slide it onto a pencil or other "stick."

If the knitter is weary the baby will have no new bonnet.

Irish Proverb

STEP 1

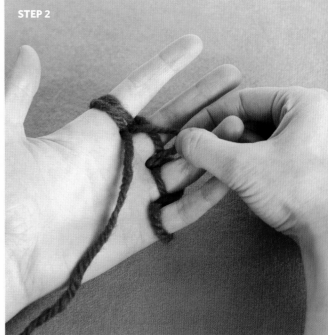

STEP 2

STEP 3

COMPLETE!

Mother-Daughter Duos

I love it when people share their wonderful memories of who taught them to knit and what their first projects were. Nearly without fail and with varying degrees of pride (or embarrassment) knitters describe the color of the yarn, the size of the needles, and how their first project turned out. Many pieces are still in use after decades; others were never finished. Some knitters became obsessed from day one; many others have come back to knitting after not touching needles for years. Many describe the mismatched socks, mysteriously "growing" sweaters, and scarves with radically different widths at each end — where did those extra stitches come from, or where did those missing stitches go to?

Not surprisingly, many of us were taught by our mothers, grandmothers, or favorite aunts, and many say that their most meaningful experience has been to teach others — especially a daughter or granddaughter. And for many there's no more joyful memory than mother-daughter time spent pouring over knitting pattern books or sharing gossip, tea, and knitting. Australian knitter Sasha Ozanne offers this description of sitting with her grandmother and mother, three generations of knitters, "quietly turning the pages of the new knitting book I received for Christmas — a book on intricate ethnic sock designs — sharing the moment together, discussing ideas and preferences, hot tips, and memories of items knit."

One of the best-known mother-daughter pairs is Elizabeth Zimmermann and Meg Swansen. Through her delightful, encouraging, and witty books, Elizabeth Zimmermann has influenced and inspired several generations of knitters. According to Meg, three thousand people are knitting Elizabeth's Baby Surprise Jacket at any one time! Meg has continued not only to publish classically beautiful books that include her own as well as other designers' patterns but to manage her famous knitting camps, under the auspices of her company, Schoolhouse Press. The camps have been held each summer since the 1970s, and Meg describes these retreats as "gatherings of old friends, but we welcome new campers to join us as we network and zig and zag through knitting minutiae and what is happening in the knitting world." Early retreats were small, and there was only one each summer. Now, holding four sessions still isn't enough for the many applicants, and the waiting list is long. (For more about Meg, see page 147.)

Getting started. Fat, colorful yarn and big needles are a good choice for young beginners.

LEARN MELANIE FALICK ON TEACHING CHILDREN TO KNIT

Want to help a child learn to knit? "If the child is interested, that's the first step," advises Melanie Falick, author of *Kids Knitting: Projects for Kids of All Ages*. "You just have to be really patient, and be the rock of calm if the kid gets frustrated."

Falick taught her own son finger knitting and spool knitting before moving to needles. For children she likes US size 6 to 10 needles, depending on the type of yarn to be used, and a needle length of 10 inches. She favors wooden needles because they're smooth, light, and maneuverable.

And don't just hand children old scraps of unwanted yarn, she adds; let them choose from an appealing array of nice yarns in various colors.

Falick recalls teaching one after-school program composed mainly of third-grade boys. "The teachers were shocked by how much they wanted to knit and how much they enjoyed it." Probably 99 percent of children who try to knit pick it up easily, she says. "It's amazing how happy they are when they get this misshapen fabric!"

MORE FOR MY KIDS-KNIT LIFE LIST

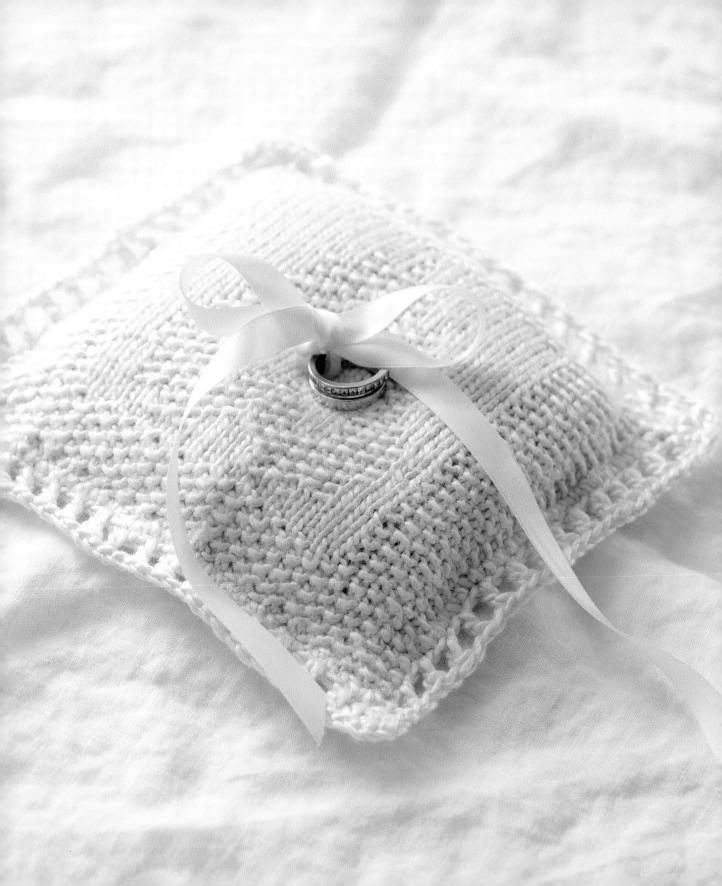

THE Home Dec LIFE LIST

Imagine temperatures hovering at about 0°F; a crackling fire in the woodstove; some nice music to set the scene; and, to make the moment really complete, a soft, oversize, hand-knit throw or afghan to cuddle up in. (On a really cold night, you might want to pull on one of your hand-knit hats and fingerless mittens as well!)

You can expand the options for your home-dec knitting beyond afghans by exploring other fibers, such as linen and cotton, and knit up some handmade table coverings or even panels for your windows — weavers and lacemakers shouldn't have all the fun! If you're not up for a completely hand-knit tablecloth or curtains, consider adding knitted edgings to a fabric center. Kitchens and bathrooms are also in need of touches from your knitting needles. Impressively absorbent, bamboo and bamboo blends are great yarn choices for washcloths, dishcloths, and dishtowels. Linen is another wonderful fiber to consider for these items: it softens beautifully with use, washing, and time. And knitted felt is perfect for placemats (dependable cushioning), coffee- and teapot "cozies" (insulation), and pot holders and heat pads (protection).

LIFE

THE

KNITTER'S

LIST

Lean it · Explore it · Do it · Check it off!

HOME DEC

MEET

- Jared Flood
- Shannon Okey
- Barbara Walker

DISCOVER

- Discover "scrumbling" by visiting the International Freeform Fiberarts website.
- Learn about the amazing things that can be done with "mathematical knitting."
- Use up yarn odds and ends to create modular-knit home dec articles.
- Read Barbara Walker's award-winning book, *Woman's Encyclopedia of Myths and Secrets.*
- Use your knitting time as a chance to catch up on books about you've always intended to read, but haven't gotten to yet.
- Face up to your tolerance level for UFOs, ranging from (1) don't start anything new until you've finished what you're knitting to (2) keep all your UFOs together so that they at least don't get forgotten.

DO/TRY

- Knit sofa pillow covers.
- Knit covers for seat cushions.
- Knit an afghan or throw.
- Knit a window valance or curtains.

- Knit placemats — and a table runner to match.
- Knit napkins and napkin rings.
- Knit (and stuff to make heat-proof) pot holders.
- Knit hanger covers.
- Knit heat pads.
- Knit coffeepot and teapot cozies.
- Knit dishcloths.
- Knit a bath mat.
- Knit spa items, such as washcloths and soap covers: felt the soap cover right to a bar of soap.
- Knit an old-fashioned coverlet.
- Knit pillowcase edgings.
- Knit (and felt?) a hot-water-bottle cover.
- Knit edgings for bath towels.
- Knit (and felt) for your electronic gadgets (laptop, Netbook, iPad, etc.)
- Knit Christmas stockings for everyone in the family.
- Knit a Christmas tree stand cover.
- Knit Christmas tree ornaments.
- Knit for weddings: edging for chuppah, "ribbon" for bouquets, ring-bearer pillow.
- Wrestle your yarn stash into a system that makes sense to you: for instance, all of the same colors together or all of the same weights together.

- Collect all your needles in one place and inventory them: keep track in a notebook, on your computer, or with an app.
- Buy an inexpensive file box for single patterns.
- Use see-through containers to avoid the out-of-sight-out-of-mind syndrome.
- Knit a covering for something out of the ordinary in your home: for instance, a door handle, mirror or picture frame, bowl, TV remote, or chair.
- Go outdoors and cover a tree trunk or the pole for your neighborhood street sign with your handknit.
- Knit a cover for the knob of your gear shift.
- Knit (and felt) a comfy seat cover for your bike (thank you, Nan Koenig!)
- Work Jared Flood's Hemlock Ring Blanket.
- Encourage any men you know who would like to knit.
- Make a multi-cabled afghan or throw.
- Work a bath mat that features bobbles.
- Use Barbara Walker's stitch dictionaries to create your own home dec designs.
- Find out how to contribute swatches to the online Walker Treasury Project.

- Create a lace edging and attach it to the edges of a linen square for a table covering.

LEARN

- Learn to knit backwards!
- Use intarsia to create a throw that uses at least 15 different-color yarns.
- Learn to speak a foreign language (à la Holly Golightly) as you knit.
- Create and knit from a "magic ball."
- Experiment with scale by making the same pattern in several wildly different yarn weights.
- Learn to cable without holding stitches aside on a cable needle.
- Knit potholders or a pillow cover made of mitered squares.
- Use variegated yarn to knit mitered squares following Vivian Høxbro's suggestions.
- Introduce yourself to entrelac by making a set of pot holders.
- Play with entrelac for a pillow design.
- Work a monogram in intarsia for a seat cushion.
- Learn to make yarn butterflies for better yarn management.
- Use Kaffe Fassett's method for handling multiple yarns.

- Make a pillow cover using shadow knitting.
- Find out about "illusion knitting" on the Web.
- Work at least five swatches in mosaic knitting from Barbara Walker's collection of 380 stitch patterns.
- Explore Barbara Walker's other stitch dictionaries and knit at least five from each.
- Use plied fringe on a project.
- Use beaded fringe on a project.
- Use knotted fringe on a project.
- Use three-strand braid on a project.
- Use four-strand braid on a project.
- Use square braid on a project.
- Use Kumihimo braid on a project.
- Use knitted fringe on a project.

EXPERIENCE

- Choose ten movies from the list on pages 244–245 and put them in your Netflix queue.
- Find some Wensleydale wool and knit something from it as you watch a Wallace and Gromit movie. (Thanks, Deb Robson, for that suggestion!)
- Listen to some Edith Piaf recordings while you knit.
- Set aside a simple afghan project just for movie watching.

- Notice geometric patterns in the world around you, and use these as inspiration for your knitting.
- Choose a group of at least 20 colors from the same line of yarn to create a palette for intarsia.

EXTRA CREDIT

- What famous singer was a dedicated knitter?
- What fictional woman mistook house plans for her knitting project?
- What is "mathematical knitting"?
- Where can you find out what it means when one of Jane Austen's characters knits?

MORE FOR MY HOME DEC LIFE LIST

On Getting Organized

It's lovely to beautify our homes with our handknits, but the serene and superorganized home workplace that we sometimes envision is often seriously threatened by all the yarns, needles, stitch gauges and measuring tapes, scissors and snips, favorite books and precious patterns torn from 10-year-old magazines, along with the many other irresistible "notions" that we accumulate over the years. The truth is that most of us are not as super at organizing our creative lives as we'd like to be. Wouldn't it be great to know what we have tucked away (and just where it is), as well as have a clutter-free workspace when we start pulling things out to begin a new project? Being organized can actually make space in our brains for greater creativity — sort of like unclogging the drain! Here are a few suggestions from one organizer maven:

Shannon Okey is a big fan of Lexie Barnes's foldable storage cube. These versatile boxes are covered with spill-resistant, wipeable fabric, and she says, "They're cute! . . . Major points for cute." The leopard print is her favorite. She advises that storage space be well lit (dark corners make it hard to retrieve things), easily accessible, and, if possible, behind a closed door (especially if you have "incredibly naughty cats"). She also likes to use lockable plastic tubs and zippable heavy-duty plastic bags (like those that comforters and pillows are sold in): you can see what's inside without opening them, they're lightweight, and you can stash them anywhere.

A major culprit of disorganization is often the dreaded UFO. Most knitters know I'm not referring to a mysterious item from outer space, but that other much-less-mysterious item you may have hiding in your closet or in the bottom of your knitting bag: an UnFinished Object. Judy Becker, known for her clever invisible cast on, refers to the UFO as her "sidebar of shame." She reports, "I am really very much a process knitter rather than a project knitter, and I am easily distracted by that next bright, shiny project. Thus the number of UFOs that lie forlornly about." Although at one point she resolved to finish everything she'd already started, once the decision was made, she admits, "the first thing I did was cast on a new project, which is still unfinished. My head is bloody but unbowed!"

I confess it would be hypocritical for me to offer any further advice on this subject.

DID YOU KNOW **FEELING SUBVERSIVE?**

From Houston to Boston, Stockholm to New York, Monaco to Mexico, guerrilla knitters have made tagging a knitting-group action game and taken "home dec" outdoors. Also referred to as *knitting graffiti, yarn bombing,* and *yarnstorming*, this street art form features knit "sleeves" for lampposts, street signs, parking meter posts, railings, trees, and a whole assortment of other likely (and unlikely) targets. London's iconic red phone boxes and a bus in Mexico City were no mean feats to fit out with knits. One of the most impressive is an entire abandoned service station (including the gas pumps) in Syracuse, New York. This yarn-graffiti masterpiece is covered with over-the-top colorful knitted fabric, contributed from knitters all over the world. The movement even inspired a book, complete with patterns for creating your own knitting graffiti: *Yarn Bombing: The Art of Crochet and Knit Graffiti,* by Mandy Moore and Leanne Prain. In London the Yarn Corp "organizes" urban graffiti happenings under the name Knit the City.

Berkeley whimsy. High-spirited yarn bombers have here hit Berkeley, California: on Addison Street outside the Berkeley Repertory Theatre (*left*) and on College Avenue (*right*).

EXPLORE SPOTTED AT THE MOVIES

Some evenings nothing sounds better than curling up with a movie classic and your knitting (and forget worrying about lack of organization in your fiber world). There's some debate about what kinds of movies go with which kind of knitting: nothing too complex on your needles if you've chosen a complicated thriller, and most knitters can't manage subtitled films and knitting lace at the same time.

What makes the watching even more fun is if you spot knitters in the action. From murders and tragedies (*Chicago* and *A Cry in the Dark*) to comedies and cartoons (*Foul Play* and *Wallace and Gromit*), there's a lot to choose from. Here are some plot descriptions for a few films in which knitting is an integral part of the plot, followed by a longer list of flicks that are just plain fun for knitting-spotting. Add your own gotta-see movies to this list of old and new favorites. Many of these films were based on novels, so you might want to check out the books as well. (For websites with more leads, see the appendix.)

▷ BREAKFAST AT TIFFANY'S. When free-spirited Holly Golightly decides to abandon her high-end New York "escort" business for the promise of a respectable life with a wealthy Brazilian ranch owner, she sets herself to learning not only Portuguese but also how to knit. She admits, however, that her knitting project may not quite work out, because she may have confused the knitting pattern with her fiancé's ranch blueprint. (1961; based on a novel by Truman Capote)

▷ DANCING AT LUGHNASA. A dark Irish tale starring Meryl Streep, in which five sisters struggle with poverty, depending for their income on knitting gloves, until their livelihood is threatened when a knitting factory is opened nearby. (1998)

▷ HOW TO SUCCEED IN BUSINESS WITHOUT REALLY TRYING. Pretending to share his boss's passion for knitting, an aspiring ad man tries to win favor with this line that knitters love to quote: "I feel sorry for men who don't knit — they lead empty lives." (1967)

▷ LA VIE EN ROSE. The real life of the internationally famous French singer Edith Piaf was anything but rosy, as the bio-pic *La Vie en Rose* illustrates. This unhappy but determined woman was also a dedicated knitter. Asked by her lover, "What do you do when you're not singing?" she replied, "I knit." (2007; Oscar for Best Actress)

▷ LIKE WATER FOR CHOCOLATE. In this Mexican love story, Tita is devastated when her mother insists that her sister marry Tita's boyfriend, Pedro. Whenever she's upset (which is almost always after this marriage), Tita works on her crocheted bedspread, ultimately creating a fantastically long piece. (1992; based on a novel by Laura Esquivel)

◇ **PREPAREZ VOS MOUCHOIRS (GET OUT YOUR HANDKERCHIEFS).** In this French romantic comedy, Gérard Depardieu (Raoul) and Patrick Dewaere set out to cheer up Raoul's wife Salonge, who prefers knitting to lovemaking. (1978; Oscar for Best Foreign Film)

◇ **WALLACE AND GROMIT: A CLOSE SHAVE, AND OTHERS IN THE SERIES.** If you're a knitter with a sense of humor, you don't have to be under 10 to love this Wallace and Gromit film. Gromit is a knitter, and Wallace is in love with Wendolene Ramsbottom, the owner of a local yarn shop. His new Knit-O-Matic machine, a wool shortage, and Wendolene's sheep-nabbing dog combine to create hilarious chaos. Wallace and Gromit's favorite cheese was Wensleydale, and the popularity of this movie is said to have saved the real-life Wensleydale cheese factory in England from bankruptcy. (1995; Oscar for Best Animated Short)

. . . and there's more:

Alex & Emma
America's Sweethearts
Babette's Feast
Birthday Girl
Brokeback Mountain
Calendar Girls
Captain Corelli's Mandolin
Charlie and the Chocolate Factory
Chicago
Cold Mountain
Cry in the Dark
Delicatessen
Disney's *Robin Hood*
Fargo
Foul Play
Hot Shots Part Deux
Jane Austen Book Club
Ladies in Lavender

Little Women
Monty Python's The Meaning of Life
Mr. Lucky
Murder Ahoy
Murder Most Foul
My Life as a Dog
The Quiet Man
Raising Helen
Runaway Bride
Shadowlands
The Shipping News
The Story of the Weeping Camel
A Tale of Two Cities
Wait Until Dark
Witness

Time out. In this 1955 photo, Humphrey Bogart and Lauren Bacall relax on board a yacht. (She's knitting!)

Contemporary Takes on Tradition

Some of today's designers are riffing on classic and vintage home dec items, interpreting old-fashioned patterns and usages in fresh, new ways. Jared Flood's translation of crocheted doilies into knitted afghans is just one brilliant example that can inspire and spark up our knitting repertoire. Other knitters are abandoning patterns and rules altogether to create playful fabrics that are often works of art in a form known as freeform knitting and crochet.

Dallying with Doilies

Jared Flood describes the origin of his popular 4-foot-diameter wool Hemlock Ring Blanket this way: "This project was born from my love of working heavyweight lace and my desire to spruce up my new place." (He adds that a sale on Cascade EcoWool didn't hurt, either.) Jared converted a doily pattern published in 1942 by the Canadian Spool Cotton Company, which included vintage accents that begged to be played around with, into an afghan knit with worsted-weight yarn — same pattern, different yarn, completely different look (for the pattern, see the appendix).

Inspiration in pattern. Jared Flood is "drawn to pattern designing that requires geometry, as in lace and colorwork, where there is a mini structure happening in a larger structure, little systems inside a bigger system."

MEET JARED FLOOD

A SUMPTUOUS ONE-OF-A-KIND YARN from Italy, the intricacies of a new cable pattern, stitch definition — these are what's on Jared Flood's mind as he steps into a yarn store. Around him, though, people are inevitably thinking about something else: the sight of a 20-something man who knits. "You're under a microscope at all times," says Jared, a designer from Brooklyn, New York, who began knitting at 21 and has quickly gained recognition for his work. "I don't like walking into a yarn shop and finding everyone's looking at me because I'm an oddity," he admits. And Jared knows he isn't that unusual: he's discovered that many men are part of the online knitting world, even if they don't show up at knitting groups and trunk shows. Still, being a male knitwear designer in a female-dominated arena has worked to his advantage, he says, helping him promote his work and make a living at it.

Flood, a native of Washington State, was studying art at the University of Puget Sound when one of his housemates took up knitting, and he found himself riveted. "She taught me knit and purl, and I quickly became a nuisance to her," he recalls, laughing. "I didn't want to make a garter stitch scarf; I wanted to make a sweater. From that point on it was a self-education, using both books and the Internet."

Jared, also a professional photographer with a strong background in two-dimensional art and graphic design, has been interested in art as long as he can remember, and he credits his parents for their creative influence. His mother is a skilled knitter and seamstress; his father hand-built toys for Jared and his two brothers and once constructed a backyard play structure for them using all salvaged materials, from scrap telephone poles to old tires.

Moving to Brooklyn after college, Jared soon started a blog to connect with other knitters and share his work. More recently, Jared has published *Made in Brooklyn*, a book of patterns; has created his own line of yarn; and continues to teach. He's also keeping his eye on the future of the hand-knitting community. "I feel very strongly that the hand-knitting industry can and needs to be pushed into a more respectable place," he says. "Hand-knitting is not taken seriously in fashion and other industries." But he believes that stereotypes like "dumpy fashions," which have sometimes been applied to hand-knitting, are being driven away by the renewed interest in the craft. "It's fun to imagine how hand-knitting will be perceived in five years."

Freeing Up Your Inner Knitter

If you're willing to let go of patterns altogether, you might want to try freeform knitting. Some days you just don't feel like following a pattern. Your stash is getting more awesome by the minute, yet you never seem to have enough of any one yarn to complete a project. You love colors and textures, and you sometimes get bored with repetitive stitch patterns. Take all these feelings as a sign: you're ready to try freeform knitting. British authors Sylvia Cosh and James Walters promoted the technique for crocheters back in the 1970s, and a number of contemporary proponents continue to teach and write about "scrumbling," the whimsical term coined to describe the process.

Scrumbling involves designing small, irregularly shaped pieces as you go by using random yarns, colors, and stitch patterns (even making up stitches) with an eye to maximizing texture. When you attach these pieces, the result is a unique fabric with a one-of-a-kind design. Author and designer Jenny Dowde calls the process "taking your yarn for a walk." Although the process started with crocheters, knitters don't have to be left out. In fact, you'll find a number of recent books showing how to combine knitting and crochet taking a freeform approach.

One of the fun projects a number of members of the Scrumbling and Freeform Crochet and Knitting group on Ravelry recently took up was to knit from a "magic ball." They created their balls by tying short lengths of different yarns together, rolling the piece into a ball as they went. When the ball was satisfactorily fat, they started knitting.

Many fiber artists who enjoy working in this style add buttons and beads to their creations as well, and some move their work from flat to three-dimensional. The International Freeform Fiberarts guild has a website and sponsors an annual show. There are also several groups on Ravelry. In addition to Jenny Dowde, several other designers teach and write about freeform knitting and crochet; these include Prudence Mapstone and Myra Wood. You'll find a listing of their books and websites in the appendix.

A related group of fiber enthusiasts share ideas for what they call "mathematical knitting." These retired UK teachers focus on creating knitted (or crocheted) objects based on mathematical or scientific principles and modular or geometric techniques. For information about their fascinating (and addictive) work, check out their website Woolly Thoughts.

Scrumbling! Jenny Dowde, an enthusiastic promoter of freeform knitting (often called "scrumbling") contributed this colorful, textured swatch as an example of her work.

Techniques for Home Dec Knitting

As satisfying as it is to shape garments and accessories to fit all kinds of body shapes, you sometimes yearn for a project that doesn't matter whether it fits or where to make the increases and decreases — or which ones to use. Because many of the items you might choose to knit for your home are flat, you'll find lots of scope for exploring knitting techniques you haven't tried before.

Among your choices is lace, which works for everything from afghans to table coverings (see page 172). Intarsia, as well as entrelac and other modular techniques, are especially well suited to afghans and throws. Throws and coverlets are also the ideal training ground for cables, traveling stitches, and other textural designs, such as those used in Aran and Shetland knits (see page 112). It can be fun to play with scale in any of these projects by experimenting with the same stitch pattern knit with lighter-weight yarns on small needles and also with bulky yarn and large needles. Vivian Høxbro's development of modular knitting techniques (what she calls "domino knitting"), as well as her innovative shadow knitting, are ideal for all kinds of household items, from pot holders and pillows to afghans and throws. Kaffe Fassett's brilliant colorwork, especially with intarsia, and Edie Eckman's and Nicky Epstein's inventive edgings all provide inspiration that will keep you knitting for as long as you can hold needles.

Modular Madness

The mitered squares that Vivian Høxbro popularized in her *Domino Knitting* and *Knit to Be Square* are one form of modular knitting. To create a square you begin with one stitch at a corner, increase on either side of it row by row until you reach the desired diagonal measurement, then decrease back to the corner opposite the beginning. Fabric is created by joining one square to another as you knit.

Another equally engrossing modular technique is entrelac, which is created by knitting small squares or rectangles one by one across a row; you join this series of small pieces as you knit to create the next row of rectangles. Each small shape is set on a point, creating a series of diamond-like patterns. Depending on the way you use color, entrelac can look a bit as if you've interwoven narrow widths of knitted fabric basketry style.

Both mitered squares and entrelac offer all kinds of opportunity to explore complex color and pattern combinations. A large part of their fascination is the small-bite approach. You construct your fabric by working a series of comparatively small squares or rectangles, and as your work develops it's easy to become captivated by the structure and color patterns that evolve under your fingers, piece by piece. Each technique has some of the fascination and possibilities of quilting, because you can completely change an overall design by the way you arrange the colors of the components. Once you get in the swing, it's very hard not to want to make "just one more square." (How often have you said, "Wait until I finish this row"? This is worse than rows — even more addictive.)

Many fans of variegated and hand-painted yarns find modular techniques particularly appropriate, because the pooling that can be an annoyance or lead to disappointment when working with variegated yarns isn't usually a problem and, in fact, multicolor yarns often create a fabric with unexpected and delightful design elements that appear much more complicated than the knitting really is. Modular knitting is also an ideal way to make use of small bits and pieces of yarn leftovers from other projects, and it can be a very fun challenge to create interesting color combinations just from what's at hand.

SWATCHING | *Mitered Knit*

SWATCHING | *Entrelac*

Inch-by-inch, row-by-row. Both mitered knitting (*above*) and entrelac (at right) involve working small units, and then picking up along one side of a unit to develop adjacent units. Both are ideal for creating color effects, though with quite different outcomes.

Modular approaches are also perfect for exploring new color pathways you haven't tried in the past. Color lover and expert Kristin Nicholas suggests starting with a group of at least 20 colors, all from the same line of yarn. "That way, it's likely that the same person has picked them all and they will work together," she says. With that many colors you have choices among major color groups. "Drawing all your yarn from one line also means the texture and weight are uniform," she notes.

EXPLORE **MEET THE MULTITASKERS**

Heather Ordover, who hosts CraftLit: A Podcast for Crafters Who Love Books, has the solution for knitters who don't want to make the choice between two things they love to do: read and knit. As she notes, "Knitters like books — or at least we like to be entertained when we're working endless stockinette on a cardigan back or a never-ending K2, P2 sock cuff." Heather's podcast comes to the aid of this "knitting-obsessed-but-book-loving audience by marrying crafts to a chapter or two of a work of classic literature."

One of the surprises Heather has learned from her listeners is that they're likely to take on more than two tasks at once: some even mention knitting a sock while listening to the podcast while also working out on a treadmill. She notes that, "Although you don't *need* to work that hard to listen, it's always nice to be able to share a good book while the needles are flying." (For CraftLit's Web address, see the appendix.)

SWATCHING | *Cables*

Another kind of cable. In this pattern from Barbara Walker, the cables don't cross, but instead create a lovely undulating surface that she calls "Shadow Cable."

"Humans make patterns because we live in a world that is teeming with them."
TEXTILE MUSEUM OF CANADA

LEARN WHEN BACKWARD THINKING IS A GOOD THING

A function of modular knitting, especially of entrelac, that can become an annoyance is the need to turn your work frequently.

If you're one of those who get impatient with the twists and turns, it's time to try out backward knitting. It sounds weird, and it may seem weird when you begin to learn it, especially when you're used to sailing along at high speed going forward. But if turning is annoying enough to you, backward knitting is worth a try. You may be pleasantly surprised at how quickly it becomes natural to you. The following instructions are for plain stockinette: the rows you knit backwards would ordinarily be purled.

When you complete a knit row, leave your hands and needles right where they: stitches on the right, receiving needle on the left. You may hold your yarn in either your left or right hand, whichever is more comfortable for you.

Insert your left-hand needle into the first stitch from left to right behind your right-hand needle. Wrap the yarn clockwise around the left-hand needle, draw the stitch on the right-hand needle over the wrapped yarn to make the stitch on the left-hand needle, and drop the stitch off the right-hand needle.

Note: Wrapping the yarn clockwise puts the back leg ahead of the front leg when you're ready to knit forward again. To avoid twisting the stitches, knit into the back legs when you knit forwards again. Alternatively, you can wrap the yarn counterclockwise as you make the stitch. Perhaps because I hold my working yarn in my left hand, I find the counterclockwise wrap slightly more awkward, and I'm just as happy to make the adjustment on the forward row. The approach is entirely up to you and your comfort level. Try both ways to see which works best for you — just be sure that when you knit forward you don't twist the stitch.

Backward knitting is useful whenever you have to knit back and forth on just a few stitches, including entrelac and other modular techniques but also when working bobbles.

Backward knitting. Insert left-hand needle into the first stitch from left to right behind your right-hand needle; wrap yarn clockwise (A).

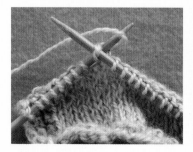

Draw the stitch on the right-hand needle over the wrapped yarn, making a stitch on the left-hand needle (B), and drop the stitch off the right-hand needle.

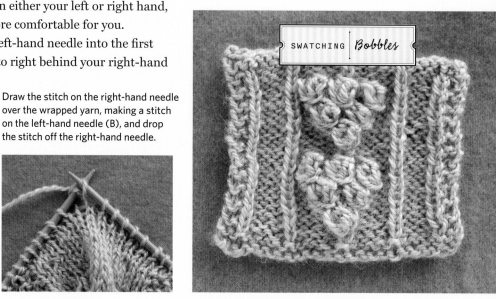

SWATCHING | *Bobbles*

MEET BARBARA WALKER

Barbara Walker's stitch collections and other books have been indispensable references for knitters and knitting designers for decades, but Barbara herself didn't get interested in knitting until she was in her mid-thirties. What drew her in was a fascination with stitch patterns, both color and texture. She began collecting patterns, first from Mary Thomas and James Norbury, then moved on to inventing her own stitches — more than a thousand in all.

She also improved on several common knitting techniques, including the slip-slip-knit decrease (ssk). She liked to envision the look of a design by writing it out on paper, so she strongly advocated the charting of patterns and devised a comprehensive array of symbols to represent stitch maneuvers. When set down as charts, in contrast to written-out instructions, "the patterns are visible at a glance," she explains, "which is especially helpful when working cables."

Barbara created a new way of working color patterns using slip stitches. She published the technique and patterns in her 1976 *Mosaic Knitting*, which contained 157 charted designs; a new edition featuring 116 new designs was published in 2006. The complex multicolor designs are achieved by knitting alternating pairs of rows in contrasting colors and developing the color patterning by slipping stitches from one row to the next. No need to carry two yarns at once across a row as in stranded knitting!

She personally knitted every one of the hundreds of swatches shown in her books, which include the mosaics book, *A Treasury of Knitting Patterns* (and the three subsequent releases in the series), *Knitting from the Top*, and *Learn-to-Knit Afghan Book*. Most of the patterns are shown in black-and-white photos, but you can find many swatches of Barbara's patterns online at the Walker Treasury Project, a volunteer effort to collect examples worked in color. (The patterns are not included, but the photos are referenced to the specific books where the patterns appear.)

Fans may not realize that she has an equally impressive "other life." In addition to her books on knitting, she has published many articles and a dozen other books dealing with such subjects as comparative religion and mythology, rituals, symbols, feminist history, mineral lore, the Tarot, the *I Ching*, and the image of the "Crone" in European tradition, plus an autobiography, a novel, and a collection of original *Feminist Fairy Tales*. Her *Woman's Encyclopedia of Myths and Secrets* won a Book of the Year award in 1986 from the *Times* (London). Her most recent book, a collection of her lectures in essay form, is entitled *Man Made God*. She's pleased to note that her newest book is available on Kindle, even though she prefers to write out her manuscripts in longhand. As an artist, Barbara created 78 original paintings for the "Barbara Walker Tarot Deck" and 64 original paintings for her "I Ching of the Goddess" cards.

Picture It with Intarsia

Stranded knitting is one way to incorporate multiple colors into your knitting. But *intarsia* is another multicolor knitting method that allows you to create sections of a color without having to carry the yarn of that particular color along the entire width of the fabric. Really, the sky is almost the limit for intarsia. You can include representations of humans, animals, or plants; lettering; large nonrepetitive abstract graphics — in fact, just about any design you can dream up. Whether you'd like to monogram your purse or show off a favorite pictorial design, intarsia may be the way to go. Kaffe Fassett's designs are often worked in intarsia, and whether he creates floral images or geometric patterns, his use of color in these designs is well known and always inspiring.

With intarsia, instead of carrying the non-working yarn along the back of the fabric until needed again, you drop it and use the next color. Each color yarn that you leave behind is then waiting for you when you work back across the next row, ready to be picked up and knit with once again. The key to successful intarsia is to wrap the old working yarn around the new yarn as you take the first stitch with it. If you fail to do this, a telltale hole will very likely appear at this spot. Intarsia is more suitable for flat than for circular knitting, although with some maneuvering, it's not impossible to work it in the round. (In her *Knitting in the Old Way*, Priscilla Gibson-Roberts presents several ways to work intarsia in the round.)

For efficient yarn management many knitters wind a small bobbin or "butterfly" of yarn for each area of color required along the row. Kaffe Fassett recommends a somewhat unorthodox method, but one that is particularly useful when there are a great many small areas of colors. For butterflies see the illustration (on facing page); for Kaffe's method, see Kaffe Fassett's Tips for Intarsia (also on facing page).

> SWATCHING | *Intarsia*

Endless potential. Intarsia is your chance to spell out messages or sketch pictures with your yarns. Use graph paper to plan your images, and then use the result as a chart to knit from. An enlarged version of these punctuation marks would make a fun set of pillows.

Butterfly Tie

The butterfly tie is a tried-and-true technique when working intarsia, especially if the areas of each color are rather large. If you're right handed, hold your left hand so that your palm faces you. Leaving the beginning tail hanging down about 4 inches, wrap the yarn figure-8 fashion around your left thumb and little finger. Keep the width of the developing bundle to no more than about 4 inches. If you spread your fingers apart, the butterfly will be too wide and thus likely to tangle. When you have about 20 wraps, pinch the bundle in the middle where the strands cross (the "waist"), and slide the bundle off your thumb and finger. Wrap the yarn you've been winding around the waist of the bundle, then cut the yarn and make a half hitch around the waist to fasten off. As you knit draw your yarn supply from the beginning tail, allowing only as much as you need for a few stitches.

Kaffe Fassett's Tips for Intarsia

Kaffe, the knitting designer known for his adventurous color work, has created his own practical technique for handling the dozens of colors he uses in his patterns: use short lengths of yarn to avoid tangles and allow them to simply hang behind your work. He also recommends weaving yarn ends into your knitting as you go, rather than facing long end-weaving sessions when you've finished a project. He ignores certain knitting conventions to get the look he wants, using, for instance, an assortment of yarn weights and fibers in a single project. He adds this advice: "When in doubt, add 20 more colors."

Borrowing designs. Kaffe Fassett's stitch pattern design for a vest is just as appropriate adopted for a cozy throw.

A Shadowy Concept

A simple technique with many possibilities, shadow knitting is created by alternating two rows of a light-colored yarn with two in a dark color. The background is generally stockinette stitch, and the subtle design (the "shadow") is created by working a combination of knits and purls in specified areas in the second (wrong-side) row of a color. Characteristically, the design isn't apparent when you look at the fabric straight on but shows subtly when viewed from an angle, making it particularly fruitful when playing with color effects.

The technique is ideal for all kinds of household projects, from throws to pillows and even tableware, as well as for garments. Vivian Høxbro's book *Shadow Knitting* includes instruction about the method as well as patterns to explore. Pat Ashforth and Steve Plummer of Woolly Thoughts have drawn some techniques from shadow knitting to develop an unusually dramatic and exciting approach that they call "illusion knitting." For patterns and a look at some of their work, which includes everything from the depictions of the Mona Lisa to Harry Potter, go to their website (see the appendix for the Web address).

Mosaic Knitting

If you enjoy the play of contrasting colors in your knitting but don't like having to carry two or more colors of yarn across a single row, you might like to try Barbara Walker's mosaic knitting. In *Mosaic Knitting*, complex multicolor designs are created by knitting alternating pairs of rows in contrasting colors and developing the color patterning by slipping stitches from one row to the next. You have the option of working the patterns in stockinette or garter stitch. The keys to success with this technique: always slip stitches purlwise (with the needle positioned as if you were purling the stitch) and always keep the working yarn on the wrong side of the work when you're slipping.

SWATCHING | Shadow Knitting

Fooling the eye. It's amazing what one can do with two colors and just knit and purl stitches. The fabric created with shadow knitting subtly changes color as you see it from different angles.

SWATCHING | Mosaic

Only one at a time. If you love playing with color patterns, but don't really enjoy stranded knitting, slip-stitch techniques offer the chance to create multicolor designs without having to work with more than one color yarn in any one row.

Living on the Edge

Half the fun and much of the impact of knitted throws and other home dec items is how you choose to finish the edges. The most obvious choices are knitted or crocheted edgings and fringe.

Over the Border

One way to go is to pick up stitches along an edge and either knit or crochet a border in the project yarn or a contrasting color. In Nicky Epstein's *Knitting on the Edge*, she writes that edgings and borders are "the icing on the cake." The book includes her own as well as traditional designs, drawn from many different cultural traditions. For knitters ready to experiment and blend their knitting with crochet, Edie Eckman's *Around the Corner Crochet Borders* offers dozens of choices. And as the title indicates, she even shows you how to get around the corners without ruffling or "cupping" your work. As in Nicky's book, Edie's designs are all shown in wool, but they can easily be used with other fibers, as desired.

Fringe Elements

Whether working thick-knit woolly afghans or delicate linen placemats, you may want something other than, or in addition to, a knitted or crocheted edge. This is where fringes come in: having a supply of methods up your sleeve for creating fringe will stand you in good stead over and over. Fringe can be seen as a sort of yarn version of hair extensions. It might be as simple as unadorned strands of yarn, either reserved "tails" or tied on. Or you can decorate the fringe

with beads, twist it, knot it, or braid it. It's particularly important to consider how to handle a fringe of loosely spun singles or other somewhat delicate yarn, which can easily tangle or disintegrate if not strengthened or protected by braiding, twisting, or some other method that helps stabilize it.

To trim the ends of a scarf, shawl, or afghan with simple applied fringe, first cut pieces of yarn twice the length you want your fringe to be. You may tie the yarn onto the edge doubled or in groups, depending on the look you want. For example, for a 6-inch-long fringe grouped in bundles of eight, cut 12-inch strands of yarn. Hold four strands together, and fold them in half. Insert a crochet hook into the edge of your fabric (for stability you should usually take up the entire bound-off or cast-on row and not just a single strand), then insert the hook through the loop at the middle of the folded strands. Draw the loop through the knitted edge for about 1 inch. Next, draw the cut ends of the fringe through the loop, creating an overhand knot at the edge of the fabric. Take care always to work from the same side of the fabric, so the knots face in the same direction.

Continue across the edge, spacing the fringe as close together as desired (see the Varsity Scarf in Knitting the Classics . . . and Beyond, pages 156–157, for another method for making fringe). When the edge is completely fringed, you can leave it as is, or proceed to ornament it in one of the following ways.

PLY IT. Decide on the thickness you'd like your plied fringe to have. For the eight-strand fringe just described, take a group of four adjacent strands of fringe in each hand. You're going to twist each group separately in order to "ply" them together. Examine the yarn, and turn so the twist you create goes in the same direction as it was plied. Continue twisting until the bundle is tightly bound. It's helpful to fasten the edge of the fabric to something stable (or have a friend hold it for you) so you can keep the fringe bundles fairly taut while you're twisting.

When both bundles of fringe are twisted, place the cut ends together. Tie a knot a short distance from the end to hold the twist. When you let go, the two bundles will twist around each other. (They're actually trying to untwist, but in doing so they embrace and lock into place.) Measure to ensure that each fringe bundle is the same length. (If you make a lot of plied fringe, you might want to invest in a mechanical fringe twister.)

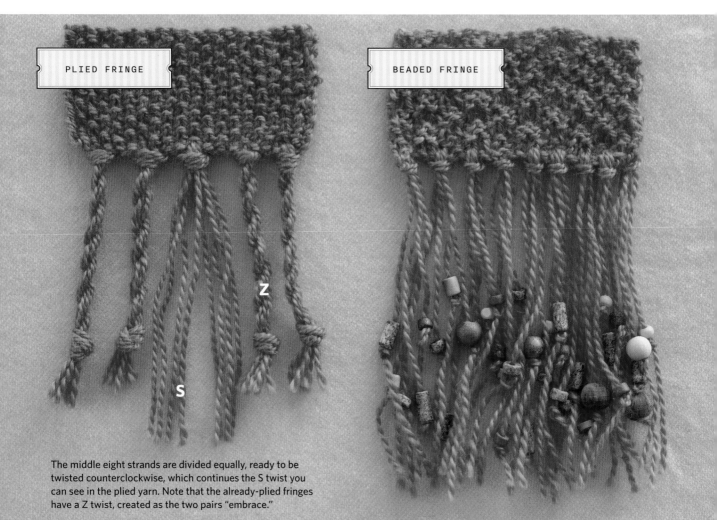

PLIED FRINGE

BEADED FRINGE

The middle eight strands are divided equally, ready to be twisted counterclockwise, which continues the S twist you can see in the plied yarn. Note that the already-plied fringes have a Z twist, created as the two pairs "embrace."

BEAD IT. Adding beads to the ends of the fringe also adds weight, which can be especially useful on a scarf or shawl that needs some help to get it to drape nicely. Beads, of course, also add some fun and glitter. Knot one bead at the end of a strand of fringe, or space two or more beads the length of the strands. You can bead every strand or space them out.

KNOT IT. For a vintage look why not knot your fringe macramé style? You'll need to make your original fringe at least half again as long as you want the final edging to be, because the knotting takes up quite a bit of length. To ensure evenly spaced knots, pin the edge of your fabric to a firm pillow or a piece of foam, and continue to pin the rows of knots as you work.

Make a square knot in two adjacent strands of fringe 1 inch away from the edge of the fabric and pin the knot through its center to your pillow. Do the same with the next pair of strands, and continue across to the edge. Make another row of knots 1 inch down from the first, this time using one strand from each of the preceding knots to create a knotwork lattice. Continue making rows of knots until you get the fringe

KNOTTED FRINGE

BRAIDED FRINGE

length you like. You can add beads at any of the knots, as well as at the ends of the fringe when you've finished knotting. For lightweight yarns, you may want to knot together more than one strand.

BRAID IT. Braid-making goes back centuries; in fact, probably to 800 BCE or even earlier in both Incan and Japanese cultures. The impetus for making braids was to make threads (whether plant or animal based) both stronger and more decorative. Jacqui Carey offers history, instructions, and dozens of different braids in her two books: *200 Braids to Twist, Knot, Loop, or Weave* and *Japanese Braiding: The Art of Kumihimo.*

KNIT IT. Here's a very simple way to create a knitted fringe that you can then attach to the end or side of a scarf, shawl, or afghan. Cast on the number of stitches you need for a width about

twice as long as the fringe you want. (For example, in the swatch shown below, the stitch gauge is 5 stitches to an inch; to obtain a 5-inch fringe, I cast on 12 stitches.) Knit in garter stitch to the length needed to span the area you're fringing. Bind off four or five stitches, then unravel the rest. You can leave the loops uncut, or trim them and treat them like any of the fringes just described. Attach the piece to your knitted item. You could also begin with the fringe, picking up along the selvedge, and working an afghan, scarf or other item from there.

Referring to knitting: "Scarcely any kind of work is susceptible of so much variety, or can be applied to so many ornamental fabrics or uses in domestic economy."

MARGARET VINCENT, *The Ladies' Work-Table Book* (1844)

KNITTED FRINGE

bind off

EXPLORE **KNITTING OUT LOUD**

KATHY GOLDNER SAYS of her website *Knitting Out Loud,* "I record books I love — books of knitting stories, essays, histories and interviews, which I find inspiring. Knitters, some famous, some not, write about the importance of knitting in their lives. Some stories are funny, some about difficulties overcome, but all of them changed the way I thought about knitting, and some of them changed the way I thought about life." The following are Kathy's descriptions. Choose any to curl up with, knitting in hand — or not. (For Kathy's website, see the appendix.)

◊ AMERICA KNITS, *by Melanie Falick.* An inspiring group of interviews with people who followed their dreams and became pioneers in the fiber world.

◊ ARCTIC LACE: KNITTING PROJECTS AND STORIES INSPIRED BY ALASKA'S NATIVE KNITTERS, *by Donna Druchunas.* Description of knitting and designing lace, especially with qiviut, along with insights into the culture of the native people.

◊ THE ART OF FAIR ISLE KNITTING, *by Ann Feitelson.* A history of knitting on Fair Isle, which explores the myths and folklore of the origins of this style.

◊ A HISTORY OF HAND KNITTING, *by Richard Rutt.* Explores the origins and history of hand knitting, with emphasis on knitting in literature: how Shakespeare uses the word "knit," what it means when a Jane Austen character knits.

◊ KNITKNIT: PROFILES + PROJECTS FROM KNITTING'S NEW WAVE, *by Sabrina Gschwandtner.* This series of interviews with artists who knit changed the way I think about knitting.

◊ KNITTING LESSONS: TALES FROM THE KNITTING PATH, *by Lela Nargi.* On September 11, 2001, women came into Lela Nargi's local yarn shop to knit, inspiring her to travel across the country to talk with knitters.

◊ KNITTING MEMORIES: REFLECTIONS ON THE KNITTER'S LIFE, *edited by Lela Nargi.* Wonderful essays, including one on knitting a map of Paris.

◊ KNITTING YARNS AND SPINNING TALES: A KNITTER'S STASH OF WIT AND WISDOM, *edited by Kari Cornell.* Inspiring stories, including one by Meg Swansen, to feed the knitter's soul.

◊ MASON-DIXON KNITTING OUTSIDE THE LINES, *by Kay Gardiner and Ann Shayne.* Stories from the book and their famous blog by these funny and witty knitting raconteurs.

◊ NO IDLE HANDS: THE SOCIAL HISTORY OF AMERICAN KNITTING, *by Anne L. Macdonald.* The often hair-raising stories, found in diaries and letters, of women's courage and determination as they knit through major events of our history.

◊ THE SECRET LANGUAGE OF KNITTERS, *by Mary Beth Temple.* A useful and very funny dictionary of knitting terms, including SEX, frog, and WIP.

◊ STITCH 'N BITCH: THE KNITTER'S HANDBOOK, *by Debbie Stoller.* A very funny "how to" book.

◊ WILD FIBERS: FIVE YEARS OF FAVORITES, *by Linda Cortright.* The editor and publisher of *Wild Fibers* travels from the Himalayas to Puget Sound talking with the devoted people who tend unusual fiber animals.

Chapter 11

THE
Fiber-
Lover's
LIFE LIST

Once you're bitten by the color-and-fiber bug, there comes a time when knitting's just not enough, so, this chapter raises some chicken-or-egg-first questions: Did you first crochet and then get drawn into knitting? Are you yearning to learn to weave, just to have another outlet for your love of fiber? Do you want to customize your yarns by spinning and/or dyeing your own originals? Would you like to add some needle felting to a favorite hat? Although some people do "stick to their knitting," many more at least dabble in related fiber crafts. (For a list of suggested books on these topics, especially if you're entry level, see the appendix.)

Hand carders (front) and wool combs (back)

263

LIFE

THE
KNITTER'S
LIST

Learn it · Explore it · Do it · Check it off!

FIBER LOVER'S

MEET
- Jeannine Bakriges
- Gail Callahan
- Edie Eckman
- Bev Galeskas
- Kristin Nicholas
- Kathleen Taylor
- Christine White

DISCOVER
- When you're ready to buy your own spinning wheel, try out a number of different kinds first.
- Choose a portable wheel if you're likely to want to spin on the go.
- Plan what you're going to do with your handspun yarn before you begin to spin.
- Discover the differences among batts, roving, and top.
- Examine the amazing intricacy of a spider web.
- Look up Chekhov's, Nietzsche's, and A. A. Milne's re-telling of Ariadne's story.
- Read Tennyson's "Lady of Shalott."
- Choose some animal fiber, in fleece or yarn form, and dye it in a kettle.
- Use food-safe dyes to color protein fiber.
- Heat-fix your color using a microwave or Crock-Pot.
- Use fiber-reactive dyes to color plant fibers.
- Dye some silk yarn in several brilliant colors.
- Collect plants to process into dye solutions.
- Dye small batches of fleece different colors, then blend them together with hand cards or combs, on a carding drum, or with a hackle.
- Dye roving before spinning it.
- Hand-paint a skein of yarn.

DO/TRY
- Learn to spin.
- Buy, borrow, or make a hand spindle and teach yourself to spin.
- Take a spinning class or find a spinning group to join.
- Learn how to process raw fleece.
- Learn about the characteristics of different sheep (and other fiber plants and animals) and the fiber they produce.
- Learn to weave.
- Crochet a button band on a hand-knit cardigan.
- Use crochet for the front and back of a sweater, then pickup stitches around the armholes and knit the sleeves.
- Embellish your knitting with crocheted flowers.
- Make crocheted buttons to complement a hand-knit jacket or sweater.
- Crochet a lacy collar for a hand-knit sweater.
- Decorate the edge of an afghan or throw with a bold crochet border.
- Use crochet to adjust poorly fitting necklines or shoulders.
- Use crochet to join two or more hand-knit pieces.
- Attach crocheted pockets to a knit garment.
- Use a crochet cast on.
- Choose felted knitting for a sturdy bag, placemat, hat.
- Make felted shoes, slippers, or clogs for everyone on your holiday list.
- Make a hat or bowl using the wet felt technique.
- Create a "painting" in your wet felt, using different colored fleece.
- Design and make a nuno felt scarf or wrap.
- Use fleece and a felting needle to create a freeform "sculpture" of your choice.
- Attach yarn or fleece to a handknit using the needle-felting technique.
- Use a strategically placed bit of embroidery to hide a stitch error.
- Use bold embroidery stitches in a variety of yarn colors to accent your handknits.
- Learn chain stitch.
- Learn running stitch.
- Learn buttonhole stitch.
- Learn feather stitch.
- Learn the lazy daisy stitch.

GO

◇ Find paintings and drawings that depict some of the ancient, fiber-related myths and stories.

EXPERIENCE

◇ Blend several different fibers together to create a very custom-made yarn.

◇ Spin, and then spin some more, just for the sheer pleasure of it.

◇ Buy or borrow a rigid-heddle or small table loom to try out weaving.

◇ Look for small hand-held looms, such as a Weavette or a loom designed for continuous strand weaving to build your weaving skills.

◇ Listen to Ariadne-inspired music by Haydn, Strauss, Sondheim, and/or Led Zeppelin.

◇ Listen to music while you work: choose the style by your mood and what you're working on.

◇ Watch the film version of *Cabaret.*

◇ Listen to folk songs by such performers as Norman Kennedy, Bob Dylan, Jean Redpath, and the Clancy Brothers and Tommy Makem.

◇ Don't worry if your yarn isn't perfect!

◇ Don't be afraid of color!

◇ Notice your own distinctive color palette developing.

◇ Base your color choices on your favorite colors in nature.

◇ Find color inspiration in ethnic textiles, your favorite artists, pottery, and animals.

◇ Catch up on books you've never had a chance to read by listening to audiobooks while you knit.

MORE FOR MY FIBER-LOVER'S LIFE LIST

◇ _____

◇ _____

◇ _____

◇ _____

◇ _____

◇ _____

◇ _____

◇ _____

◇ _____

◇ _____

◇ _____

◇ _____

◇ _____

◇ _____

◇ _____

◇ _____

◇ _____

DID YOU KNOW SPINNING AND WEAVING LINGO

Because many of the terms that describe techniques and equipment used by spinners, weavers, and dyers originated way back when those crafts were more widely practiced, you may find some of the language a bit esoteric (not to say archaic) when you first encounter them. One of the charms of spinning and weaving is this seemingly arcane vocabulary. Here's a little crib sheet to help get you over the newbie hump.

Boat (back) and stick (front) shuttles, with spinning bobbins

BATT (OR BATTING). Fleece that has been prepared on hand cards or a drum carder to form a thick, soft blanket to spin from. *See also* Carding.

BEAM. On a loom the back and front beams are the horizontal rails on which the warp threads are supported.

BOBBIN. The part of the spinning wheel onto which the yarn is wound as it's being spun; also the (smaller) device on which yarn is wound and placed in a shuttle for weaving. (See photo, bottom left.)

CARDING. The process of opening up the fibers to prepare the fleece for spinning. It can be done with a pair of hand cards, which consist of handles and a square or rectangular wooden base that is covered with a piece of leather into which dozens of short wire pins are embedded. The person who is carding places small amounts of fleece on one of the cards, then uses the second card to brush the fleece. Drum carders have the same leather-and-pin arrangement, but in this case the leather pieces are wrapped around a large and a small drum. The carder hand-cranks the drums, drawing the fleece in and allowing it to collect on the larger drum. In the resulting batt, the fibers are not parallel to one another. *See also* Batt. (For hand cards, see photo, page 262.)

CASTLE. A style of spinning wheel in which the flyer and spindle are stacked over the wheel, in an upright, compact design. Also the upright part of a loom that holds the shafts.

CRIMP. The waviness or kinks in strands of fiber, which can be expressed as number of crimps per inch.

DRAFT. The process of drawing out and controlling a specific amount of fiber as you begin the spinning process.

FLYER. The part of the spinning wheel that winds the spun yarn onto the bobbin during the spinning process.

FOOTMAN. The part of the spinning wheel that attaches the treadle to the wheel and, with the assistance of a crank at its upper end, causes the drive wheel (the big, identifiable wheel) to turn.

HANDSPINDLE. A tool (usually wood) with a shaft and a whorl used for handspinning; the whorl can be at the top or bottom. (See photo, page 269.)

HEDDLE. Arranged on a frame, heddles are the part of a loom through which the warp is threaded. *See also* Shaft.

LAZY KATE. A frame in which to set bobbins filled with spun yarn as you wind off the yarn to form skeins or balls or to ply two or more strands together.

LOCK. Fibers in the raw fleece that form a close-set group.

MAIDEN. The upright posts on a spinning wheel that hold the flyer in place.

NIDDY-NODDY. A handheld device used for winding off spun yarn into a skein. (See photo, at right.)

RAW FLEECE. Unwashed fleece directly shorn from the sheep.

REED. The part of the loom through which the warp threads run; the reed is used both to space the warp threads and to beat each new length of weft yarn against the developing woven fabric.

ROVING. Washed and carded fiber ready to spin. *See also* Top.

SCOUR. The process of washing fleece.

SHAFT. The part of the spinning wheel that holds the bobbin; also, on a loom, the frame that holds the heddles.

SHED. On a loom, the opening that appears as shafts are raised to provide the path for the yarn.

SHUTTLE. A weaving tool that holds the weft yarn and is used to carry it across the warp. Some

Niddy-noddy (left) and umbrella swift (right)

shuttles, called "boat shuttles," hold a bobbin around which the weft yarn has been wound; on stick shuttles, the yarn is wrapped directly on the shuttle itself. (See photo, page 266.)

STAPLE. The length of the individual wool fibers.

SWIFT. A tool used to hold a skein of yarn as you wind it off into a ball; an umbrella swift may be adjusted to a wide range of skein diameters. (See photo, page 267.)

THROW. In weaving the action of running a shuttle through the shed.

TOP. A fiber preparation that uses wool combs to arrange the fibers in a smooth, parallel direction. *See also* Roving.

WARP. In weaving, the yarn that is threaded on the loom from back to front (or front to back) and through which the weft travels.

WEFT. In weaving, the yarn that is interlaced across the warp.

WHORL. The (usually) round weight on a hand spindle; also the pulley on a spinning wheel.

WOOL COMBS. Tools used to align fibers in a parallel direction in preparation for spinning. (See photo, page 262.)

WOOLEN SPUN. Fiber spun from a carded preparation; fibers are every which way, rather than aligned parallel, thus providing an elastic, airy yarn.

WORSTED SPUN. Fiber spun from a combed preparation; the parallel fibers result in a smooth, less elastic yarn than woolen spun yarn. (Note that this is a separate meaning from that of worsted-weight yarn, which refers to a specific yarn weight.)

Spinning a Yarn

If you're someone who loves the journey as much as, if not more than the ending, you're very likely to find yourself tempted into creating your own yarns. This is Jenny Bakriges' experience. Jeannine Bakriges, known as Spinning Spider Jenny, has long been an avid spinner, dyer, and knitter. Creating your own yarns, she says, isn't just about the pleasure: it's also the control. If you want to knit with wool, you can start your journey by choosing a fleece that has the exact "hand" (feel) and color you have in mind. Maybe you want a color that doesn't grow naturally on a sheep's back: dye it, and do so at whatever stage you want (from raw fleece to spun yarn), using whatever dyeing techniques give you the results you're looking for.

"You get to scour the fleece as gently as you'd like and prepare it in such a way that will let you have a glorious spinning experience," she explains. You can blend it with other fibers if you wish, decide what size yarn to make, ply it or not, make it smooth or textured. "All this, and you haven't even knit a stitch yet! That's a lot of bang for the buck from a journey standpoint. And you could have even started by raising the sheep!"

Jenny articulates what many spinners have discovered: creating your own yarns from scratch not only makes your knitted items unlike anyone else's, but the process can be immensely absorbing and relaxing. Once you open the door, you're likely to discover that spinning is one of those crafts that offers endless possibilities.

Shades of sherbet. A handspindle and several lengths of hand-dyed roving ready for spinning.

THE TOOLS. Although some spinning wheels can be pricey, you can learn to spin with a relatively inexpensive spindle or even with one you can make with a discarded CD or DVD and a dowel. When you decide to move up to a wheel, it's ideal if you can try out a number of different kinds before making the investment. You may be lucky enough to have a dealer or yarn store nearby that carries a selection of wheels, but if not, fiber festivals are a great place to start looking: as you wander among vendors and demonstrators, you're sure to find friendly spinners more than willing to let you sit down and spin — as well as give you some advice on how to spin if you're a complete beginner. Yarn stores that carry spinning equipment may demonstrate and help you get started, and they may also have spinning classes or spinning groups where you can try out other spinners' wheels and chat about features important to them. Each spinner has his or her own, likely strong, likes and dislikes.

Brilliant braids. This partially blended hand-dyed roving was braided, showing it off to great advantage and making it easy to store and ready to spin.

On the go. Andean hand-spinners are so adept at their craft that they are able to spin as they go about other activities.

It's possible to teach yourself, but it's awfully nice to get some coaching, either at a spinning or knitting retreat or festival or at a yarn store or other local craft center. Find out if there's a spinning guild in your area; members are likely to be excellent sources of advice and inspiration. Like knitting, spinning can be a terrific social activity, where you can not only get some great tips but also enjoy a relaxing time chatting with other spinners. In fact, if you think you're likely to want to spin on the go, one consideration when you choose a wheel may be its portability.

THE FIBERS. Fleece in a variety of forms is much easier to locate now than it was 10 or 15 years ago: many yarn stores carry it, you can order online, or you can go to a fiber festival. Do some research on the characteristics of various fleeces, as well as the kind of processing it has had and the form it comes in (for example, "raw" or "in the grease," batts, roving, top), so you choose the best fleece for creating the kind of yarn you like to knit with.

Because each fiber has its own very special characteristics, once you get acquainted with them, you can make the best choices for whatever project you have in mind. If you're a spinner, you can also blend two or more fibers to take advantage of the specialness of each. Margaret Radcliffe, who says she saves her perfectionism for her knitting but loves to spin as a hobby, describes a handspun yarn that is her favorite: she first spun three different fibers separately: bombyx silk, angora, and a very fine Merino. She then plied the three together to create a yarn that gets sheen from the silk, elasticity from the Merino, and a halo from the angora — it was beautiful, she remembers.

One exceptional store specializes in supplying spinners: Beth Smith may well put up a sign in front of her shop near Ann Arbor, Michigan: "Beware: This store is full of temptation." Although the Spinning Loft has very little ready-to-knit yarn, there is a great deal to explore. Beth specializes in wool breeds and teaching others how to use each of the wide variety of wools she carries. Depending on the season, her "Wall O'Fleece" displays between 50 and 75 different fleeces from local shepherds, as well as from those farther afield in North America and even internationally. This impressive array plants the spinning seed in everyone who ventures in, including knitters who never had any intention of spinning.

Beth demonstrates how to customize yarns to specific projects in a way that mill-spun yarn can never be tailored, since mass-produced yarn must be spun to appeal to a wide number of knitters and to work for a variety of projects. Choosing the right wool for a specific project and deciding on the correct spinning technique for it presents endless, irresistible possibilities. Combine that with the calm and meditative qualities of spinning, and the surrender begins. If you're not lucky enough to live nearby, you can visit Beth's shop online (see the appendix).

LEARN | JILLIAN MORENO: PERFECTION ISN'T ALWAYS PERFECT

When Jillian Moreno first tried spinning nearly two decades ago, it didn't last long. As she admits, "I couldn't get into a groove. I was very hung up on making 'perfect yarn' that looked like it came from a yarn store, which made it decidedly unfun, so the wheel went into the basement." Even so, she kept taking spinning classes here and there, reading about spinning, going to fiber festivals and, of course, buying fiber. Then one day four or five years ago, she woke up, she recalls, "with a burning desire to spin my own yarn. I didn't care if it was perfect; I wanted it to be fun. And lo and behold, it was and is, and I spin every day now. And no, I still haven't made perfect yarn."

EXPLORE RHYTHM AND RHYME

WHEN IT COMES TO THE BEST MUSIC to knit by, your taste, your project, and your mood each influence whether you choose loud and fast or quiet and soothing or something in between. Knitters' tastes range from German industrial rock to those other Germans, Bach and Beethoven, and almost anything in between. It's always fun to find references to knitters, spinners, or weavers in music. Here are some tunes you might like to search out.

FROM THE MUPPETS. In a Muppets' *Fraggle Rock* episode, Jim Hensen's Doozers try (unsuccessfully) to keep busy by knitting, because "it's neat and it's sweet . . ./Knittin' socks for little feet."

FROM A MUSICAL. The title song from the 1960s musical *Cabaret* urges us to "Put down the knitting/The book, and the broom" and take a holiday at the cabaret. (Hmmm . . . most knitters might like to *take* their knitting to the cabaret.)

FROM POETRY. From 1915 a poetic image by Jessie Pope of knitting for the troops: "Soldier lad, . . ./Can't you hear a little clicketty sound/Stealing across on the breeze?/It's the knitting-needles singing their song/As they twine the khaki or blue . . ."

FROM THE CLASSICAL WORLD. A century ago, the Russian composer Anatoly Konstantinovich Lyadov set several Russian folktales to music for orchestra, including *Kikimora*, Op. 63 (1909). Kikimora is a Slavic house spirit, said to harass housekeepers who don't keep their homes clean and to fly about at night continually spinning flax — all the time with evil in her heart.

SONGS ABOUT SPINNING AND WEAVING. In addition to the suggestions below, you'll find websites for downloads or purchases of recordings of songs about weaving and spinning in the appendix).

Waulking Songs, Bannal

"The Band of Shearers," sung by Carla Sciaky on *Her Infinite Variety: Celtic Women in Music & Song;* also her *Spin the Weaver's Song.*

"Four Loom Weaver," *Silly Sisters,* June Tabor and Maddy Prior

"Golden Loom," *The Bootleg Series,* Vols. 1–3, Bob Dylan

"The Hand-Loom Weaver's Lament," sung by Harry Boardman on *Deep Lancashire: Songs, Ballads, and Verse from the Industrial North West of England*

"Maid at the Spinning Wheel," *Mist and Stone,* Maggie Sansone

"Nancy Whiskey," *Nancy Whiskey,* Switchback

"Sheep Shearing Days," *Wild Mountain Thyme,* The Revels

Old Songs Festival albums featuring Norman Kennedy, an accomplished (and award-winning) handweaver and a storyteller and singer of traditional songs

"The Gallant Weaver," *Songs of Robert Burns,* Vol. 7, Jean Redpath

"The Weaver and the Factory Maid," *Parcel of Rogues,* Steeleye Span

"The Work of the Weavers," *The Best of the Clancy Brothers and Tommy Makem*

Ins and Outs of Weaving

The simplest form of weaving involves setting up a group of parallel warp threads, and inserting a weft thread under one, then over one warp thread across the width of the warp. From this simple system weavers have devised countless other combinations of warp-weft interlacements, aided by looms with structural devices that allow the warp threads to be raised and lowered in different combinations, by hand, by foot treadles, or even by computerized programs.

If you're first and foremost a knitter, think of it this way: knitting taken to the basics is just two stitches, knit and purl. But the way you manipulate these stitches, as well as the way you choose the colors, types of fibers, size of the needles and number of stitches per inch, and multiple other factors, allows for endless outcomes using your "sticks and string." Weaving takes a similar simple set of basics (under warp threads or over them) to an infinitely complex and fascinating range of possibilities.

There's one thing that often surprises beginning weavers: once you have your loom set up, much weaving goes extraordinarily fast compared to knitting. Even across a very wide warp, one quick, confident throw of your shuttle through the path of the raised and lowered warp threads can cover the same ground that a whole row of painstakingly knit stitches does. If the pattern is straightforward and the yarn is fairly heavy, you can weave an inch in a matter of minutes. I remember being disappointed when my first hand-woven project was completed just when I was getting into the swing of it. Another feature of weaving is that yarn disappears really fast. You may sometimes feel as if your yarn is

EXPLORE LIFE AS A YARNIE

Liz Gipson comes at all the fiber disciplines being yarn centric. She explains, "I like making yarn do tricks. I gravitate towards weaving because it is fast: you work row by row, not stitch by stitch. The process of weaving involves gross motor movements — big sweeping throws of the shuttle and beater are pretty darn satisfying, even on a small, portable rigid heddle like the Schacht Cricket (shown below). I put my yarn skills to work where they are the most appropriate: When I want to make a garment, I knit, but I turn to weaving to make goods for my home. It is the perfect medium for hand towels, curtains, rugs, table linens, pillows, blankets, and the like. I often use knitting for joins or to add trims to handwovens. I'm also an unashamed scarf maker. You will be amazed at how many scarves you can crank out with a loom. A yarnie's life is a good life."

literally being eaten by your loom. It's said that it takes six spinners to keep up with one weaver's hunger for yarn.

Although a floor loom can be expensive and a real space consumer, you can accomplish amazing things with smaller table looms, such as rigid heddle looms. An excellent way to test the weaving waters, rigid heddle looms are also satisfying for weavers with larger looms who want to experiment with something new or carry their weaving along on the go. Most are also quite portable, so you can take them right along to your Wednesday night knitting or spinning group just as easily as you carry your knitting bag. A number of manufacturers, such as Ashford, Kromski, Louet, and Schacht have designed looms especially popular with knitters who are interested in transitioning to weaving; and recent books, such as Liz Gipson's *Weaving Made Easy* and Jane Patrick's *The Weaver's Idea Book*, feature weave structures and techniques, as well as patterns for simple projects to get you going. Handheld looms, such as the old-fashioned Weave-It looms, Weavettes, and Hillcreek Fiber Studio's continuous strand looms are other possibilities for people who crave the under-over flow of weaving but don't have the space or inclination for a large loom just now (see appendix for addresses).

All about color. Traditional Andean weaving with hand-dyed alpaca fiber, photographed in Awana Kancha, Peru.

MEET BARBARA ELKINS

THE WEBS BILLBOARD ALONG INTERSTATE 91 in Northampton, Massachusetts, invites shoppers to "America's largest yarn store." Large barely begins to describe WEBS. The 25,000-square-foot store is a fiber enthusiast's paradise, stocked to the gills with yarns of every type for knitting, weaving, and crocheting, plus felting and spinning fibers and more — from hand-dyed to undyed, from alpaca to bamboo.

WEBS boasts its own line of yarns, an in-house designer, and a booming online business. It has books, classes, workshops, and a staff of talented knitters who can advise shoppers of every skill level. It's a destination for knitters all around the Northeast.

But large — never mind largest — wasn't even on the radar when Barbara Elkins and another stay-at-home mom opened their store in Amherst, Massachusetts, in 1974. All Barbara and her friend Donna Muller wanted from their little basement weaving shop was a bit of spending money. "We were weavers. We wanted money to support our habit," Barbara explains, chuckling.

So they traveled to Harrisville Designs in Harrisville, New Hampshire. There, they bought 20 kit looms to rent and give lessons on while their professor-husbands were at work and the children were at school. At first, they did workshops; later, they added yarns for both weaving and knitting and moved into progressively larger quarters. Barbara's passion is weaving; knitting, which she taught herself at age five, has never been as interesting to her. But she soon recognized that knitting — a more affordable and portable craft — had a greater audience.

In the late 1980s Muller left the business, and WEBS relocated to its first downtown storefront, a large Victorian house. "The college kids came in. They were knitting Lopi sweaters for their boyfriends," Barbara recalls.

She and her husband, Art, who by then had retired from his post at the University of Massachusetts Isenberg School of Management to help with the business, saw the market growing. "We were intrigued with the idea of seeing how far we could grow. We took a lot of chances, a lot of risks," she says.

After three years at their new Amherst storefront, they needed even more room and moved WEBS to its current location in Northampton, in a former telephone company garage. Then in 2001 the Elkins' son Steve and his wife, Kathy, took over the business.

Barbara is no longer involved in day-to-day operations but is in the store every day, available to help customers and answer questions. Freed from the responsibilities of running a business, she spends time each day on numerous weaving projects, such as the one shown below, experimenting with design ideas on the many looms set up just outside her office. "Nothing," she says, "is more satisfying than winding a warp."

EXPLORE IT'S GREEK TO ME!

Knitting with a friend or friends has always been a perfect time for sharing stories, real and imagined. But knitters, spinners, and weavers have also often been the subjects of legends and myths in many different cultures. In Mayan tradition, for instance, Ixzaluoh was the goddess of water and is said to have invented weaving. Many of these legends have a dark side to them, and Greek mythology has some of the most imaginative — and goriest — stories of all.

ARACHNE, one of the most famous weavers of all time, got into serious trouble with the goddess of the weaving arts (Athena in Greek mythology and Minerva in Roman), by boasting that she, Arachne, was the better weaver. The goddess, disguised as an old woman, challenged Arachne to a weaving contest. Versions of what happened next include Athena's changing Arachne into a spider, Arachne's hanging herself, and, in the Roman poet Ovid's account, Athena's changing the hanging rope into a web when she changed Arachne into a spider. Velazquez's famous painting *The Spinners* illustrates Ovid's version. Arachnida, the scientific class that includes spiders, takes its name from this legend.

ARIADNE. Again from the Greeks: When Ariadne's lover Theseus entered the Minotaur's labyrinth with the assignment to kill the monster that demands human sacrifice, Ariadne lent him a ball of yarn that she spun. (Many retellings of the legend actually specify that the yarn was red!) He was to let it out behind him as he went, so that he could retrace the yarn and find his way out. Over time Ariadne's story inspired a number of painters, authors (including Chekhov, Nietzsche, and A. A. Milne), and composers (including Haydn, Strauss, Sondheim, and Led Zeppelin).

PHILOMELA. According to one Greek myth, Philomela, daughter of the king of Athens, was raped by Tereus, the king of Thrace, who was escorting her on a trip to Thrace. When she threatened to tell on him, he cut out her tongue, but she wove her story into a tapestry that she sent to Tereus's wife, who in turn took revenge on him by . . . but that's an even grimmer story!

PENELOPE. Homer told Penelope's familiar story: During Odysseus's 20-year absence, his wife, Penelope, fended off more than a hundred suitors, thus becoming a memorable symbol of fidelity and ingenuity. One of her techniques for discouraging these would-be new husbands was to claim that she couldn't remarry until she finished weaving a funeral shroud for her father-in-law, Laertes; all the while she was secretly unraveling part of the piece each night.

LADY OF SHALOTT. Alfred, Lord Tennyson's ballad tells the story of the "Lady of Shalott," a beautiful weaver who was cursed to remain in a castle that stood on an island in the river that flowed into Camelot. She was to weave constantly but never look directly outside. She viewed the world through a mirror, until the day Lancelot rode by. She immediately fell for him, left the castle, and pushed off in a boat down the river. Unfortunately, when she escaped, the curse took effect, and she died before she reached the palace at Camelot.

THE THREE FATES. In Homer's *Illiad* Moera spun the thread of each man's life at his birth. In later legends "Moera" morphed into the three fates, known as the Moirae: Clotho spun the thread of life, Lachesis measured it, and Atropos cut it, which determined how and when death would come. Other traditions, including Norse and Baltic, also have their spinning-fate goddesses. Although the legends surrounding them vary, these women have often been depicted as frighteningly austere and harsh.

Penelope at her weaving. Romare Bearden's *The Return of Ulysses,* from the collection of the Smithsonian American Art Museum, Washington, D.C.

Art © Romare Bearden Foundation/Licensed by VAGA, New York, NY

Dyeing for Fun

It's not that there isn't a dazzling array of colors in commercial yarns, but dyeing is so much fun! It's easy and magical, and like spinning, dyeing gives you the chance to make your knitted (or woven or felted or crocheted) projects completely unique, starting with the yarn. You do have a few important choices about the dyes and dye processes to use, and these depend in large part on the kind of fiber you are dyeing. Commercial dyes come with instructions for how to use them, and many excellent books are available on the dye process. The following overview gives you an idea of some of the things you can consider.

Color blends. These handspun yarns all started with white or natural-colored fleece dyed in small batches, then lightly blended on a drum carder before spinning and plying.

Choosing the Right Dye

Dyes can be either natural (usually plant material) or chemical. It is fascinating to make your own dye solutions by collecting and steeping plant material that grows right outside your door or down the street. You can also purchase processed natural dyes, in which case you may have a wider (and more predictable) range of colors. Purchased natural dyes include dye stuff made from insects (cochineal for shades of red, for instance) or various woods (logwood for purple). These colors aren't as easy to find in North American fields and gardens, which offer in greater abundance the more common golds, greens, and browns. Other natural dye materials include lichens and mushrooms, which require some special techniques for success, but which also offer a wide range of colors.

When you use natural dyes, whether you grow your own dye material or purchase it, you may need to treat the fiber with a mordant before, during, or after the dye process. The mordant helps the fiber accept the dye. Alum is a common mordant that is readily available and relatively safe. You use heat to set natural dyes.

If you're just beginning to think of dyeing and are reluctant to invest in supplies you don't already have, or you have concerns about some of the safety considerations with commercial dyes and mordants, you can achieve some lovely colors by simply using ordinary food coloring or even unflavored drink mixes, which, by the way, are also acid dyes (see appendix for resources). The dye you choose is also dependent on the kind of fiber you're dyeing.

PLANT FIBER. One method for dyeing plant fibers (linen, cotton, bamboo, and so on; see pages 33–35) is to use fiber-reactive dyes. These dyes require a controlled air temperature and soda ash to make the process work properly.

ANIMAL FIBER. Fiber from sheep, llamas, alpacas, mohair goats, angora rabbits, and other animals is protein. In most cases when you're working with animal fibers, in order to set the dye (that is, to make the dye bond with the fabric), you need acid. Don't let the word "acid" scare you off: the acid can be as simple as white vinegar. (You can also use granular citric acid, which is less expensive and less smelly than vinegar, considerations if you end up doing a lot of dyeing.)

Plant partners. Natural dye made from chillca plant leaves produces a dark green in the alpaca wool (Chinchero, Peru).

The other thing you need to set the dye is some kind of heat, either from steam or immersion in a dye bath. The heat source can be anything from your stovetop to a microwave oven, electric fry pan, or Crock-Pot. (Note that once you've used a utensil for dyeing, you should reserve it for only that purpose, unless you're using a food-safe dye such as food coloring or a drink mix.)

SILK FIBER. Although silk may be dyed with either acid or fiber-reactive dyes, the silk is less likely to be damaged by acid than it is by the chemicals needed for fiber-reactive dyeing (see Silk: In a Class by Itself, page 31, for further information).

Applying the Dye

The dyer has several choices for how and when to apply the color, and each of those choices results in a different effect on the final yarn.

If you're a hand spinner, you may choose to dye the fleece before making yarn. In most cases the fleece is first washed to remove plant material and dirt, and possibly scoured, which removes lanolin, suint, and other grease and oils. If the entire fleece is dyed at this point, you'll get a fairly even hue, but depending on how much of the natural oil was removed during scouring, you may find that the color modulates, with some parts of the fleece absorbing more dye than others. Many spinners and knitters enjoy this subtle shading. (This effect is even more likely if you dye the fleece before washing it.)

Another approach to dyeing fleece is to dye batches in two or more different colors, then blend the dyed fleeces with hand cards or combs, on a carding drum, or with a hackle. If the fleeces are only lightly blended, you can achieve a tweedy or marled yarn when you spin

LEARN GAIL CALLAHAN: KANGAROO DYER

Gail Callahan has explored a whole variety of fiber arts during her creative career, first as a quilter, then a weaver, then felter, and now, hand-dyer. She demonstrates a number of techniques in her book, *Hand Dyeing Yarn and Fleece;* dyes several lines of yarn for WEBS in Northampton, Massachusetts; and offers her own lines of yarn through her website and her Etsy store. Gail's choice of a kangaroo as part of her creative name references her love of her children and of carrying them with her — just like a kangaroo mom. Her affinity to color and texture has been a driving force throughout her life. All her work over the years has led to deep knowledge and appreciation of various yarns. Her advice to all knitters is to "be aware of what the yarn can tell you, so that you know how best to use it." Gail's clear colors in the photo at the left came from McCormick's food coloring.

it. If you blend them very thoroughly, you'll get an entirely new color, almost like mixing different paint colors (for example, yellow and red make orange, blue and yellow make green, and red and blue make purple). But take care: if you mix all three of the primary colors (red, yellow, blue) together, whether the dyes themselves or dyed fleece, you'll get a neutral, most likely gray or beige. Although you may be happy with this result, it can also be rather dull.

You can also dye roving or top, either by immersing the entire piece or by hand-painting sections of it. There are ways to ply the spun yarn so that same-colored sections align, or you can simply let the chips fall where they may for a mixed-color yarn that includes sections of marled yarn and sections where the individual plies match fairly closely with one another. And of course you can also dye the finished yarn. The yarn in the photo at the right was spun from hand-painted roving, which you can see in the basket.

LEARN JENNY BAKRIGES ON THE GIFTS OF COLOR

Jenny Bakriges has studied, used, and taught natural dyeing for many years. She shares her passion with these thoughts: "I don't think I'll ever look at a plant and not wonder what colors could be extracted from it. Each plant holds the 'gift' of color! Natural dyeing, quite literally, put this born-and-bred Detroiter more in touch with nature. I soon learned that whatever options or variables I used technique-wise would affect the outcome, and not always predictably." She notes that "'playing'" in natural dyeing became the name of the game. "The more fun I had and the more adventurous I became, often the better the results!"

Not Your Granny's Crochet

Crocheting is a natural sister to knitting, but surprisingly few knitters say that they also crochet. Yet developing some crochet skills gives knitters multiple opportunities to enhance their knitting, whether it's simply to crochet firm button bands down the front of a cardigan sweater or to create a more elaborate meld by, say, crocheting the whole front and back of a sweater and then adding knitted sleeves. The key to a successful blend of the two lies in recognizing the strengths of each: crochet can be airy and firm at the same time, for instance, whereas knitting usually has more stretch. Ignoring one to devote yourself only to the other is maybe on a par with saying, "I never use my oven; I use only my stovetop" — in which case, you're missing out on a whole lot of good food.

"Knitting loves crochet" is Candi Jensen's motto, and each craft has its strengths. For instance, she notes, "A knitted ribbing is so much better than a crocheted one; the elasticity you get from knitting is really great." On the other hand, crochet works better for edging sweaters, for embellishments such as flowers, and any kind of sculptural work that requires picking up stitches. Crochet has gotten a "bad rap" when it comes to garments, believes Candi, but the secret to creating soft, stretchy sweaters and other garments in crochet is to use sport-weight yarn. That way, you get more stitches to the inch, and the fabric is more flexible.

Edie Eckman advises knitters who are ready to experiment and blend their knitting with crochet that sometimes a crocheted edging really is the best choice for a knitted project. You can choose a border that complements the item — whether it's a delicate lace trim on a lightweight cardigan or a flamboyant and sturdy frame on an afghan. Once you're happy with your smooth foundation round, you can continue with more decorative additional rounds, remembering to make increases or decreases as appropriate for the shape of the edging. Edie's *Around the Corner Crochet Borders* offers dozens of choices. For knitters who aren't crocheters, Edie offers advice for how to pick up along an edge, as well as 150 designs to choose from.

Crochet is also a great tool for solving structural and fit problems in a knitted garment. Using cotton yarn, which doesn't stretch, you can tighten up a stretched-out neckline or too-wide shoulders by working a line of crochet slip stitch on the wrong side of the garment. Or for extra stability use crocheted trim in place of knitted ribbing.

Lively finishing touches. A square motif for a pocket, a crochet edging up the center-front opening, and crocheted buttons transform a plain stockinette sweater.

LEARN GETTING STARTED WITH A CROCHETED EDGE

Edie Eckman describes how easy it is to work a crocheted edge:

* To begin, make a slipknot on your hook.
* Insert the hook into the knitted fabric in the same place you would to pick up and knit a stitch, yarn over and draw up a loop, then yarn over and pull through both loops on the hook. You've made one single crochet!
* Continue inserting your hook and drawing a loop through as above along the edge until you've reached the end.

   Note: If you are working around a piece (such as an afghan or front and bottom edges of a sweater), make sure that the edging lies flat when you turn the corners, as well as all along the straight edge. In some cases, in order to keep the edging flat, you may need to space your crochet stitches a bit further apart (or closer together) than one crochet stitch for every knit stitch or row. Place increases at outside corners and decreases at inside corners in order to get the stitching to lie flat.

First row, single crochet. Be sure to pick up both legs of the knitted stitch as you form the single crochets.

Second row, double crochet. Here a row of double crochet is being worked over the single crochet. Notice the extra single crochet stitches taken at the corner to keep the piece from buckling.

MEET CANDI JENSEN

TENS OF THOUSANDS OF YOUNG PEOPLE descended upon San Francisco's Haight-Ashbury district in 1967, tie-dyes and patchwork peasant skirts adorned with peace signs, to join in the infamous "Summer of Love." For one reveler, Candi Jensen, it was also the Summer of Crochet. Around her, young people were experimenting wildly with everything from communal living to embroidery. Candi, then 18 and a new mother, reached for a crochet hook.

"I really wanted to make a blanket for my baby," she says. Already a proficient knitter, Candi taught herself to crochet and was rewarded with the joy of bundling her baby in the colorful blanket she had envisioned.

"You didn't have money, so you did it yourself," Candi reminisces. In a world gripped by political unrest and the unraveling of social conventions, inventive designs were emerging everywhere, and it was energizing. "Everyone went to a thrift store and bought stuff, and then you'd cut off the sleeves and make something," she says. "It was a sign of creativity."

Candi, who had learned to knit as a child and loved the rhythm and motion of the needles, immediately took to crochet and developed her own technique, which became her future, stitch by stitch.

"I think every knitter should learn crochet," says the Bay Area author, designer, and needlework show producer. "My feeling is, even if you are an avid knitter and you learn some basics of crochet, it will enhance what you're doing."

Since her early days in San Francisco, Candi has worked in public relations for the yarn industry and written more than a dozen books and many magazine articles, along with her television work. But all these years later, she still looks back fondly on the summer of 1967, for its sense of abundant possibility and creativity. The popularity of stitching ebbed in the 1980s but revived in the late 1990s, bringing forth — to Candi's delight — everything from felted garments to knitted footstool covers. As the crafting renaissance continues, she's continually inspired by the work she sees. Recently, she happened upon some crocheted squid, created by a young San Francisco designer majoring in science. Candi couldn't resist buying one, and it resides on her fireplace mantel, basking in attention from her houseguests.

"It just blew me away," she says. "To look at a squid and say, 'I can crochet that.'"

Posies for tanks. Candi's easy-to-crochet flowers are the perfect embellishment for tees, as well as handknits.

I Just Felt Like It

Like knowing how to crochet, having some felting tricks up your sleeve can add a great deal of interest to your knitting. And even if you don't combine felting and knitting in a single item, felting is yet another excuse to get your fingers into wool or other animal fibers. Felting can take you in several directions, each of which gives a different effect. Note that the words "fulling" and "felting" have different meanings to different people and in different contexts, some of which are explained below. For instance, in some resources, including some Scandinavian references, fulling is the first stage in the felting process, and felting refers to the entire process as well as to the second stage, which results in the "hard" felt.

Knitted "Felt"

You may have heard of knitted felt, but this technique is more accurately called *fulling*. To full a knitted fabric, you subject it to the very things we're taught to avoid when washing our favorite wool sweater: hot water and agitation. You'll need a yarn consisting of animal fiber that hasn't been treated to be "washable." (Most fibers from sheep, llama, alpaca, or mohair goat, for instance, will felt, but you may need to experiment — a.k.a. swatch!) Your gauge should be loose enough to give the strands room to blossom and bond together when fulled.

When the item is complete, you immerse it in hot water and vigorously swish it around (by hand or in a washing machine) until the fabric thickens and becomes as dense as desired. If agitation alone doesn't do the trick, you may need to add some other material, such as old blue jeans, to the water to provide some extra friction that speeds the process along. After fulling, if

Cool it! Felting a knitted bottle bag gives it more insulation power, making it perfect to keep a nice bottle of wine at just the right temperature.

you brush up a "nap" on the surface, you'll discover that the individual stitches are even more completely disguised and the fabric takes on a smooth, coherent look.

It pays to check the item frequently during this process. Be aware that you can always full it more after it dries, if necessary, but you can never go in reverse and loosen it up! Remember, too, that as the piece fulls, it also draws in, so it will have considerably smaller dimensions than the piece you started with.

Wet Felt

Christine White, a felt artist, teacher, and author in western Massachusetts, offers the following description and advice about traditional, non-woven felt: Working with loose fibers, rather than knitted (or crocheted) fabric, which has internal structure (that is, stitches), the felt-maker wets and soaps the arranged fleece and gently rubs or rolls it. During this stage (which is sometimes inaccurately called "felting"), the pressure of rubbing encourages the scaly fibers to entangle. This produces a weak but coherent soft cloth called *prefelt*. *Fulling* is the next stage, during which the prefelt is rolled and worked with increasing energy and vigor, then sometimes finished on a washboard or shaped by hand with simple tools.

The developing felt can be molded into a wide array of three-dimensional shapes, including bowls, hats, and shoes. Some felt workers create "paintings" with their felt, using different-colored fleece to build their designs.

Citrus Picnic Blanket. Chris White's throw begins with commercially prefelted fabric, which she joins and then felts to create a sturdy throw.

KATHLEEN TAYLOR. Author and designer Kathleen Taylor emphasizes that felting knitted fabric is an art, not a science. Felting a swatch can give you a feel for how much a specific yarn shrinks. The size and weight of a larger item, like a bag, affects the final outcome, however, and sometimes the finished size is radically different from what you were expecting. It's good to remember that felt is a fabric, which means that it can be cut and sewn and reshaped if the felting process doesn't have the results you were looking for.

BEV GALESKAS wrote that one of knitting's special challenges is achieving the right size and shape so it comes out perfect when felted. "If knitters remember just one of my patterns, I hope it is my Felt Clogs. These are one of my favorite holiday gifts, and many people request a new pair every few years, so I know I am making something they really want."

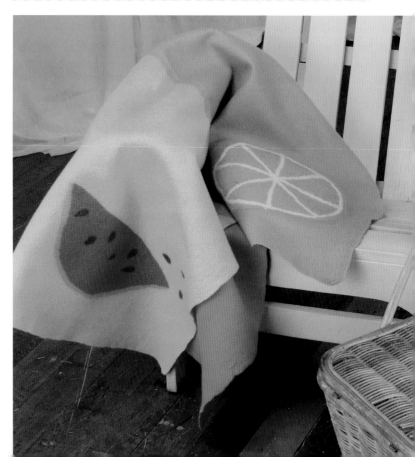

Another technique, known as *nuno felting*, involves placing thin layers of a lightweight fleece on a piece of woven fabric, such as silk. When the combination of fabric and fleece is subjected to agitation in the presence of water and soap, the fleece fibers migrate through the fabric and interlock around its threads. The fabric provides a support for the fibers as they felt, but although the fabric pulls up some (producing an effect known as *ruching*), the interaction between fabric and fiber keeps the felt from drawing in as much as usual in a felting process, thereby becoming compact. Instead, the fabric locks and halts the fulling process, and the result is an unusually lightweight, textural cloth that drapes surprisingly well. (For further information about Christine's work, see the appendix.)

Needle Felting

This may be the technique you'll find most useful to combine with your knitting. Because of the structure of the individual wool fibers, which are comprised of scales that lock onto each other as they are agitated (sometimes described as acting like Velcro), yarn and even unspun fleece can be affixed to fabric by needle felting. The equipment you need is simple: a thick (at least 2 inches) piece of foam and a special felting needle, which has a series of fine barbs along its shaft. These needles come in several sizes and styles. If you ever get into needle felting in a big way, you'll probably want a needle with a handle, but for small or occasional use, an inexpensive single shaft is just fine.

To apply your yarn or fleece to knitted (or woven) fabric, position it where you want the decoration, then repeatedly stab through the fiber until it becomes firmly embedded in the fabric. You'll find that this happens fairly quickly

but also that you can remove the decoration by simply pulling it off. When the finished piece is in use, the decoration almost always becomes more firmly joined to the background. The leaves and leaf veins on the wine bottle bag shown on page 285 were needle felted to the knitted felt fabric. (The grapes were made using the wet felt process.)

It's completely engrossing to experiment with this technique, and it couldn't be easier to learn. In addition to ornamenting other fabrics, you can also sculpt whole three-dimensional figures from fleece that you shape with the use of the needle. And for the practical minded, needle felting is a great way to recycle those little odds and ends of yarn leftover from another project.

Winter wonderland. Fat balls of fleece are needle-felted together, then accented with dyed fleece, also needle felted in place.

The Fine Art of Embroidery

Whether it's fine embroidery using silk threads or tapestry work such as bargello and needlepoint or counted thread work, we're still talking needles and string/thread/yarn here! And the fascination of wielding a needle and making stitches is no less compelling in any of these ancient crafts, with all their many permutations.

Even if you're not interested in tackling a whole set of needlepoint seat covers for your dining room chairs, you may discover that a strategically placed embroidered flower is just the touch for customizing an otherwise plain stockinette-knit hat or sweater. Adding a few simple embroidery stitches to your fiber-working toolbox can transform your knitting and give you lots of opportunities to play with color and texture. And like needle felting, embroidery is an excellent way to use up odds and ends of yarn leftovers.

Embroidery has another strategic purpose. Have you ever completed a garment and only then discovered a nasty ill-knit stitch in an all-too-obvious spot? If you're lucky, this might be just the right place for a flower, bauble, or "spider web," and the error suddenly becomes a design feature!

"In the rhythm of the needles, there is music for the soul."

FROM AN OLD SAMPLER

SWATCHING | *Embroidery*

Embroidery swatch. From left to right, columns of feather stitch, lazy daisy with French knot center, chain stitch, blanket stitch.

MEET KRISTIN NICHOLAS

MAYBE IT'S HER MOTIFS, reminiscent of Persian tiles and Indian fabrics, blooming extravagantly across a sweater and surrounded by sizzling stripes. Perhaps it's the embroidery she uses — simple, bold flowers scattered on a striped ground; sturdy French knots embellishing a border. Or maybe it's the color. Lots of designers use color. When you become familiar with the work of designer Kristin Nicholas, however, you discover that her palette is nearly unmistakable, featuring late-summer hues of fuchsia, sunflower, coleus, and eggplant, as well as deep blues, soft olive greens, and chartreuse, to name a few.

"I think it may be the way I put combinations together," says Kristin, who's been known, for example, to tweak the traditional guidelines for color-scheme pairings by using a poppy red with a yellow-green, then adding in a bit of purple as an accent. "Also, there are colors I use a lot, like chartreuse."

Chartreuse, which she made more prominent in the knitting scene as creative director for Classic Elite Yarns in the 1980s and 1990s, is one of the colors that make up her signature line of yarn, Julia, a wool, alpaca, and mohair blend named for her daughter and distributed by Nashua Handknits. The Julia colors are inspired partly by the landscape of western Massachusetts, where Kristin lives with her husband and daughter. From one window of their antique Cape-style home, she can gaze upon a hillside of dark pine green, dark brown bark, and light green buds. She also draws inspiration from ethnic textiles, the Bloomsbury artists of the early twentieth century, antique pottery, her garden, and even the feathers of her heirloom-breed chickens.

In addition to creating knitwear patterns for her books, and her website, http://kristinnicholas.com, Kristin also brings her distinct color sense to her handmade pottery, paintings, painted lampshades, and other work.

"Very rarely do I water anything down with white," notes Kristin. She avoids both black and white in her work, preferring neutrals such as deep brown and soft wheat.

If her color combinations are easy to spot, it's not because there's a formula behind them. She doesn't have any particular methods for choosing project colors beyond what pleases her eye. And she pays no attention to color rules, like keeping "warm" or "cool" colors together, for example. As for color theory books, "it's been so long since I even looked at them," she says. Teaching classes, however, she finds that many knitters are at the opposite end of the spectrum, fearful of using multiple colors and trying new combinations. Students may come in with shades of blue and green too close to show off pattern work to any advantage. Kristin nudges them toward bolder choices. "I teach a lot of that," she reflects. "You need to free yourself of what you're afraid of, colorwise."

Who's Who

IN THIS COMMUNITY OF KNITTING EXPERTS

I'm awed by and grateful for the warmth, generosity, and knowledge of the knitters and designers who have shared their ideas and contributed advice about knitting and their passion for fiber in general. Meet them here through these brief introductions, then get to know more about them as you read the book. You'll find their own books and other publications in the appendix, organized as relevant to various chapters.

PAM ALLEN. A leading figure in the knitting industry for more than 25 years, Pam was editor of *Interweave Knits* and more recently creative director for Classic Elite Yarns. In 2010, in partnership with Bob Rice and Carrie Hoge, Pam founded Quince & Co., a Maine-based yarn company committed to sustainable production and rich colors and designs. (www.quinceandco.com)

SARAH ANDERSON. A self-taught spinner since 1973, Sarah now loves to teach spinning techniques to others. She has written for *Spin-Off* magazine and contributed designs to *All New Homespun Handknit.*

SUSAN B. ANDERSON. Describing herself as a wife, mother, knitter, and writer, Susan has published three books, featuring toys and garments for babies and children. (http://susanbanderson.blogspot.com)

JEANNINE BAKRIGES. Jeannine is a hand spinner, dyer, and knitter. Her recent book, *Spinning Around: Spinning, Dyeing & Knitting the Classics*, features Elizabeth Zimmermann's designs worked with Jeannine's handspun and hand-dyed yarns. (http://thespiritualspider.blogspot.com)

JUDY BECKER. Judy writes about knitting and other interests on her blog. Her inventive method for casting on for toe-up socks (and other center-starting projects), Judy's Magic Cast On, has intrigued and aided knitters since first published in *Knitty* in 2006. (www.persistentillusion.com/blogblog)

DEBBIE BLISS. Debbie has published more than two dozen books, many of which feature knit-wear designs for babies and children. She also frequently lectures and offers workshops in the United States, Canada, and other countries. She publishes a magazine, and her own Debbie Bliss branded yarn is sold worldwide. (www.debbieblissonline.com)

CAT BORDHI. Cat teaches both writing and knitting workshops. She finds the possibilities of the knit stitch endlessly fascinating and delights in exploring the Möbius construction in particular. She writes both young adult fiction and pattern books for knitters. (www.catbordhi.com)

BETH BROWN-REINSEL. Beth writes about knitting, designs and markets her own patterns, and teaches workshops both in the United States and abroad. Her website offers a wealth of information on and patterns for classic styles, such as gansey, Fair Isle, Aran, and Scandinavian knitting. (www.knittingtraditions.com)

ANN BUDD. In *The Knitter's Handy Book of Patterns* and in much of her other work, Ann shows herself to be someone who always likes to know how things work and why, and she thus has become an authority on creating and tailoring patterns. (www.annbuddknits.com)

NANCY BUSH. Nancy is a specialist in the knitted lace of Estonia, about which she has written several books. She teaches at conferences throughout the year, offering workshops on knitting Estonian lace and other Estonian knitting traditions, knitting socks with traditional "top-down" construction, and more. She also runs an online mail-order yarn and supply business, the Wooly West. (www.woolywest.com)

GAIL CALLAHAN. Calling herself the "Kangaroo Dyer," Gail creates several lines of yarn, which she dyes in her western Massachusetts studio and sells on her website and at her Etsy shop. Color and textures are her priorities, and her book *Hand Dyeing Yarn and Fleece* describes her dye techniques, as well as her ideas about color. (www.kangaroodyer.com)

LILY CHIN. Lily is not only a master knitter, but she has held the title of "the world's fastest crocheter." Her designs have been published in books and magazines, and she designs for yarn companies as well as offers her own line of yarn. (www.lilychinsignaturecollection.com)

MICHAEL COOK. A recognized authority on silk making and silkworms, Michael lectures and teaches frequently and writes about many issues related to silk at his website. (www.wormspit.com)

LINDA CORTRIGHT. Linda is the editor and publisher of *Wild Fibers* magazine, whose mission is "to educate and promote all aspects of the natural fiber industry with special emphasis on sustainable practices and responsible use of natural resources throughout the world." (www.wildfibersmagazine.com)

DONNA DRUCHUNAS. Combining her interest in knitting with her experience and skill in writing how-to directions, Donna contributes to a number of knitting magazines and has also published several knitting books. (http://sheeptoshawl.com)

JUDITH DURANT. One of the founding editors of *Interweave Knits* magazine, Judith has published several books on knitting, and her designs and articles on both knitting and beading have appeared in *Interweave Knits*, *Beadwork*, and *Piecework* magazines. (www.judithdurant.com)

JIL EATON. A knitting designer, author, and teacher, Jil has her own line of yarns and is well known for her Minnowknits designs. She regularly contributes to *Vogue Knitting*. (www.minnowknits.com)

EDIE ECKMAN. A former yarn shop owner, Edie teaches, writes, edits, and designs in both the knit and crochet worlds. She has published several books of crochet patterns and contributes regularly to a number of fiber magazines. (http://edieeckman.com)

BARBARA ELKINS. Co-founder of WEBS, the well-known yarn store in Northampton, Massachusetts, Barbara now devotes herself to her great love: teaching about and designing handwovens. Her designs appear frequently in *Handwoven* magazine.

MELANIE FALICK. Author and editorial director of STC Craft, Melanie wrote *Knitting in America* in 1996 (reissued in paperback as *America Knits*), ushering in an era of a new appreciation for contemporary knitters and designers and their varied lifestyles.

KAFFE FASSETT. Known foremost for his lushly colorful designs, Kaffe demonstrates how to see color and pattern all around and to transform that inspiration into fabric. He has published his designs widely, not only in books about knitting, but also quilting, needlepoint, and even mosaics. (www.kaffefassett.com)

JARED FLOOD. Knitting designer and photographer Jared Flood loves designs, such as those in lace and colorwork, that depend on geometry for their structure. His work is regularly published in magazines, and he has written a book of patterns for Classic Elite yarns (*Made in Brooklyn*), as well as created a line of his own yarns called Shelter. (http://brooklyntweed.blogspot.com)

BEV GALESKAS. Bev, who passed away in 2010, was the owner of Fiber Trends, a widely distributed pattern company. Her own special design interest was knitted felt. (www.fibertrends.com)

KAY GARDINER. A lawyer by training, Kay Gardiner met her coauthor Ann Shayne through an online knitting message board. Their conversation morphed into the popular books *Mason-Dixon Knitting: The Curious Knitter's Guide* and *Mason-Dixon Knitting Outside the Lines*. (www.masondixonknitting.com)

KATE GILBERT. Knitting designer Kate Gilbert's goal is to create patterns that are not only great when completed but also fun to knit. She is editor-in-chief of the online magazine *Twist Collective*, which is published three times a year. (www.twistcollective.com; www.kategilbert.com)

LIZ GIPSON. Liz Gipson is a self-described yarnie. Not only does she raise cashmere goats, but she weaves, spins, and dyes, and her "day job" is Sales and Marketing Director for Schacht Spindle Company, a loom and spinning wheel manufacturer. (www.lizgipson.com)

ROBIN HANSEN. A folklorist by training, Robin offers a wealth of information about traditional designs and techniques in her books and articles, especially topics related to mittens.

VICKIE HOWELL. Designer, author of a number of books, and a voice for this generation's craft movement, Vickie hosted DIY's *Knitty Gritty*. Her passion is to show how crafts, including knitting, can be a path to self-sufficiency and community. (http://vickiehowell.com)

VIVIAN HØXBRO. An embroidery and knitting designer for more than 25 years, Vivian is well known for her promotion of "domino" and shadow knitting techniques. She is also a colorist and worked with Harrisville Designs to develop a new line of yarns for them. (www.viv.dk)

MARIANNE ISAGER. Danish designer Marianne Isager has published a number of books inspired by design traditions in various parts of the world, including Africa, Japan, and South America. Her signature yarn is now available in the United States. (www.isagerknit.com)

CANDI JENSEN. A designer in the craft and needlework industry for more than 25 years, Candi has had more than three hundred designs published in national magazines, as well as 11 books to her credit. She is the producer of PBS's *Knit and Crochet Today*. (http://knitandcrochetnow.com)

LINDA LIGON. Founder and now creative director of Interweave Press, Linda's special personal interest is weaving. Under her leadership, Interweave grew from a small regional publication to a diverse media company that publishes six craft magazines and has more than 150 craft books in print.

BRANDON MABLY. Brandon designs knitwear patterns for Vogue Knitting and Rowan Yarns and leads workshops in knitwear design and use of color throughout the world. As studio manager for the Kaffe Studio in London, Brandon has worked closely with Kaffe Fassett in many aspects of the studio's creative life. (www.brandonmably.com)

BETSY MCCARTHY. Leaving a successful career in the health-care world behind in the 1990s, Betsy has since then focused on her true love: writing about, designing, and teaching knitting. (http://betsymccarthyknits.com)

JILLIAN MORENO. In addition to coauthoring books with Amy Singer, Jillian is ad manager of *Knitty* as well as editor of *Knitty*'s "little sister" section on spinning, dubbed Knittyspin. Jillian is an enthusiastic spinner as well as a knitter. (www.knitty.com; http://knittingfrau.blogspot.com)

MELISSA MORGAN-OAKES. Melissa has made knitting socks two-at-a-time her specialty and has published two books of patterns, one dealing with top-down and the other with toe-up methods. She teaches regularly at workshops and retreats. (www.melissaknits.com)

LUCY NEATBY. As a teacher, designer, and writer, Lucy delights knitters worldwide with her knowledge and uniquely colorful designs. Her passion is to nurture and empower knitters so they're in control of their art. (www.lucyneatby.com)

KRISTIN NICHOLAS. Kristin is a knitwear, stitchery, and textile designer, as well as author of stitchery and knitting books. She lives with her family on a farm in western Massachusetts, along with border collies, cats, chickens, pigs, and 150 sheep. (http://getting-stitched-on-the-farm.blogspot.com; http://kristinnicholas.com)

SHANNON OKEY. Shannon heads up a publishing company and is owner of a yarn shop. She teaches and speaks nationwide and is author of several books, including the Knitgrrl series. (www.knitgrrl.com)

CLARA PARKES. Clara has worked in both print and online publishing and has written several books on yarn and fiber. She founded and writes the weekly online magazine for fiber enthusiasts, *Knitter's Review.*
(www.knittersreview.com)

STEPHANIE PEARL-MCPHEE. Best known as the Yarn Harlot, Stephanie has a passion for all things fiber, and she uses her enthusiasm and wit to entertain yarn fanatics through her blog, books, and speaking appearances.
(www.yarnharlot.ca)

MARGARET RADCLIFFE. Margaret offers knitting classes on everything from beginner's basics to design and is particularly interested in promoting creativity and independence in all knitters. She has written several books on knitting techniques.
(www.maggiesrags.com)

DEBORAH ROBSON. Deb's work in the fiber world includes serving as editor of *Spin-Off* magazine, contributing articles to many books and magazines, and coauthoring a book on fleece and fiber. She is also the founder and publisher of Nomad Press.
(http://independentstitch.typepad.com and www.drobson.info)

CHARLENE SCHURCH. Teacher, knitting designer, dyer, and spinner, Charlene has published numerous books and contributes widely to fiber magazines.

AMY R. SINGER. Amy is a full-time writer and the founder and editor of the online magazine *Knitty.* With a particular interest in nonwool fibers, she has published several books and has a regular column in *Interweave Knits* magazine.
(www.knitty.com)

ALICE STARMORE. Alice is a professional needleworker, photographer, and author of books on needlework, with a particular interest in traditional knitting of Scandinavia and the British Isles.
(www.virtualyarns.com)

DEBBIE STOLLER. Co-founder of *BUST* magazine, Debbie is known in the knitting world for her series of Stitch 'n Bitch books, which support her firm belief in the traditional social qualities and values of knitting.

MEG SWANSEN. A designer and writer, Meg also heads Schoolhouse Press, produces a semiannual booklet ("Wool Gathering"), imports and distributes wool from abroad, and runs four sessions of the annual summer Knitting Camp, which her mother, Elizabeth Zimmermann, began in 1974.
(www.schoolhousepress.com)

KATHLEEN TAYLOR. Along with her love of knitting and spinning, Kathi has written six mysteries, five knitting books, and lots of designs and reviews; she's also interested in paper dolls.
(http://kathleen-dakotadreams.blogspot.com)

BARBARA WALKER. Not only has Barbara written a dozen knitting encyclopedias and pattern books, which include stitch patterns and mosaic knitting, but she's also author of another dozen books on topics dealing with religion, cultural anthropology, spirituality, and mythology.

SANDI WISEHEART. Describing herself as an avid knitter, spinner, and beader, Sandi also makes forays into crochet, weaving, sewing, quilting, and, in fact, almost anything fiber related. She was the founding editor of Interweave's online magazine *Knitting Daily.*
(http://sandiwiseheart.wordpress.com)

An Invitation to the Knitting Trip of a Lifetime

3-Hour Sweater
www.lrvictor.bravepages.com/Free/3-HOUR. htm
A vintage pattern from the 1930s that has been a popular knit-along project

Hemlock Ring Blanket
theraineysisters
http://theraineysisters.com/?cat=51
Jared Flood's adaptation of a vintage doily pattern from the Canadian Spool Cotton Company (1942) is reprinted with Jared's permission on the Rainey Sisters blog

Flow
Berroco
www.berroco.com
Berroco Pattern Booklet, Norah Gaughan, Vol. 2

Clapotis
Knitty
http://knitty.com/ISSUEfall04/PATTclapotis. html
Kate Gilbert's scarf pattern may be downloaded here

Baby Owl Sweater and Bonnet
http://strakerclassics.com
Penny Straker's pattern is available in yarn shops and online. Look for pattern number B818, Baby Owl & Bonnet

Baby Surprise Jacket
Schoolhouse Press
www.schoolhousepress.com/patterns.htm
Elizabeth Zimmermann's pattern is available in baby, child, and adult sizes through Schoolhouse Press. Look for pattern A-B-C-SJ

Chapter 1: The Yarn Life List

Books and Magazines

Bliss, Debbie. *The Knitter's Year: 52 Make-in-a-Week Projects — Quick Gifts and Seasonal Knits*. Trafalgar Square, 2010.

Budd, Ann. *The Knitter's Handy Book of Patterns: Basic Designs in Multiple Sizes & Gauges*. Interweave, 2001.

——. *Knitting Green: Conversations and Planet Friendly Projects*. Interweave, 2010.

Callahan, Gail. *Hand Dyeing Yarn and Fleece: Custom Color Your Favorite Fibers with Dip-Dyeing, Hand-Painting, Tie-Dyeing, and Other Creative Techniques*. Storey Publishing, 2010.

Ekarius, Carol, and Deborah Robson. *The Fleece and Fiber Sourcebook*. Storey Publishing, 2011.

Fassett, Kaffe. *Family Album: More Glorious Knits for Children and Adults*. Taunton, 1999.

——. *Glorious Knits: 35 Designs for Sweaters, Dresses, Vests, and Shawls*. Random House, 1995.

——. *Kaffe Fassett's Pattern Library: Over 190 Creative Knitwear Designs*. Taunton, 2003.

——. *Kaffe Knits Again: 24 Original Designs Updated for Today's Knitters*. Potter Craft, 2007.

——. *Kaffe's Classics: 25 Favorite Knitting Patterns for Sweaters, Jackets, Vests and More*. Little Brown, 1993.

Finlay, Victoria. *Color: A Natural History of the Palette*. Random House, 2003.

Høxbro, Vivian. *Domino Knitting*. Interweave, 2002.

——. *Knit to be Square: Domino Designs to Knit and Felt*. Interweave, 2008.

——. *Shadow Knitting*. Interweave, 2004.

Isager, Marianne. *Classic Knits*. Interweave, 2009.

——. *Inca Knits: Designs Inspired by South American Traditions*. Interweave, 2009.

——. *Japanese-Inspired Knits*. Interweave, 2009.

——. *Knitting Out of Africa*. Interweave, 2006.

Mably, Brandon. *Brilliant Knits: 25 Contemporary Knitwear Designs from the Kaffe Fassett Studio*. Taunton, 2001.

——. *Knitting Color: Design Inspiration from around the World*. Sixth & Spring, 2006.

Menz, Deb. *Color Works: A Crafter's Guide to Color*. Interweave, 2004.

Nicholas, Kristin. *Color by Kristin: How to Design Your Own Beautiful Knits.* Sixth and Spring, 2009.

———. *Kristin Knits: 27 Inspired Designs for Playing with Color.* Storey Publishing, 2007.

Okey, Shannon, and Sasha Gulish. *Alt Fiber: 25+ Projects for Knitting Green with Bamboo, Soy, Hemp, and More.* Ten Speed, 2008.

Parkes, Clara. *The Knitter's Book of Wool: The Ultimate Guide to Understanding, Using, and Loving This Most Fabulous Fiber.* Potter Craft, 2009.

———. *The Knitter's Book of Yarn: The Ultimate Guide to Choosing, Using, and Enjoying Yarn.* Potter Craft, 2007.

Radcliffe, Margaret. *The Essential Guide to Color Knitting Techniques.* Storey Publishing, 2008.

Robson, Deborah. *Handspun Treasures from Rare Wools.* Interweave, 2002.

Seiff, Joanne. *Fiber Gathering: Knit, Crochet, Spin, and Dye More Than 25 Projects Inspired by America's Festival.* Wiley, 2009.

Singer, Amy R. *No Sheep for You: Knit Happy with Cotton, Silk, Linen, Hemp, Bamboo & Other Delights.* Interweave, 2007.

Wild Fibers magazine. 207-594-9455; www.wildfibersmagazine.com.

Online Resources

Cashmere and Camel Hair Manufacturers' Institute
617-542-7481
www.cashmere.org

Craft Yarn Council
www.craftyarncouncil.com

Michael Cook
www.wormspit.com

Sources for Breed-Specific Yarns

The following businesses represent only a sampling of breed-specific yarns now available. Search online by breed for additional sources.

Beaverslide Dry Goods
406-472-3283
www.beaverslide.com
Montana; Merino

Bloomin Acres Farm
479-848-3060
www.bloominacresfarm.com
Arkansas; Icelandic

Frelsi Farm
207-793-4640
www.frelsifarm.com
Maine; Icelandic

Marr Haven Wool Farm
269-673-8800
www.marrhaven.com
Michigan; Merino, Rambouillet

Morehouse Farm
866-470-4852
www.morehousefarm.com
New York; Merino

Mostly Merino
802-254-7436
www.mostlymerino.com
Vermont; Merino

Mt. Bruce Station
810-798-2568
www.sheepstuff.com
Michigan; Corriedale, Moorit, Jacob

Solitude Farm
540-554-2312
solitudewool.com
Virginia; many breeds

Sweet Grass Wool
888-222-1880
www.sweetgrasswool.com
Montana; Targhee

Swift River Farm
978-724-3525
www.swiftriverfarm.com
Massachusetts; Shetland

Thirteen Mile Lamb & Wool Co.
406-388-4945
www.lambandwool.com
Montana; mainly Border Leicester, Corriedale, Romeldale crosses

Other Yarn Sources

Catskill Merino Sheep Farm
845-772-1050
www.catskill-merino.com
New York

Ellie's Reclaimed Cashmere
www.elliesreclaimedcashmere.com

Fleece Artist
www.fleeceartist.com

Foxfire Fiber & Design
413-625-6121
www.foxfirefiber.com
Massachusetts

Full Belly Farm
530-796-2214
www.fullbellyfarm.com
California

Good Karma Farm and Spinning Co.
207-322-0170
www.goodkarmafarm.com
Maine

Habu Textiles
212-239-3546
www.habutextiles.com

Holy Myrrhbearers Monastery
607-432-3179
www.holymyrrhbearers.com
New York

Island Fibers
360-468-2467
www.islandfibers.com
Washington

The Spinning Loft
517-540-1344
www.thespinningloft.com
Michigan

Stitchuary, Inc.
866-991-7057
www.stitchuary.com
New Jersey

New England Textile Mills

Green Mountain Spinnery
802-387-4528
www.spinnery.com
Vermont

Harrisville Designs
800-338-9415
www.harrisville.com
New Hampshire

Quince & Co.
877-309-6762
www.quinceandco.com
Maine

Still River Mill
860-974-9918
www.stillrivermill.com
Connecticut

Fiber Festivals

See also www.spinweave.org/news/
festivals.html for a listing of fiber festivals as well as fiber guild–sponsored
activities, retreats, classes, and other
fiber-related getaways. Knittersreview
.com also lists upcoming events, as does
the "Festival Fans" group on Ravelry (go
to Forums, search for Festival Fans, then
the "groups" tab for their page; listings
are sorted by United States, Australia,
Canada, and United Kingdom). The following festivals are listed in alphabetical
order by state.

Southwest Fiber Festival
Amado, Arizona
www.southwestfiberfestival.com

California Wool & Fiber Festival
Boonville, California
www.fiberfestival.com

Lambtown Fiber Fair
Dixon, California
www.lambtown.com

Estes Park Wool Market
Estes Park, Colorado
www.estesnet.com/events/woolmarket.htm

Sheep, Wool & Fiber Festival
Vernon/Rockville, Connecticut
www.ctsheep.com

Snake River Fiber Fair
Idaho Falls, Idaho
www.srfiberarts.org

Midwest Fiber & Folk Art Fair
Grayslake, Illinois
www.fiberandfolk.com

Hoosier Hills Fiberarts Festival
Franklin, Indiana
http://hoosierhillsfiberartsfestival.com

Southern Indiana FiberArts Festival
Corydon, Indiana
www.southernindianafiberarts.com

Iowa Sheep & Wool Festival
Adel, Iowa
www.iowasheep.com

The Kentucky Sheep and Fiber Festival
Lexington, Kentucky
www.kentuckysheepandfiber.com

Common Ground Country Fair
Unity, Maine
www.mofga.org

Denmark Sheepfest
Denmark, Maine
www.denmarksheepfest.com

Maine Fiber Frolic
Windsor, Maine
www.fiberfrolic.com

Maryland Sheep & Wool Festival
Columbia, Maryland
www.sheepandwool.org

Massachusetts Sheep & Woolcraft Fair
Cummington, Massachusetts
www.masheepwool.org

Michigan Fiber Festival
Allegan, Michigan
www.michiganfiberfestival.info

**Shepherd's Harvest Sheep & Wool
Festival**
Lake Elmo, Minnesota
www.shepherdsharvestfestival.org

World Sheep & Fiber Arts Festival
Bethel, Missouri
www.worldsheepfest.com

Big Sky Fiber Arts Festival
Hamilton, Montana
www.bigskyfiber.com

**New Hampshire Sheep and Wool
Festival**
Contoocook, New Hampshire
www.nhswga.com

Sheep & Fiber Festival
Hunterdon County, New Jersey
www.njsheep.org

**Best of the Southwest Fiber Arts
Festival**
Farmington, New Mexico
www.woolfestivalsw.meridian1.net

Fiber Arts Fiesta
Albuquerque, New Mexico
www.fiberartsfiesta.org

Sheep Is Life Celebration
Tsailé, New Mexico, Navajo Nation
www.navajolifeway.org

Wool Festival at Taos
Taos, New Mexico
www.taoswoolfestival.org

Finger Lakes Fiber Arts Festival
Hemlock, New York
www.gvhg.org/fest.html

New York Sheep & Wool Festival
Rhinebeck, New York
www.sheepandwool.com

Southeastern Animal Fiber Fair
Fletcher, North Carolina
www.saffsite.org

Fiber Arts Festival
West Fargo, North Dakota
www.fiberartsfest.com

Great Lakes Fiber Show
Wooster, Ohio
www.greatlakesfibershow.com

Black Sheep Gathering
Eugene, Oregon
www.blacksheepgathering.org

Oregon Flock & Fiber Festival
Canby, Oregon
www.flockandfiberfestival.com

Waynesburg Sheep and Fiber Festival
Waynesburg, Pennsylvania
www.sheepandfiber.com

North Country Fiber Fair
Watertown, South Dakota
www.northcountryfiberfair.org

Middle Tennessee Sheep, Wool and Fiber Festival
Dickson, Tennessee
www.tnfiberfestival.com

DFW Fiber Fest
Dallas, Texas
www.dfwfiberfest.org

Great Basin Fiber Arts Fair
South Jordan, Utah
www.greatbasinfiberartsfair.org

Vermont Sheep and Wool Festival
Tunbridge, Vermont
www.vermontsheep.org

Blue Ridge Llama & Alpaca Show
Charlottesville, Virginia
www.llamalife.com

Fall Fiber Festival & Montpelier Sheep Dog Trials
Montpelier Station, Virginia
www.fallfiberfestival.org

Alpacapalooza
western Washington
www.alpacawa.org

Shepherds' Extravaganza
Puyallup, Washington
www.shepherds-extravaganza.com

Eastern Angora Goat and Mohair Association
Lewisburg, West Virginia
www.angoragoats.com

Wisconsin Sheep & Wool Festival
Jefferson, Wisconsin
www.wisconsinsheepandwoolfestival.com

Australian Sheep & Wool Show
Bendigo, Australia
www.sheepshow.com

Olds College Fibre Week
Olds, Alberta
www.oldscollege.ca

Victoria Fibre Fest
Victoria, British Columbia
www.victoriafibrefest.com

Wonderwool Wales
Llanelwedd, Powys, Wales, United Kingdom
www.wonderwoolwales.co.uk

Woolfest
Cockermouth, United Kingdom
www.woolfest.co.uk

Class Acts
Stitches East, West, Midwest, and South
www.knittinguniverse.com

Vogue Knitting Live
www.vogueknitting.com/live

Chapter 2: The Know-How Life List
Reading List

Chin, Lily. *Lily Chin's Knitting Tips & Tricks: Shortcuts and Techniques Every Knitter Should Know*. Potter Craft, 2009.

Galeskas, Bev. *The Magic Loop: Working Around On One Needle — Sarah Hauschka's Magical Unvention*. Fiber Trends, 2002.

Mably, Brandon. *Brilliant Knits: 25 Contemporary Knitwear Designs from the Kaffe Fassett Studio*. Taunton, 2001.

———. *Knitting Color: Design Inspiration from Around the World*. Sixth & Spring, 2006.

Modesitt, Annie. *Confessions of a Knitting Heretic*. ModeKnit Press, 2004.

Radcliffe, Margaret. *The Knitting Answer Book: Solutions to Every Problem You'll Ever Face, Answers to Every Question You'll Ever Ask*. Storey Publishing, 2005.

Wong, Andrea. *Portuguese Style of Knitting: History, Traditions, and Techniques*. Andrea Wong Knits. Also, three DVDs, including *Learn How to Knit Portuguese Style*; *All about Socks Portuguese Style*; and *Portuguese Style of Knitting II* (to order, see www.andreawongknits.com).

Stitch Dictionaries and General Reference

365 Knitting Stitches a Year: Perpetual Calendar. Woodinville, WA: Martingale, 2002.

400 Knitting Stitches: A Complete Dictionary of Essential Stitch Patterns. Potter Craft, 2009.

Budd, Ann. *The Knitter's Handy Book of Patterns: Basic Designs in Multiple Sizes & Gauges*. Interweave, 2002.

———. *The Knitter's Handy Book of Sweater Patterns: Basic Designs in Multiple Sizes & Gauges*. Interweave, 2004.

Online Resources

For more knitters' vocabulary, see www.knitlist.com.

For World Wide Knit in Public Day, see www.wwkipday.com

Museums

For information about more museums, go to www.fibreartsonline.com/res/museum/index.htm

UNITED STATES

American Textile History Museum
Lowell, Massachusetts
978-441-0400
www.athm.org

Nordic Heritage Museum
Seattle, Washington
206-789-5707
www.nordicmuseum.org

Texas Museum of Fiber Arts
Austin, Texas
512-784-5651
www.texasfiberarts.org

Textile Museum
Washington, DC
202-667-0441
www.textilemuseum.org

Versterheim Norwegian-American Museum
Decorah, Iowa
563-382-9681
www.vesterheim.org

CANADA

Textile Museum of Canada
Toronto, Ontario
416-599-5321
www.textilemuseum.ca

UNITED KINGDOM

Shetland Museum
Lerwick, United Kingdom
+44-1595-695057
www.shetland-museum.org.uk

Victoria and Albert Museum
London, United Kingdom
+44-20-7942-2000
www.vam.ac.uk

NORWAY

Museum of the Norwegian Knitting Industry
Salhus, Norway
+47-61-21-77-20
www.olavsrosa.no
Click on the British flag at the top for English, then put "knitting" in the "quick search" window.

SWEDEN

Bohus Museum
Uddevalla, Sweden
+46-0522-65-65-00
www.bohuslansmuseum.se

Fiber Workshops

The following workshops are listed in alphabetical order by state.

Golden Gate Fiber Institute
Bonita Point, San Francisco, California
www.goldengatefiberinstitute.org

Mendocino Art Center
Mendocino, California
800-653-3328
www.mendocinoartcenter.org

North House Folk School
Grand Marais, Minnesota
888-387-9762
www.northhouse.org

Split Rock Arts Program
Minneapolis Forestry Center, Minnesota
612-625-1976
www.cce.umn.edu/splitrockarts

Ozark School of Creative Arts
Joplin, Missouri
www.ozarkschoolofcreativearts.com

Peters Valley Craft Center
Layton, New Jersey
973-948-5200
www.petersvalley.org

Harrisville Designs
Harrisville, New Hampshire
603-827-3996
www.harrisville.com

John C. Campbell Folk School
Brasstown, North Carolina
800-365-5724
www.folkschool.org

Penland School of Crafts
Penland, North Carolina
828-765-2359
www.penland.org

Arrowmont School of Arts and Crafts
Gatlinburg, Tennessee
865-436-5860
www.arrowmont.org

Nordic Knitting Conference
Seattle, Washington
206-789-5707
www.nordicmuseum.org/conference.aspx

Knitting with Jean
Vancouver, British Columbia
www.knittingwithjean.com

Chapter 3: The Sweaters Life List

Reading List

Brown-Reinsel, Beth. *Knitting Ganseys.* Interweave, 1993. Also, two DVDs available through her website (www.knittingtraditions.com).

Budd, Ann. *The Knitter's Handy Book of Sweater Patterns: Basic Designs in Multiple Sizes & Gauges.* Interweave, 2002.

Bush, Nancy. *Folk Knitting in Estonia: A Garland of Symbolism, Tradition, and Technique.* Interweave, 2000.

———. *Knitted Lace of Estonia: Techniques, Patterns, and Traditions.* Interweave, 2008.

Chynoweth, Therese. *Norwegian Sweater Techniques for Today's Knitter.* Hoboken, NJ: Wiley, 2010.

Dandanell, Birgittat, and Ulla Danielsson. *Twined Knitting: A Swedish Folkcraft Technique*. Translated by Robin Orm Hansen. Interweave, 1989.

Druchunas, Donna. *Arctic Lace: Knitting Projects and Stories Inspired by Alaska's Native Knitters*. Fort Collins, CO: Nomad Press, 2006.

——. *Ethnic Knitting Discovery: The Netherlands, Denmark, Norway, and the Andes*. Fort Collins, CO: Nomad Press, 2007.

——. *Ethnic Knitting Exploration: Lithuania, Iceland, and Ireland*. Fort Collins, CO: Nomad Press, 2009.

Falick, Melanie. *America Knits*. Paperback edition of *Knitting in America*, published in 1996. New York: Artisan, 2005.

Feitelson, Ann. *The Art of Fair Isle Knitting: History, Technique, Color and Pattern*. Interweave, 2009.

Erlbacher, Maria. *Twisted-Stitch Knitting: Traditional Patterns & Garments from the Styrian Enns Valley*. English edition. Schoolhouse Press, 2009.

Fanderl, Lisl. *Bäuerliches Stricken*. Rosenheimer Verlagshaus, 2001.

Fassett, Kaffe. *See* Chapter 1 Reading List, page 295.

Gaughan, Norah. *Knitting Nature: 39 Designs Inspired by Patterns in Nature*. STC Craft, 2006.

Gibson-Roberts, Priscilla. *Knitting in the Old Way: Designs and Techniques from Ethnic Sweaters*. Fort Collins, CO: Nomad Press, 2005.

Guy, Lucinda. *Northern Knits: Designs Inspired by the Knitting Traditions of Scandinavia, Iceland, and the Shetland Isles*. Interweave, 2010.

Handberg, Mette. *Norwegian Patterns for Knitting: Classic Sweaters, Hats, Vests, and Mittens*. Trafalgar Square, 2010.

Hiatt, June Hemmons. *The Principles of Knitting: Methods and Techniques of Hand Knitting*. Simon and Schuster, 1988.

Hisdal, Solveig. *Poetry in Stitches: Clothes You Can Knit*. Oslo, Norway: N.W. Damm & Søn, 2000.

Hollingworth, Shelagh. *Traditional Aran Knitting*. Mineola, NY: Dover, 2006.

Keele, Wendy. *Poems of Color: Knitting in the Bohus Tradition*. Interweave, 1995.

Khmeleva, Galina, and Carol R. Noble. *Gossamer Webs: The History and Techniques of Orenburg Lace Shawls*. Interweave, 1998.

——. *The Gossamer Webs Design Collection: Three Orenburg Shawls to Knit*. Interweave, 2003.

Knight, Erika. *Cable and Arans* (The Harmony Guides). Interweave, 1997.

Kosel, Janine. *Norwegian Handknits: Heirloom Designs from Versterheim Museum*. Minneapolis, MN: Voyageur, 2009.

Leszner, Eva Maria, trans. *Knitted Lace Designs of Herbert Niebling*. Berkeley: Lacis, 2009.

Lewandowski, Marcia. *Andean Folk Knits: Great Designs from Peru, Chile, Argentina, Equador, and Bolivia*. New York: Lark, 2006.

McGregor, Sheila. *Traditional Fair Isle Knitting*. Mineola, NY: Dover 2003.

——. *Traditional Scandinavian Knitting*. Mineola, NY: Dover 2004.

Niebling, Herbert. Translated by Eva Maria Leszner. *Knitted Lace Designs of Herbert Niebling*. Lacis, 2009.

Norbury, James. *Traditional Knitting Patterns: from Scandinavia, the British Isles, France, Italy and Other European Countries*. Mineola, NY: Dover, 1973.

Pearson, Michael. *Michael Pearson's Traditional Knitting: Aran, Fair Isle, and Fisher Ganseys*. New York: Van Nostrand Reinhold, 1984.

Starmore, Alice. *Alice Starmore's Book of Fair Isle Knitting*. Mineola, NY: Dover, 2009.

——. *Aran Knitting*. Interweave, 1997.

——. *The Celtic Collection: Twenty-Five Knitwear Designs for Men and Women*. North Pomfret, VT: Trafalgar Square, 1992.

Swansen, Meg. *Armenian Knitting*. Schoolhouse Press, 2007.

——. *A Gathering of Lace*. XRX Books, 2005.

——. *Meg Swansen's Knitting: 30 Designs for Hand Knitting*. Interweave, 1999.

Szabo, Janet. *Aran Sweater Design*. Kalispell, MT: Big Sky Knitting Designs, 2006.

——. *Cables: The Basics*. Kalispell, MT: Big Sky Knitting Designs, 2007.

Thomas, Mary. *Mary Thomas's Book of Knitting Patterns*. Mineola, NY: Dover, 1972.

——. *Mary Thomas's Knitting Book*. Mineola, NY: Dover, 1972.

Thompson, Gladys. *Patterns for Guernseys, Jerseys and Arans*. Mineola, NY: Dover, 1971.

Walker, Barbara. *See* Reading List for chapter 10.

Wright, Mary. *Cornish Guernseys and Knit-Frocks*. Worcestershire, UK: Polperro Heritage, 2008.

Zimmermann, Elizabeth. *Elizabeth Zimmermann's Knitter's Almanac: Projects for Each Month of the Year*. Mineola, NY: Dover, 1981.

——. *Elizabeth Zimmermann's Knitting Workshop*. Schoolhouse, 1981.

——. *Knitting Around*. Schoolhouse, 1989.

——. *Knitting without Tears: Basic Techniques and Easy-to-Follow Directions for Garments to Fit All Sizes*. New York: Scribner, 1971.

——. *The Opinionated Knitter*. Schoolhouse, 2005.

Online Resources

Beth Brown-Reinsel
Patterns and DVDs
www.knittingtraditions.com

Moray Firth Project
www.gansey-mf.co.uk

Penny Straker patterns
http://strakerclassics.com

Susan Sarabasha
www.spinningbunny.com

The Walker Treasury Project
http://thewalkertreasury.wordpress.com

Knitting Retreats

The following retreats are listed in alphabetical order by state.

Knitaway in the Rockies
Boulder, Colorado
www.cheryloberle.com

Knitting and Yoga Adventures
Monhegan Island, Maine
http://knittingandyogaadventures.com

**Knitting Cruise on Schooner
J. & E. Riggin**
Rockland, Maine
www.mainewindjammer.com

Getting Stitched on the Farm
Leyden, Massachusetts;
http://getting-stitched-on-the-farm.blogspot.com
Kristin Nicholas

Moontide Lace Knitting Retreat
Wellfleet, Massachusetts
www.moonriselaceknitting.com

Knitter's Review Fall Retreat
Williamstown, Massachusetts
www.knittersreview.com

Squam Art Workshops
Squam Lake, New Hampshire
www.squamartworkshops.com

Knitaway in Taos
Taos, New Mexico
www.cheryloberle.com

Knitters Connection
Columbus, Ohio
www.knittersconnection.com

Mindful Knitting Retreat
Greensboro, Vermont
www.tarahandknitting.com

Acorn Street Retreat
Leavenworth, Washington
www.acornstreet.com

Madrona Fiber Arts Winter Retreat
Tacoma, Washington
www.madronafiberarts.com

Meg Swansen's Knitting Camps
Marshfield, Wisconsin
http://www.schoolhousepress.com/camp.htm

Sheep in the City Get-Away
Milwaukee, Wisconsin
*http://web.mac.com/jmassie1/
Sheep_in_the_City*

Chapter 4: The Socks Life List

Reading List

Bordhi, Cat. *New Pathways for Sock Knitters: Book One.* Friday Harbor, WA: Passing Paws Press, 2007.
——. *Personal Footprints for Insouciant Sock Knitters: Book Two in the New Pathways for Knitters Series.* Friday Harbor, WA: Passing Paws Press, 2009.
——. *Socks Soar on Circular Needles: A Manual of Elegant Knitting Techniques and Patterns.* Friday Harbor, WA: Passing Paws Press, 2001.
Budd, Ann. *Getting Started with Socks.* Interweave, 2007.
Bush, Nancy. *Folk Socks: The History & Techniques of Handknitted Footwear.* Interweave, 1994.
Galeskas, Bev. *The Magic Loop: Working Around On One Needle: Sarah Hauschka's Magical Invention.* Fiber Trends, 2002.
Ligon, Linda, ed. *Homespun Handknit: Caps, Socks, Mittens & Gloves.* Interweave, 1987.
Macdonald, Anne L. *No Idle Hands: The Social History of American Knitting.* Ballantine, 1990.
McCarthy, Betsy. *Knit Socks! 17 Classic Patterns for Cozy Feet.* Storey Publishing, 2010.
Morgan-Oakes, Melissa. *Toe-Up 2-at-a-Time Socks.* Storey Publishing, 2010.
——. *2-at-a-Time Socks.* Storey Publishing, 2007.
Neatby, Lucy. *Cool Socks, Warm Feet.* Nimbus, 2003.
Pearl-McPhee, Stephanie. *Knitting Rules: The Yarn Harlot Unravels the Mysteries of Swatching, Stashing, Ribbing & Rolling to Free Your Inner Knitter.* Storey Publishing, 2006.
Rutt, Richard. *A History of Hand Knitting: The Compelling History of This Ancient Craft.* Interweave, 2003.
Schurch, Charlene. *More Sensational Knitted Socks.* Woodinville, WA: Martingale, 2007.
——. *Sensational Knitted Socks.* Woodinville, WA: Martingale, 2005.
Schurch, Charlene, and Beth Parrott. *Sock Club: Join the Knitting Adventure.* Woodinville, WA, WA: Martingale, 2010.
Strawn, Susan M. *Knitting America: A Glorious Heritage from Warm Socks to High Art.* St. Paul, MN: Voyageur, 2007.
Zilboorg, Anna. *Simply Socks: 45 Traditional Turkish Patterns to Knit.* Asheville, NC: Lark, 2001.

Online Resources

Judy's Magic Cast On
www.persistentillusion.com/blogblog
(Click on "Techniques." Cat Bordhi has also prepared a video demonstrating Judy's Magic Cast On, with Judy Becker's permission, that can be viewed on YouTube. The original article is in the Knitty.com archives for spring 2006.)

Historical Knitting

*http://knittinghistory.typepad.com/
historic_knitting_pattern*

Antique Pattern Project

www.antiquepatternlibrary.org

Evelyn Clark's Flower Basket Shawl

Pattern #5-2014
www.fibertrends.com

Knitting for a Cause

The following are only a few of the
organizations that sponsor knitting for
a cause. For additional suggestions for
charitable projects, see www.knitting-
forcharity.org. Also, Betty Christiansen's
*Knitting for Peace: Make the World a
Better Place One Stitch at a Time* (STC
Craft, 2006) includes many of the following organizations as well as others.

Afghans for Afghans

www.afghansforafghans.org

Chemo Caps

www.chemocaps.com

Hats for the Homeless

www.hats4thehomeless.org

Operation Toasty Toes

www.operationtoastytoes8.gobot.com

Project Linus

www.projectlinus.org

Shawl Ministry

www.shawlministry.com

Warm Up America

www.craftyarncouncil.com/warmup.html

A Winter Weather Craft Tradition: "Knit Your Bit"

American Red Cross Museum
www2.redcross.org/museum/exhibits/knits.asp
Red Cross patterns for knitting for the
troops

Chapter 5: The Scarves & Shawls Life List

Reading List: Patterns

Armstrong, Adrienne, and Vickie Howell.
*Aware Knits: Knit & Crochet Proj-
ects for the Eco-conscious Stitcher.*
New York: Lark Books, 2009.

Allen, Pam. *Scarf Style: Innovative to
Traditional, 31 Inspirational Styles
to Knit and Crochet.* Interweave,
2004.

Baber, M'Lou. *Double Knitting: Reversible Two-Color Designs.* Schoolhouse
Press, 2008.

Barr, Lynne. *Knitting New Scarves: 27
Distinctly Modern Designs.* New
York: Stewart Tabori & Chang,
2007.

———. *Reversible Knitting: 50 Brand-
New, Groundbreaking Stitch Pat-
terns.* New York: Stewart Tabori &
Chang, 2009.

Bordhi, Cat. *A Second Treasury of Magical Knitting.* Friday Harbor, WA:
Passing Paws Press, 2005.

———. *A Treasury of Magical Knitting.*
Friday Harbor, WA: Passing Paws
Press, 2004.

Bush, Nancy. *Folk Knitting in Estonia:
A Garland of Symbolism, Tradition
and Technique.* Interweave, 2000.

———. *Folk Socks: The History & Techniques of Handknitted Footwear.*
Interweave, 1994.

———. *Knitted Lace of Estonia: Techniques, Patterns, and Traditions.*
Interweave, 2008.

———. *Knitting on the Road: Sock Patterns for the Travelling Knitter.*
Interweave, 2001.

———. *Knitting Vintage Socks: New
Twists of Classic Patterns.* Interweave, 2005.

Chin, Lily. *Power Cables: The Ultimate
Guide to Knitting Inventive Cables.*
Interweave, 2010.

Cornell, Kari, ed. *Knitting Yarns and
Spinning Tales: A Knitter's Stash of
Wit and Wisdom.* Stillwater, MN:
Voyageur Press, 2005.

Cortright, Linda. *Wild Fibers: Five Years
of Favorites.* Audio book. Stockton
Springs, ME: Knitting Out Loud,
2010.

Druchunas, Donna. *Arctic Lace: Knitting Projects and Stories Inspired by
Alaska's Native Knitters.* Fort Collins, CO: Nomad Press, 2006.

———. *Successful Lace Knitting: Celebrating the Work of Dorothy Reade.*
Woodinville, WA: Martingale, 2010.

Falick, Melanie. *America Knits* (First
published as *Knitting in America,*
Artisan, 1996). Artisan, 2005.

———. *Handknit Holidays: Knit-
ting Year-Round for Christmas,
Hanukkah, and Winter Solstice.*
Stewart,Tabori and Chang, 2005.

———. *Kids Knitting: Projects for Kids of
All Ages.* Artisan, 2003.

———, and Kristin Nicholas. *Knitting for
Baby: 30 Heirloom Projects with
Complete How-to-Knit Instructions.*
STC Craft, 2008

———. *Weekend Knitting: 50 Unique
Projects and Ideas.* STC Craft, 2009.

Gardiner, Kay, and Ann Shayne. *Mason-
Dixon Knitting: The Curious Knitter's Guide: Stories, Patterns, Advice,
Opinions, Questions, Answers, Jokes,
and Pictures,* rev. ed. Potter Craft,
2010.

———. *Mason-Dixon Knitting Outside
the Lines: Patterns, Stories, Pictures,
True Confessions, Tricky Bits, Whole
New Worlds, and Familiar Ones,
Too.* Potter Craft, 2008.

Gschwandtner, Sabrina. *KnitKnit: Pro-
files & Projects from Knitting's New
Wave.* New York: Stewart, Tabori &
Chang, 2007.

Howell, Vickie. *Craft Corps: Celebrating
the Creative Community One Story
at a Time.* New York: Lark Books,
2010.

——. *Knit Aid: A Learn It, Fix It, Finish It Guide for Knitters on the Go.* New York: Sterling, 2008.

——. *New Knits on the Block: A Guide to Knitting What Kids Really Want.* New York: Sterling, 2005.

——. *Not Another Teen Knitting Book.* New York: Sterling, 2006.

——. *Vickie Howell's Pop Goes Crochet: 36 Projects Inspired by Icons of Popular Culture.* New York: Lark Books, 2009.

Jensen, Candi. *Knit Scarves! 16 Cool Patterns to Keep You Warm.* Storey Publishing, 2004.

Khmeleva, Galina, and Carol R. Noble. *Gossamer Webs: The History and Techniques of Orenburg Lace Shawls.* Interweave, 1998.

——. *The Gossamer Webs Design Collection: Three Orenburg Shawls to Knit.* Interweave, 2003.

Moreno, Jillian, and Amy Singer. *Big Girl Knits: 25 Big, Bold Projects Shaped for Real Women with Real Curves.* Potter Craft, 2009

——. *More Big Girl Knits: 25 Designs Full of Color and Texture for Curvy Women.* Potter Craft, 2009.

Nargi, Lela. *Knitting Lessons: Tales from the Knitting Path.* New York: J. P. Tarcher / Putnam, 2003.

——, ed. *Knitting Memories: Reflections on the Knitter's Life.* St. Paul, MN: Voyageur Press, 2006.

Noble, Carol Rasmussen, and Margaret Leask Peterson. *Knits from the North Sea: Lace in the Shetland Tradition.* Woodinville, WA: Martingale, 2009.

Oberle, Cheryl. *Folk Shawls: 25 Knitting Patterns and Tales from around the World.* Interweave, 2000.

Schreier, Iris. *Iris Schreier's Reversible Knits: Creative Techniques for Knitting Both Sides Right.* Asheville, NC: Lark, 2009.

Sowerby, Jane. *Victorian Lace Today.* Sioux Falls, SD: XRX, 2008.

Singer, Amy R. *No Sheep for You: Knit Happy with Cotton, Silk, Linen, Hemp, Bamboo & Other Delights.* Interweave, 2007 (includes Amy Singer's Tuscany Shawl)

Stoller, Debbie. *Son of Stitch 'n Bitch: 45 Projects to Knit and Crochet for Men.* Workman, 2007

——. *Stitch 'n Bitch: The Knitter's Handbook.* New York: Workman, 2003.

——. *Stitch 'n Bitch Crochet: The Happy Hooker.* Workman, 2006.

——. *Stitch 'n Bitch Nation.* Workman, 2004.

——. *Stitch 'n Bitch Superstar Knitting: Go Beyond the Basics.* Workman, 2010.

Swansen, Meg. *A Gathering of Lace.* Sioux Falls, SD: XRX, 2005.

Temple, Mary Beth. *The Secret Language of Knitters.* Kansas City, MO: Andrews McMeel Publishing, 2007.

Thies, Sheryl. *Nature's Wrapture: Contemporary Knitted Shawls.* Woodinville, WA: Martingale, 2010.

——. *Ocean Breezes: Knitted Scarves Inspired by the Sea.* Woodinville, WA: Martingale, 2007.

Editors of *Vogue Knitting* magazine. *Vogue Knitting: Shawls and Wraps.* Sixth & Spring, 2009.

Walker, Barbara. *The Craft of Lace Knitting.* New York: Scribner, 1971.

Reading List: Books with References to Knitting

For more suggestions of books that have some reference to knitting in them, see www.woolworks.org/bookref.html and www.hipforums.com/newforums/archive/index.php/t-147076.html. (No edition is listed here for classic books or series.)

Bartlett, Anne. *Knitting.* Boston: Houghton Mifflin, 2006.

Christie, Agatha. *The Miss Marple* mysteries

Conrad, Joseph. *Heart of Darkness*

Deitch, Joanne Weisman, ed. *The Lowell Mill Girls: Life in the Factory.* Carlisle, MA: Discovery Enterprises, 1998.

Dickens, Charles. *A Tale of Two Cities*

Dreiser, Theodore. *An American Tragedy*

Ferris, Monica. *Blackwork*; *Thai Die*; *Unraveled Sleeve*

Goldenbaum, Sally. *Death by Cashmere.* New York: New American Library, 2009.

Graver, Elizabeth. *Unravelling.* Boston: Houghton Mifflin, 1999.

Hood, Ann. *The Knitting Circle.* New York: W. W. Norton, 2008.

Jacobs, Kate. *The Friday Night Knitting Club* series

Kingsolver, Barbara. *The Lacuna.* New York: HarperCollins, 2009.

Krueger, Mary. *Died in the Wool*; *Knit Fast, Die Young*

Lenhard, Elizabeth. *Chicks with Sticks* series

Macomber, Debbie. *Blossom Street* series

Paterson, Katherine. *Lyddie.* New York: Puffin, 2004.

Proulx, Annie. *The Shipping News.* New York: Scribner, 1999.

Sefton, Maggie. *Dropped Dead Stitch*; *Knit One, Kill Two*; *Needled to Death*

Shields, Carol. *Small Ceremonies.* New York: Penguin, 1996.

Shreve, Anita. *Fortune's Rocks.* Boston: Back Bay Books, 2001.

Sijie, Dai. *Balzac and the Little Chinese Seamstress.* Translated by Ina Rilke. Garden City, NY: Anchor, 2002.

Wharton, Edith. "Roman Fever"

Woolf, Virginia. *The Voyage Out*

Reading List: Books about Knitting

Brown, Melissa, and Martin John Brown. *Knitalong: Celebrating the Tradition of Knitting Together.* New York: Stewart Tabori & Chang, 2008.

Lydon, Susan Gordon. *Knitting Heaven and Earth: Healing the Heart with Craft.* Potter Craft, 2005.

———. *The Knitting Sutra: Craft as a Spiritual Practice*. Potter Craft, 2004.

Macdonald, Anne. *No Idle Hands: The Social History of American Knitting*. New York: Ballantine, 1990.

Murphy, Nora. *Knitting the Threads of Time: Casting Back to the Heart of Our Craft*. Novato, CA: New World Library, 2009.

Pearl-McPhee, Stephanie. *At Knit's End: Meditations for Women Who Knit Too Much*. Storey Publishing, 2005.

———. *Knitting Rules!* Storey Publishing, 2006.

———. *Stephanie Pearl-McPhee Casts Off*. Storey Publishing, 2007.

———. *Things I Learned from Knitting . . . Whether I Wanted to or Not*. Storey Publishing, 2008.

Roghaar, Linda, and Molly Wolf, eds. *KnitLit: Sweaters and Their Stories . . . and Other Writing about Knitting*. New York: Three Rivers Press, 2002.

———, eds. *KnitLit the Third: We Spin More Yarns*. New York: Three Rivers Press, 2005.

———, eds. *KnitLit (Too): Stories from Sheep to Shawl . . . and More Writing about Knitting*. New York: Three Rivers Press, 2004.

Rutt, Richard. *A History of Hand Knitting: The Compelling History of This Ancient Craft*. Interweave, 2003.

Strawn, Susan M. *Knitting America: A Glorious Heritage from Warm Socks to High Art*. St. Paul, MN: Voyageur, 2007.

Online Patterns and Other Resources

Kate Gilbert
For "Clapotis" and other patterns
www.kategilbert.com

Cheryl Marling
For "Tudora" and other patterns
www.knitty.com

Lucy Neatby
For "Bubbles," "Hugs and Kisses," and other patterns
www.lucyneatby.com

Dolly Mama Felted Doll Kits
http://thedolly-mamas.com

Canadian Knitwear Designers & Artisans (CKDA)
www.canknit.com

The Knitting Guild Association (TKGA)
www.tkga.com

Meetup
www.meetup.org

Stitch 'n Bitch
www.stitchnbitch.org

Stitch n' Pitch
www.stitchnpitch.com

Twist Collective
http://twistcollective.com

Chapter 6: The Hats Life List

Reading List

Baber, M'Lou. *Double Knitting: Reversible Two-Color Designs*. Schoolhouse Press, 2008.

Handberg, Mette. *Norwegian Patterns for Knitting: Classic Sweaters, Hats, Vests, and Mittens*. North Pomfret, VT: Trafalgar Square, 2010.

Leapman, Melissa. *Mastering Color Knitting: Simple Instructions for Stranded, Intarsia, and Double Knitting*. Potter Craft, 2010.

Ligon, Linda, ed. *Homespun Handknit: Caps, Socks, Mittens & Gloves*. Interweave, 1987.

———. *This Is How I Go When I Go Like This: Weaving and Spinning as Metaphor*. Interweave, 2004.

Moreno, Jillian, and Amy R. Singer. *Big Girl Knits: 25 Big, Bold Projects Shaped for Real Women with Real Curves*. Potter Craft, 2006.

———. *More Big Girl Knits: 25 Designs Full of Color & Texture for Curvy Women*. Potter Craft, 2008.

Radcliffe, Margaret. *The Essential Guide to Color Knitting Techniques*. Storey Publishing, 2008.

———. *The Knitting Answer Book*. Storey Publishing, 2005

Schurch, Charlene. *Hats On! 31 Warm and Winsome Caps for Knitters*. Camden, ME: Down East Books, 1999.

Square, Vicki. *Folk Hats: 32 Knitting Patterns & Tales from Around the World*. Interweave, 2005.

Chapter 7: The Gloves & Mittens Life List

Reading List

Handberg, Mette. *Norwegian Patterns for Knitting: Classic Sweaters, Hats, Vests, and Mittens*. North Pomfret, VT: Trafalgar Square, 2010.

Hansen, Robin. *Favorite Mittens: Best Traditional Mitten Patterns from Fox and Geese and Fences and Flying Geese and Partridge Feet*. Camden, ME: Down East Books, 2005.

———. *Flying Geese & Partridge Feet: More Mittens from Up North and Down East*. Camden, ME: Down East Books, 1986.

———. *Fox and Geese and Fences: A Collection of Traditional Maine Mittens*. Camden, ME: Down East Books, 1983.

Ligon, Linda, ed. *Homespun Handknit: Caps, Socks, Mittens & Gloves*. Interweave, 1987.

Nicholas, Kristin. *Kristin Knits: 27 Inspired Designs for Playing with Color*. Storey Publishing, 2007.

Radcliffe, Margaret. *The Essential Guide to Color Knitting Techniques*. Storey Publishing, 2008.

Schurch, Charlene. *Mostly Mittens: Ethnic Knitting Designs from Russia*. Woodinville, WA: Martingale, 2009.

Upitis, Lizbeth. *Latvian Mittens: Traditional Designs & Techniques*. Schoolhouse Press, 1997.

Online Resources

The following are addresses of some useful websites with general information of interest to knitters. For more specific information, check out addresses of other online resources listed under other chapter heads in this appendix.

Knitlist
www.knitlist.com
A Yahoo! group formed to share information about knitting

Knitter's Review
www.knittersreview.com
Online magazine for knitters; events, articles, published weekly

Knitty
www.knitty.com
Patterns and articles, published four times a year

Patternfish
www.patternfish.com
Buy or sell your knitting or crochet patterns as customized PDF downloads

Ravelry
www.ravelry.com
Social networking, including patterns, discussions, and knit-alongs

Twist Collective
http://twistcollective.com
Patterns and articles published three times a year

Weavolution
www.weavolution.com
Online community for handweavers to share information

Yarndex
www.yarndex.com
Directory of yarn spinning mills, searchable by brand, company name, weight, fiber type, and texture

YouTube
www.youtube.com
Search for videos of specific techniques

Chapter 8: The Bags Life List

Reading List

Allen, Pam, and Ann Budd. *Bag Style: 20 Inspirational Handbags, Totes, and Carry-alls to Knit and Crochet*. Interweave, 2007.

Durant, Judith. *Knit One, Bead Too: Essential Techniques for Knitting with Beads*. Storey Publishing, 2009.

Fassett, Kaffe. *Kaffe Fassett's Pattern Library: Over 190 Creative Knitwear Designs*. Taunton, 2003.

Pace, Maggie. *Felt It!* Storey Publishing, 2006.

Sirna, Gail Carolyn. *In Praise of the Needlewoman: Embroiderers, Knitters, Lacemakers, and Weavers in Art*. New York: Merrell, 2006.

Square, Vicki. *Folk Bags: 30 Knitting Patterns and Tales from Around the World*. Interweave, 2003.

Taylor, Kathleen. *Knit One, Felt Too: Discover the Magic of Knitted Felt with 25 Easy Patterns*. Storey Publishing, 2003.

Yarn-Friendliest Cities

These websites may help direct you to knitting-related activities in specific cities. Check out www.meetup.org, www.ravelry.com, and http://stitchnbitch.org, for contacts in cities not listed.

Boston
www.bostonknitting.com

Chicago
www.windycityknittingguild.com

District of Columbia
www.dcknitting.net

Minneapolis
Minnesota Knitters' Guild
www.knitters.org

New York
www.bakg.org

San Francisco
Craft and Folk Art Museum
www.cafam.org

California College of Arts and Crafts
www.cca.edu

Seattle
www.seattleknittersguild.org
www.theknittingschool.com

Knitting Trip Adventures

Alaska for Fiber Fanatics
www.vernhalter.com/ ToursAdventures/DreamADreamTours/ KnitandSpinTourforWomen

Behind the Scenes Adventures
www.btsadventures.com

Craft Cruises
www.craftcruises.com

Craft World Tours
www.craftworldtours.com

Fiber Summit Series Abroad
www.alpineadventureagency.com

Joyce James Tours
www.joycejamestours.com

Chapter 9: The Kids Knit Life List

Reading List

Anderson, Susan B. *Itty-Bitty Hats: Cute and Cuddly Hats to Knit for Babies and Toddlers*. New York: Artisan, 2006.

———. *Itty-Bitty Nursery: Sweet, Adorable Knits for Baby and Beyond*. New York: Artisan, 2007.

———. *Itty-Bitty Toys: How to Knit Animals, Dolls, and Other Playthings for Kids*. New York: Artisan, 2009.

Bliss, Debbie. *Baby Knits for Beginners*. North Pomfret, VT: Trafalgar, 2003.

———. *Booties, Blankets, & Bears: 20 Irresistible Hand Knits for Your Baby*. North Pomfret, VT: Trafalgar, 2009.

———. *Debbie Bliss Baby and Toddler Knits: 20 Gorgeous Jackets, Sweaters, Hats, Booties and More*. London: Cico, 2009.

———. *Design It, Knit It: Babies*. Sixth & Spring, 2010.

———. *Essential Baby: Over 20 Handknits to Take Your Baby from First Days to First Steps*. North Pomfret, VT: Trafalgar, 2007.

———. *The Knitter's Year: 52 Make-in-a-Week Projects: Quick Gifts and Seasonal Knits*. Trafalgar Square, 2010.

———. *Simply Baby: 20 Special Handknits for Baby's First Two Years*. North Pomfret, VT: Trafalgar, 2006.

———. *Special Family Knits*. North Pomfret, VT: Trafalgar, 2009.

Bordhi, Cat. *A Guide for Bringing Spinning and Knitting into Elementary through High School Classrooms*; www.catbordhi.com/documents/KnittinginSchools.pdf.

Durant, Judith. *Luxury Yarn One-Skein Wonders: 101 Small Indulgences*. Storey, 2008.

———. *Sock Yarn One-Skein Wonders: 101 Patterns that Go Way Beyond Socks*. Storey, 2010.

Eaton, Jil. *Minnies: QuickKnits for Babies and Toddlers*. Elmhurst, IL: Breckling, 2005.

———. *Pipsqueak Knits: 12 Deluxe Quick-Knits for Your Baby and Toddler*. Elmhurst, IL: Breckling, 2009.

Epstein, Nicky. *Barbie Doll and Me: 45 Playful Matching Designs for Knitting*. Sixth & Spring, 2005.

———. *Knits for Barbie Doll: 75 Fabulous Fashions for Knitting*. Sixth & Spring, 2001.

Falick, Melanie. *America Knits*. Paperback edition of *Knitting in America*, published in 1996. New York: Artisan, 2005.

———. *Kids Knitting: Projects for Kids of All Ages*. New York: Artisan, 2003.

Fassett, Kaffe. *Family Album: More Glorious Knits for Children and Adults*. Taunton, 1999.

Reading List: Stories for Kids

For additional titles see www.catbordhi.com/documents/KnittinginSchools.pdf, where Cat Bordhi includes lists of books for kids that contain information about knitting and related fiber subjects compiled by Myrna Stahman.

Blood, Charles L., and Martin Link; illustrated by Nancy Winslow Parker. *The Goat in the Rug*. New York: Aladdin, 1990.

Brett, Jan. *The Mitten*. New York: Scholastic, 1990.

Brown, Margaret Wise; illustrated by Clement Hurd. *Goodnight Moon*. New York: Harper, 1947; released as a board book by HarperFestival, 2001.

dePaola, Tomi. *Charlie Needs a Cloak*. New York: Aladdin, 1982.

Dr. Seuss. *The Lorax*. New York: Random House, 1971.

Guarino, Deborah; illustrated by Steven Kellogg. *Is Your Mama a Llama?* New York: Scholastic, 1989.

Klise, Kate; illustrated by M. Sarah Klise. *Shall I Knit You a Hat? A Christmas Yarn*. New York: Square Fish, 2007.

McCloskey, Robert. *Homer Price*. New York: Viking, 1943.

Miles, Miska. *Annie and the Old One*. Boston: Little, Brown, 1985.

Rowling, J. K. All books in the *Harry Potter* series. New York: Scholastic, 1997 to 2008.

Shaw, Nancy E; illustrated by Margot Apple. *Sheep in a Jeep* and *Sheep in a Shop*. San Anselmo, CA: Sandpiper, 1986 and 1994.

Spinelli, Eileen; illustrated by Jane Dyer. *Sophie's Masterpiece: A Spider's Tale*. New York: Simon & Schuster, 2001.

Wright, Dare. *A Gift from the Lonely Doll*. San Anselmo, CA: Sandpiper, 2001.

Zelinsky, Paul O. *Rumpelstiltskin*, adapted from the story by the Brothers Grimm. New York: Puffin, 1996.

Online Resources

Elizabeth Zimmermann's Baby Surprise Jacket pattern
www.schoolhousepress.com/patterns
Elizabeth Zimmerman's pattern is available in baby, child, and adult sizes through Schoolhouse Press. Look for pattern A-B-C-SJ.

Soaker Patterns

For a listing of sites that offer soaker patterns, see http://diaperpages.com/soaker.php. Yahoo also hosts a soaker group (http://groups.yahoo.com/group/wool_soaker_group). Here's a short listing:

The Curly Purly Soaker Pattern
Marnie Ann Joyce, Curly Purly
www.curlypurly.com/pdf/soaker.pdf

Fern & Faerie Soaker Pattern
www.fernandfaerie.com/freesoakerpattern.html

Free Tiny Birds Soaker Pattern
Jenny Rasmussen, Tiny Birds Organics
www.birdcrossstitch.com/soakers/pattern

Hand-knit Wool Diaper Cover Pattern
Crista Dovel
http://hubpages.com/hub/Hand-knit-Wool-Diaper-Cover-Pattern

Chapter 10: The Home Dec Life List

More Movie Suggestions

For more favorite films spiced up with a bit of knitting, visit these websites: Knit Flix, hAMImono (http://hamimono.wordpress.com/knit-flix) and Knitting in the Movies, Hip Forums (www.hipforums.com/newforums/archive/index.php/t-147076.html).

Reading List

Bortner, Gwen. *Entrée to Entrelac: A Build-as-You-Go Modular Approach for Knitters*. Sioux Falls, SD: XRX, 2010.

Carey, Jacqui. *Japanese Braiding: The Art of Kumihimo*. Tunbridge Wells, UK: Search Press, 2009.

———. *200 Braids to Twist, Knot, Loop, or Weave*. Interweave, 2007.

Dowde, Jenny. *Freeform Knitting and Crochet*. Bowral, NSW, Australia: Sally Milner, 2004.

———. *Freeformations: Design and Projects in Knitting and Crochet*. Binda, Australia: Sally Milner, 2006.

Drysdale, Rosemary. *Entrelac: The Essential Guide to Interlace Knitting*. Sixth & Spring, 2010.

Eckman, Edie. *Around the Corner Crochet Borders*. Storey Publishing Publishing, 2010.

———. *Beyond the Square Crochet Motifs*. Storey Publishing, 2008.

Epstein, Nicky. *Knitting on the Edge: Ribs, Ruffles, Lace, Fringes, Flora, Points & Picots*. Sixth & Spring, 2004.

Fassett, Kaffe. *Kaffe Fassett's Pattern Library: Over 190 Creative Knitwear Designs*. Taunton, 2003.

Flood, Jared. *Made in Brooklyn*. Classic Elite Yarns, 2009.

Gibson-Roberts, Priscilla. *Knitting in the Old Way: Designs and Techniques from Ethnic Sweaters*. Fort Collins, CO: Nomad Press, 2005.

Haxell, Kate. *Knit Edgings and Trims: 150 Stitches* (The Harmony Guides). Interweave, 2009.

Høxbro, Vivian. *Domino Knitting*. Interweave, 2002.

———. *Knit to Be Square: Domino Designs to Knit and Felt*. Interweave, 2008.

———. *Shadow Knitting*. Interweave, 2004.

Leapman, Melissa. *Mastering Color Knitting: Simple Instructions for Stranded, Intarsia, and Double Knitting*. Potter Craft, 2010.

Moore, Mandy, and Leanne Prain. *Yarn Bombing: The Art of Crochet and Knit Graffiti*. Arsenal Pulp Press, 2009.

Nicholas, Kristin. *Kristin Knits: 27 Inspired Designs for Playing with Color*. Storey Publishing, 2007.

Raffino, Jonelle, and Prudence Mapstone. *Freeform Style: Knit and Crochet to Create Fiber Art Wearables*. Cincinnati: North Light Books, 2009.

Walker, Barbara. *Charted Knitting Designs: A Third Treasury of Knitting Patterns*. Schoolhouse, 1998.

———. *The Craft of Cable-Stitch Knitting*. New York: Scribner, 1971.

———. *The Craft of Lace Knitting*. New York: Scribner, 1971.

———. *The Craft of Multicolor Knitting*. New York: Scribner, 1973.

———. *A Fourth Treasury of Knitting Patterns*. Schoolhouse, 2000; includes *Sampler Knitting*, originally published in 1973.

———. *Knitting from the Top*. Schoolhouse, 1996.

———. *Learn-to-Knit-Afghan Book*. Schoolhouse, 1997.

———. *Mosaic Knitting*. Schoolhouse Press, 2006.

———. *A Second Treasury of Knitting Patterns*. Schoolhouse, 1998.

———. *A Treasury of Knitting Patterns*. Schoolhouse, 1998.

Online Resources

CraftLit
http://crafting-a-life.com/craftlit

International Freeform Fiberarts Guild
www.freeformcrochet.com

Jared Flood patterns
http://brooklyntweed.net/

Jenny Dowde's blog
http://jennydowde.wordpress.com

Knitting Out Loud Audiobook Catalog
www.knittingoutloud.com
Kathy Goldner's book list

Knot Just Knitting
www.knotjustknitting.com
Prudence Mapstone

Myra Wood
www.myrawood.com

Nan Koenig
http://knitterhead.blogspot.com

The World of Illusion Knitting
Woolly Thoughts
www.illusionknitting.woollythoughts.com/potter.html

Woolly Thoughts
http://woollythoughts.com

Chapter 11: The Fiber Lover's Life List

The following is obviously only the tip of the iceberg if you're looking for books on the "sister" crafts, but the list includes some favorite basic beginner's books, as well as material written by authors and designers who contributed to this chapter.

Reading List

Bakriges, Jeannine. *Spinning Around: Spinning, Dyeing & Knitting the Classics*. Schoolhouse Press, 2010.

Callahan, Gail. *Hand Dyeing Yarn and Fleece*. Storey Publishing, 2010.

Casey, Maggie. *Start Spinning: Everything You Need to Know to Make Great Yarn*. Interweave, 2008.

Durant, Judith. *Knit One, Bead Too: Essential Techniques for Knitting with Beads*. Storey Publishing, 2009.

Eckman, Edie. *Around the Corner Crochet Borders*. Storey Publishing, 2010.

——. *Beyond the Square Crochet Motifs*. Storey Publishing, 2008.

——. *The Crochet Answer Book*. Storey Publishing, 2005.

Gipson, Liz. *Weaving Made Easy: 17 Projects Using a Simple Loom*. Interweave, 2008.

Jensen, Candi. *Knitting Loves Crochet: 22 Stylish Designs to Hook Up Your Knitting with a Touch of Crochet*. Storey Publishing, 2006.

McCuin, Judith MacKenzie. *The Intentional Spinner: A Holistic Approach to Making Yarn*. Interweave, 2008.

Menz, Deb. *Color in Spinning*. Interweave, 2005.

——. *Color Works: The Crafter's Guide to Color*. Interweave, 2004.

Nicholas, Kristin. *Color by Kristin: How to Design Your Own Beautiful Knits*. Sixth and Spring, 2009.

——. *Colorful Stitchery: 65 Hot Embroidery Projects to Personalize Your Home*. Storey Publishing, 2005.

——. *Kristin Knits: 27 Inspired Designs for Playing with Color*. Storey Publishing, 2007.

Okey, Shannon. *Spin to Knit: The Knitter's Guide to Making Yarn*. Interweave, 2006.

Pace, Maggie. *Felt It: 20 Fun & Fabulous Projects to Knit & Felt*. Storey Publishing, 2006.

Patrick, Jane. *Time to Weave: Simply Elegant Projects to Make in Almost No Time*. Interweave, 2006.

——. *The Weaver's Idea Book: Creative Cloth on a Rigid Heddle Loom*. Interweave, 2010.

Taylor, Kathleen. *Knit One, Felt Too*. Storey Publishing, 2003.

White, Christine. *Uniquely Felt: Dozens of Techniques from Fulling and Shaping to Nuno and Cobweb*. Storey Publishing, 2007.

Online Resources

Bev Galeskas's Felt Clogs
www.fibertrends.com
Pattern #AC 33

Carol Leigh's Hillcreek Fiber Studio
www.hillcreekfiberstudio.com
Frame looms

The Spinning Loft
www.thespinningloft.com
Fleeces from many different breeds

Music to Spin, Knit, and Weave By
www.allfiberarts.com/cs/music.htm
For a list of recordings of songs about weaving and spinning: Weavers & Handspinners Music & Audio Clips

Magpie Designs Felting Studio
www.magpiefelt.com
Felting author and designer Christine White's studio

Sources for Patterns of Photographed Items

Penny Straker's Baby Owl Sweater and Bonnet (page 11)
Available in yarn shops and online; pattern # B818
Handknit by Kathy Brock
http://strakerclassics.com

Habu Design's Kushu Kushu Scarf (page 36)
Silk stainless steel and merino knit felt scarf
Available as kit-78 from Habu
www.habutextiles.com

Vivian Høxbro's Navajo Jacket or Sweater (page 55)
Available as a kit from Harrisville Designs
www.harrisville.com

Kaffe Fassett's Carpet Coat (page 57)
From *Glorious Knits* (Clarkson Potter, 1985)

Kristin Nicholas's Diamond Panes Pullover and Striped Turtleneck in the Round (page 96)
From *Kristin Knits: 27 Inspired Designs for Playing with Color* (Storey, 2007)

Judith Durant's Sideways Socks (page 128)
From *Sock Yarn One-Skein Wonders: 101 Patterns that Go Way Beyond Socks* (Storey, 2010)

Margaret Radcliffe's Reversible Scarf (page 157)
From *The Essential Guide to Color Knitting Techniques* (Storey, 2008)

Cat Bordhi's Felted Möbius Basket (page 159)
From *A Second Treasury of Magical Knitting* (Passing Paws Press, 2005)

Kate Gilbert's Halliard (page 160)
Available at Twist Collective
http://twistcollective.com

Lucy Neatby's Bubbles scarf (page 162)
Available from Patternfish, pattern #492
www.lucyneatby.com

Dolly-Mama's Lucy doll (page 162)
From the Dolly-Mama's Deluxe KuKu Doll line
http://thedolly-mamas.com

Vickie Howell's Lyra Wool-Soy Cabled Baby Bonnet (page 175)
From *Luxury Yarn One-Skein Wonders: 101 Small Indulgences* (Storey, 2008)

Margaret Radcliffe's twined knitting samples (page 202)
From *The Essential Guide to Color Knitting Techniques* (Storey, 2008)

Robin Hansen's Fleece-Stuffed Mittens (page 204)
From *Fox and Geese and Fences: A Collection of Traditional Maine Mittens* (Down East Books, 1983).

Handful-of-Color Mittens (page 207)
From *Sock Yarn One-Skein Wonders: 101 Patterns that Go Way Beyond Socks* (Storey, 2010)

Kristin Nicholas's Olivia's and Celia's Mittens (page 210)
From *Kristin Knits: 27 Inspired Designs for Playing with Color* (Storey, 2007)

Kathleen Taylor's Soft-and-Thick Shoulder Bag (page 216)
From *Knit One, Felt Too: Discover the Magic of Knitted Felt with 25 Easy Patterns* (Storey, 2003)

Judith Durant's Beaded Bag (page 220)
Handknit and designed by Judith Durant (pattern not yet published)

Yankee Knitter's Bunny Sweater (page 222)
Available from Yankee Knitter, as well as from yarn stores
Handknit by Kathy Brock
www.yankeeknitterdesigns.com

Susan B. Anderson's Upside-Down Daisy hat (page 226)
From *Itty-Bitty Hats: Cute and Cuddly Caps to Knit for Babies and Toddlers* (Artisan, 2006)

Judith Durant's Alpaca-Silk Christening Blanket (page 227)
From *Luxury Yarn One-Skein Wonders: 101 Small Indulgences* (Storey, 2008)

Gitta Schrade's Baby's Bamboo Singlet (page 228)
From *Luxury Yarn One-Skein Wonders: 101 Small Indulgences* (Storey, 2008)

Elizabeth Zimmermann's Baby Surprise Jacket (page 229)
Available in baby, child, and adult sizes through Schoolhouse Press; pattern A-B-C-SJ
www.schoolhousepress.com/patterns.htm

Susan B. Anderson's Organic Cotton Bunnies (page 230)
From *Luxury Yarn One-Skein Wonders: 101 Small Indulgences* (Storey, 2008)

Silk Wedding Ring Pillow (page 238)
From *Luxury Yarn One-Skein Wonders: 101 Small Indulgences* (Storey, 2008)

Jared Flood's Celes Shetland Stole (page 247)
Available at http://brooklyntweed.net

Freeform Swatch (page 248)
Handknit and designed by Jenny Dowde

Afghan Design (page 255)
Adapted from Kaffe Fassett's Toothed-Stripe pattern in *Glorious Knits* (Clarkson Potter, 1985)

Mosaic Knitting Swatch (page 256)
From Barbara G. Walker's *Mosaic Knitting* (Schoolhouse Press, 1997)

Barbara Elkins's Atwater-Bronson Lace Runner (Valley Yarns #46) (page 275)
Available at www.yarn.com

Candi Jensen's Posies for Tanks (page 284)
From *Hooked on Crochet: 20 Sassy Projects* (Storey, 2004)

Kathleen Taylor's Wine Sack (page 285)
From *Knit One, Felt Too: Discover the Magic of Knitted Felt with 25 Easy Patterns* (Storey, 2003)

Christine White's Citrus Picnic Blanket (page 286)
From *Uniquely Felt: Dozens of Techniques from Fulling and Shaping to Nuno and Cobweb* (Storey, 2007)

Kristin Nicholas's Embroidered Fair Isle Cardigan (page 289)
From *Kristin Knits: 27 Inspired Designs for Playing with Color* (Storey, 2007)

PHOTO CREDITS

© AFP/Getty Images: 66, 85

© akg-images/RIA Novosti: 169 right

© Albert Moldvay/National Geographic/ Getty Images: 219

Courtesy Amy Singer: 185

© Arctic Images/Getty Images: 116 bottom

© Arctic Photo/Alamy: 27

© Ariel Skelley/Getty Images: 236

Designed and woven by Barbara Elkins: 275

© 2011 Bata Shoe Museum, Toronto, Canada: 130

Ben Fink/Storey Publishing: 216, 285

© blue jean images/Getty Images: 64 right

© Carol Ekarius: 21

© Chris Hartlove: 41

© Constance Bannister group/ReView/ Getty Images: 232

© Erik Svensson and Jeppe Wilkstrom/ Getty Images: 200 right

© Evan Sklar/Botanica/Getty Images: 34

© Fox Photos/Getty Images: 139 top

© FPG/Hulton Archive/Getty Images: 245

© Frank Driggs Collection/Archive Photos/Getty Images: 146

© GAB Archive/Redferns/Getty Images: 112 bottom right

© Georgianna Lane/Garden Photo World: 270 left, 274, 279

The Granger Collection, New York: 193 bottom

© hana/Datacraft/Getty Images: 91

Hilary Dionne: 162 bottom

© Hulton Archive/Getty Images: 38 top, 109 top left, 193 top, 237

© ILMARS ZNOTINS/AFP/Getty Images: 210

© Ira Garber Photography: 128

© Jane Heller: 161

© Jared Flood/Brooklyn Tweed: 46, 246, 247

© Jean-Pierre De-Mann/agefotostock: 40

© John Dolan: 284

© John Grant/The Image Bank/Getty Images: 194

© Johnny Franzen/Getty Images: 114 bottom

© Kate Sears: 175, 227, 228, 230, 238

Kevin Kennefick/Storey Publishing: 96, 210 top, 289

© Kim Werker (kimwerker.com): 117

© Kristin Duvall/Getty Images: 212

© Kristin Lee/Getty Images: 148

© Lars Dalby Photography: 54

© Laura A. Oda/MCT/Landov: 243

© Lew Robertson/BrandX Pictures/ Getty Images: 184 right

Library of Congress, Prints & Photographs Division: 192

© Lily Chin: 71

Photography by Liz Banfield, from *Itty-Bitty Hats* by Susan B. Anderson. Reprinted by permission of Artisan, a divison of Workman Publishing Inc.

© Mario Tama/Getty Images: 112 left

Mars Vilaubi/Storey Publishing: 8, 17 right, 18, 28, 30, 42, 44, 45, 53, 94, 176, 270 right, 287

© Nancy Bush: 170

© National Geographic/Getty Images: 111

© Nicholas Pitt/The Image Bank/Getty Images: 177

© Patricia S. Colony/Harrisville Designs: 25

© Peter Stackpole/Time & Life Pictures/ Getty Images: 203

© Popperfoto/Getty Images: 99

© Radius/Getty Images: 12

© Rosemary Kautzky: 33 left

© Scanpix Creative/Masterfile: 199

© Schacht Spindle (www.schachtspindle. com): 273

Knitting and photo by Meg Swansen used by permission of Schoolhousepress. com: 229

Shetland Museum and Archives: 65, 107, 109 top right, 169 left, 206

Smithsonian American Art Museum, Washington, DC/Art Resource, NY: 277

Sterling and Francine Clark Art Institute, Williamstown, MA, USA/ The Bridgeman Art Library: 215

© 1985 Steve Lovi, excerpted from *Glorious Knits* by Kaffe Fassett (Clarkson N Potter, Inc.): 57

© Sue Bundy: 23

Terra Foundation for American Art, Chicago/Art Resource, New York: 138

© Tetra/Getty Images: 124

© The Dolly-Mamas LLC: 162 top

© Tim Graham/Getty Images: 184 left

© Ulf Huett Nilsson/Getty Images: 182

© V&A Images/Victoria and Albert Museum: 64 left, 82

Wikimedia Commons: 145

© Workman Publishing: 155

© Zilli/iStockphoto.com: 75

ACKNOWLEDGMENTS

The generosity of the many people who have contributed their ideas and support to this project has been a source of inspiration and a joy.

I'm deeply grateful to Storey Publishing for having the confidence to give an editor the time to be an author, and especially to Pam Art for conceiving the idea of a knitter's life list and for her ongoing enthusiasm and vision for the project, Deborah Balmuth for her unfailing encouragement and trust, and Amy Greeman for her wise suggestions and sense of humor: each has shared the passion and been steadfastly positive and supportive as the project has taken shape.

My heartfelt thanks and admiration to Alethea Morrison, for the art direction and creative vision that brought the words to life; Mars Vilaubi, for the way he captured the spirit of the yarn and the animals through his photography at the New York Sheep and Wool Festival and also for his enthusiastic investment in finding much of the stock photography; John Polak, whose skills and understanding made the studio photography such a joy; Jennie Jepson Smith, whose patience and care in assisting in page layouts was (as always) unfailing.

Many thanks also to Nicole Cusano, whose interviews and profiles capture the talents, interests, and contributions of so many who have impacted the fiber industry in various ways; Molly Jackson, whose curiosity and persistence formed the groundwork for much of the early research for the book.

My deepest appreciation goes to those experts who read part or all of manuscript, especially to Deborah Robson, who is not only wise, with extraordinary editorial skills, but whose commitment to the fiber industry is awesome; to Kathy Brock, whose conscientious attention to detail has been a constant reassurance throughout; and to the many others who advised and contributed along the way, each so generously offering their expertise and their passion for knitting and fiber: Pam Allen, Sarah Anderson, Susan B. Anderson, Jeannine Bakriges, Judy Becker, Debbie Bliss, Cat Bordhi, Beth Brown-Reinsel, Ann Budd, Nancy Bush, Gail Callahan, Lily Chin, Michael Cook, Linda Cortright, Donna Druchunas, Judith Durant, Jil Eaton, Edie Eckman, Barbara Elkins, Melanie Falick, Kaffe Fassett, Jared Flood, Bev Galeskas, Kay Gardiner, Kate Gilbert, Robin Hansen, Vickie Howell, Vivian Høxbro, Marianne Isager, Candi Jensen, Linda Ligon, Brandon Mably, Betsy McCarthy, Jillian Moreno, Melissa Morgan-Oakes, Lucy Neatby, Kristin Nicholas, Shannon Okey, Clara Parkes, Margaret Radcliffe, Charlene Schurch, Amy R. Singer, Alice Starmore, Debbie Stoller, Meg Swansen, Kathleen Taylor, Barbara Walker, and Sandi Wiseheart.

With loving gratitude, finally, to my family — Dick; Kristin, José, and Sara; Paul and Tina; Ben and Brigid — your own creative spirits and loving support never fail to nourish and astound me.

INDEX

Page references in italics indicate illustrations or captions.